BIG WHITE LIE

John Fitzgerald is head of the School of Social Sciences at La Trobe University in Melbourne. His earlier publications include *Awakening China* (Stanford 1996), *Rethinking China's Provinces* (ed., Routledge 2002) and *The Dignity of Nations* (ed., Hong Kong University Press 2006). This is his first book on Australian history.

BIG WHITE LIE

CHINESE AUSTRALIANS in WHITE AUSTRALIA

JOHN FITZGERALD

UNSW PRESS

In memory of Jennifer Cushman (1944–86) and Joan Jack (1934–2006)

A UNSW Press book

Published by
University of New South Wales Press Ltd
University of New South Wales
Sydney NSW 2052
AUSTRALIA
www.unswpress.com.au

© John Fitzgerald 2007
First published 2007

National Library of Australia
Cataloguing-in-Publication entry

Fitzgerald, John, 1951- .
Big white lie: Chinese Australians in white Australia.

Bibliography.
Includes index.
ISBN 9780868408705 (pbk.).

1. Chinese Australians. 2. White Australia policy.
3. Australia - Social conditions. I. Title.

325.94

Design Josephine Pajor-Markus
Cover Jessie and Joe Mah with children Rene and Leslie (1936). Courtesy of M. Mar

This publication has been supported by La Trobe University.
Internet: <http://www.latrobe.edu.au/bundoora/>.

CONTENTS

PREFACE

In 1974, if I am not mistaken, I fell into an argument on the fourth floor of the Fisher Library at the University of Sydney with a fellow student who has since become adviser to the prime minister on Australian history. 'Why are you studying this stuff?' he asked, referring to my Chinese and Greek-language dictionaries. 'There's so much Australian history you don't know. Are you ashamed of your own country?' I don't recall coming up with an adequate reply at the time but since then I have never had occasion to concede that learning Chinese or Greek was an impediment to learning about Australian history. This book, which draws extensively on Chinese-language sources, is a long overdue attempt to answer the challenge laid down in Fisher all those years ago.

The book is designed to show how Chinese Australians survived the White Australia era, partly by tracing their emigration patterns, their social organisations and their business and religious lives, and partly by attending to the arguments they mounted on their own behalf for equality of treatment with white Australians. This last point is an important one. Chinese voices are barely audible among all the comments about people of Chinese descent that resonate through Australian art and letters of the late 19th and early 20th centuries. As a rule, Chinese are widely pictured in Australian writings of the time as self-interested, menial, unhealthy and generally disagreeable characters who have no rightful place alongside free white settlers under the Australian sun. While few of these claims are taken seriously today, a more refined version of the same argument still receives a regular hearing. This is the claim that, on the one side, Australia was host to a clash of national values between slavish, dependent and hierarchical exiles from an unchanging Chinese empire, and, on the other, individualistic, egalitarian and patriotic white settlers, fresh from doing battle with the tyrannies of Old Europe. On the basis of this highly-principled claim, old impressions of what it meant to be Australian in White Australia still sustain a case for the exclusion of Chinese Australians from their rightful place in Australian history as Australians. Some of them grew tired of waiting and left but many are still waiting to be heard.

To listen to what Chinese Australians were saying is to stumble across a big white lie at the heart of Australian history: that different peoples have different national values and that these differences have justified discrimination of one kind and another in Australian history. The notion that Chinese had to be excluded from Australia to keep it free and equal, for example, is often raised to explain anti-Chinese discrimination in White Australia. Arguments that trace legal discrimination or popular prejudice to an underlying clash of values elevate racial discrimination to a matter of high principle. When we consult Chinese-Australian sources it becomes clear that no high principles were at stake in the clash of cultures between white and Chinese Australia. Even a cursory examination of what Chinese Australians were saying and doing reveals that they were no less committed to freedom, equality and fraternal solidarity than were other Australians.

The book illustrates this argument historically. Chapter 1 highlights a number of assumptions about the place of Chinese immigrants in Australian history and shows that, to the extent that these assumptions are misleading, they serve to exclude Chinese from Australian history as Australians. The biggest of these assumptions is that a particular set of principles – or national values – served to distinguish white Australians from other Australians to the point of denying Chinese claims to be acknowledged as Australians. Chapter 2 considers the place of Australian values in Australian history. The argument mounted here is that individualism, egalitarianism and mateship were local Australian idiom for the modern ethical principle that people are born free and equal. This universal principle was understood and appreciated by Chinese Australians. The national appropriation of universal values as Australian values facilitated the exclusion of Chinese from the country on the ground that they professed a body of Chinese values that were alien to the white settlements into which they happened to stray.

Chapters 3 and 4 introduce the underground Yee Hing (*Yixing*) brotherhood, the most important fraternal network through which Chinese labourers were recruited to work in Australia, and around which they plotted to transform China into an egalitarian democracy and struggled for recognition within Australia itself. Chapter 5 offers a brief intellectual history of Chinese Australia at the time of federation, focusing particularly on the appeal of egalitarian ideals.

Chapter 6 identifies the distinctively Australian features of one of the major Chinese fraternal organisations of the White Australia era, the Kuo Min Tang (KMT), paying particular attention to its labour orientation and to its role in representing Australians to Chinese government authorities. Chapter 7 traces the expansion of the Sydney-based KMT network into the South Pacific in the shadow of Australia's Pacific mandate after the Great War. Chapter 8 introduces the business and investment strategies of Chinese-Australian firms in the White Australia era to illustrate how they evolved from the fraternal networks established in colonial and federation Australia. It concludes with a reflection on the place of Christian networks and Christian ethics in Chinese-Australian business and community formation. Many found a compelling counterpoint to Australian national values in Paul's 'Letter to the Galatians': 'All baptised in Christ, you have all clothed yourselves in Christ, and there are no more distinctions between Jew and Greek, slave and free, male and female.'[1] Chinese Australians derived comfort from their conviction that Christian values transcended national ones.

Chapter 9 asks what it meant to be Australian in White Australia. This is not a trivial question. Many Australian historians continue to maintain a clear and unequivocal distinction between Chinese and white Australians in their reproduction of dog-eared stories of timeless, deferential and tradition-bound Chinese sojourners who had to be kept out of the country to keep it free and equal. Even today few Australians would concede that it was possible to be Chinese and Australian before the advent of multicultural Australia. By consulting Chinese Australians and placing their voices on the record, this book sets out to prove otherwise.

Chinese voices are not difficult to find in Australian history. In teaching and writing about Chinese history and politics I have often come across documents dating from the late 19th and early 20th centuries written about Australia, some in English, many more in Chinese. Among the Australian personalities mentioned in these sources I have found surprisingly few references to the outstanding figures who feature in English-language works on Chinese-Australian relations, such as the Geelong boy George Morrison, who went on to become the Peking correspondent for *The Times* of London and one of the most influential commentators on China at the turn of the 20th century. Nor do these documents dwell at any length on the Australian diplomats, missionaries and businessmen who are said to have built the foundations for bilateral relations between Australia and China over the federation and prewar eras. Chinese-language sources refer overwhelmingly to Chinese-Australian men and women who established their communities in Australia, who built substantial business networks linking Australia and China, who set up Chinese newspapers and magazines in Australia and who joined Australian chapters of Chinese community organisations abroad. These Chinese-language sources offer, I would suggest, a new perspective on Australian history.

Making the acquaintance of Chinese Australians who, over the years, became friends, opened up other perspectives. Arthur Lock Chang in Sydney and Maurice and Eunice Leong in Melbourne taught me a great deal about the communities in which they came to maturity in the 1930s, 1940s and 1950s. Other encounters were serendipitous. One morning while I was at home drafting a chapter of this book, Freda Lew Shing called by unannounced to show her daughter Johanna the home where she had grown up in the 1930s and 1940s. We got to talking. Tall and blonde, Johanna could speak the kitchen Cantonese of her mother and recite the names of vegetables and specialty dishes, but she knew little about her Chinese family background. Freda, almost 90 years of age the day she rang our doorbell, was a willing and able instructor. I learnt a great deal that day about my home and my country.

The Lew Shings were battlers who had made good. Freda was the ninth of 14 children of Catherine Pine and Arthur Lew Shing who moved to Canning Street in the inner Melbourne suburb of Carlton from Grattan Street in the same area when Freda was 9 or 10 years of age. Her father worked at the fruit and vegetable markets in the city. Her brothers played football in the amateur Sunday league for the Carlton Rovers and ran a number of sideline businesses out the back gate – chiefly, Sunday beer and bookmaking – and rented the rear stables as a boxing stadium. Along with her mother and sisters Freda was part of a dancing troupe that performed in Melbourne and toured regional Victoria under the name of the Lee Moy sisters. The family was well known in more than one local community in White Australia.

From Freda I learnt that the Lew Shings were part of a wider community of Chinese-Australian families who lived in our neighbourhood in the White Australia era. Freda attended the Rathdowne Street Public School with friends whose fathers caught a tram each morning to their stalls at the fruit and vegetable markets in the city. Also at the school was the young John Wing, who penned the letter to the Melbourne Olympic Committee suggesting a new style of closing ceremony for the 1956 Olympics, one that represented the world not as many races but, as he urged in his letter, as '1 nation'.

Further north along Rathdowne Street stood the editorial offices of a national Chinese-language newspaper, one of several published in the White Australia era. Across from the newspaper premises shone the brightly lit windows of the local Chinese restaurant. Some families left lasting mementoes of their heritage in the decorations plastered onto the facades of their single-storey terraces. Alongside terraces named 'Donegal' and 'Roseneath' in nearby Drummond Street stands a house that still bears the name 'Kimoie' on its upper facade – a romanised Cantonese rendering of 'My beloved' – dating from 100 years ago. Chinese Australians in this neighbourhood were as proud of their heritage as they were of the Carlton football club.

Many blonde Australians such as Johanna can claim a Chinese ancestry. According to Joan Jack, director of the Golden Dragon Museum in Bendigo, one in four old-time residents of that great Victorian mining city has a Chinese ancestor. Many Aboriginal Australians could say the same. Olympic gold medallist Cathy Freeman acknowledged her Chinese ancestry when she applauded the award of the 2008 Olympics to Beijing.[2] As in sport, so too in business. Sir Leslie Joseph Hooker, founder of the real estate firm of LJ Hooker, was born Leslie Joseph Tingyou but exchanged his father's name for his profession (his father was a railroad 'hooker') in 1925 to conform to White Australian expectations. With a turnover in excess of $25 billion per year, and branches throughout the Asia–Pacific region, today LJ Hooker ranks fifth in the world in commercial real estate.[3]

This should not surprise us. Men from China made up the largest group of people, apart from the English, on the Victorian goldfields of the mid-19th century, exceeding in number the men from Ireland, Scotland and Wales who worked alongside them. In Darwin, men and women from China outnumbered white Australians until well into the second decade of the 20th century, and they made up a sizeable minority in far north Queensland.[4] Legend has it that while British and Irish miners settled down in Australia, Chinese sojourners pulled up stakes and went back to China. In fact, close to half of the 100 000 men who came to the Australian colonies from China in the 19th century lived out their lives in Australia, New Zealand and the Pacific Islands. They left a legacy of family stories, business enterprise, and social and religious engagement that is little understood or appreciated in Australia.[5]

Their values did not differ greatly from those of the English, Irish, Scots and Germans among whom they settled. The first Lew Shings were aware of their rights at law. Freda's grandfather, William Lew Shing, was a See Yap native from Guangdong who emigrated to the tin mines of Garibaldi in northeastern Tasmania in the 1870s, where he settled down with an Irish woman named Bridgit Gavan.[6] The couple later moved to Melbourne where they opened a confectionary shop. In 1883 William and Bridgit became involved in a dispute in Garibaldi with the local subinspector of police, John Webster. This we know from the voluminous tales of Eric Rolls, who records that Lew Shing took Webster to court alleging 'misconduct as a constable on 23 May last, contrary to section 87 of the Police Regulations Act, by entering the dwelling of the complainant without permission while in a state of intoxication'.[7]

The accusation carried a touch of irony. Constable Webster's efforts to stamp out sly grog selling had recently earned him derision in the town. Not long before the 23 May incident, Webster contrived with another Chinese resident, Ling Gooey, to confiscate 40 cases of contraband liquor. It was not a popular move. When Webster entered Lew Shing's house drunk in the company of Bridgit Gavan on 23 May, William asked him to leave. Webster threw a punch and Lew Shing hit back. Several witnesses came forward to testify in court that they saw Webster scrambling out of the window to escape William Lew Shing's well-aimed blows. A drunken constable prone to confiscating cheap liquor and pressing his attentions on other men's wives was not especially welcome in any home in colonial Australia.

Freda's introduction to the Lew Shing family brought home to me something no institutional history of Chinese-Australian communities can afford to ignore. No institutional history of this kind can overlook the lived history of Chinese immigrants and their descendents in White Australia, including their home life, work, entertainment, loves, disputes and the values that they held dear. Australia was in many ways a hostile place for Chinese Australians in the period before the Second World War. Still, the Lew Shings do not appear to have considered themselves victims of local racism or special targets of high policy and immigration quotas. They lived out their lives as though the challenge of being Chinese and Australian was a relatively trivial one when compared with the other problems that life presented.

There were certainly problems. One of the Lew Shing children, Edna, died on her third day. Athol was only four when he was cut down by the influenza epidemic in 1919. But the family bounced back. Freda recalled a saying of her elder sister Hazel that always made her laugh. Whenever she was asked how she liked her tea poured Hazel would respond, 'I like my tea strong and my men weak.' Hazel did not come around to this way of thinking by dwelling on her fate as a 'Chinese' in White Australia. Nor did young John Wing come to imagine that international athletes should form '1 nation' out of frustration at being Chinese in White Australia. 'Greeks, Italians and Poms,' he told journalist James Button, 'got much more abuse than I ever got.'[8]

My thanks go to Freda and Johanna for introducing me to their family and to Pat Foorde for expanding on their stories.[9] For help and advice over many years of writing I wish to thank Phillip Bramble, Cai Shaoqing, Chen Hong, Jocelyn Chey, Sophie Couchman, Mark Finnane, Amaraswar Galla, Jack Gregory, Hou Minyue, Huang Yuanshen, Joan and Russell Jack, Patricia Jamieson, Paul Jones, Alastair Kennedy, Dr Kok Hu Jin, Daphne Kok, Kuo Mei-fen, Lai Chi-kong, Maurice and Eunice Leong, Liu Luxin, Li Gongzhong, Janet McCalman, Amanda Rasmussen, Lachlan Strahan, Kevin Wong-Hoy, Allen Yip, Dr John Yu, and the volunteer workers of the Clarence River Historical Society and the Richmond River Historical Society, especially Annette Potts.

A special note of appreciation is due to Gregor Benton, Judith Brett, Stuart Macintyre, Adam McKeown and Tim Wright for reading and commenting on earlier drafts. Above all, I wish to thank Antonia Finnane, for reading and improving the manuscript from beginning to end, and Siobhan, Therese, Genevieve, Bernard and Bingley for sharing my voyage of discovery with patience and good humour. Research for this study was funded with the assistance of the Australian Research Council and undertaken in the School of Social Sciences at La Trobe University.

My dealings with UNSW Press have confirmed for me why it is now regarded as the finest Australian history publisher in Australia. I especially wish to acknowledge Tracy Lee, and the contributions of Phillipa McGuinness at the Press, and of my editor, Sandra Goldbloom Zurbo, for improving the structure, the format and the clarity of the book.

Names

As far as possible all personal, institutional and place names are rendered as they were best known in their own time, in most cases through an English rendering of a Cantonese pronunciation. For the sake of consistency, where multiple English variants exist for institutional or place names, I have employed the spelling found in CF Yong's *New Gold Mountain* (1977). Mandarin *pinyin* spellings are given in italics to facilitate comparative research. Chinese characters for *pinyin* spellings are available at website: <http://www.chaf.lib.latrobe.edu.au/bwlglossary>

1

BELONGING AND EXCLUSION

I belonged to a stronger secret society than any [Chinese triads].
I was a white man on the China coast.

CW Mason 1924.[1]

The White Australia era has cast a long shadow over Australian history. It falls within living memory and the humiliations suffered by those it offended still reverberate in Indigenous politics and in Australia's relations with its neighbours. That said, Australia's restrictive immigration practices were not significantly different from those of other white-settler states on the Pacific Rim. Echoes of White Australia still generate passionate debate in 21st century Australia at a time when the expressions 'White Canada' and 'White New Zealand' have long been forgotten, and America's Chinese Exclusion Act has reverted to a subject of specialist enquiry.[2] Why does the legacy of White Australia loom larger in foreign perceptions of Australia and in the self-understanding of Australians than comparable discriminatory regimes elsewhere?

The Australian features of the immigration policies of the federation era were not the restrictions themselves, which were common enough in North America and New Zealand, nor the racial ideology that inspired them, which was widespread in Canada and the USA and in many states of Europe at the time. In 1882 the US Congress passed the Chinese Exclusion Act, which denied skilled and unskilled Chinese labourers entry into American ports and denied all Chinese the right to naturalisation. This Act, the first federal act of its kind in US history to discriminate against a category of immigrants on the basis of race, was made permanent in 1902 and not repealed until the Pacific War.[3] By contrast no Australian federal government legislated specifically against Chinese immigration.[4] Canada introduced a poll tax to restrict Chinese entry from 1885 before virtually prohibiting entry in 1923. By one estimate no more than two dozen Chinese people were given permission to stay in Canada between 1923 and the beginning of the Second World War, considerably less than Australian authorities permitted over the same period.[5] New Zealand continued to impose discriminatory poll taxes on Chinese immigrants for 50 years after the last poll taxes were eliminated from the Australian continent. The difference is that none of these countries constituted themselves as sovereign states on the back of arguments about preserving national purity by restricting Asian immigration: Australia did. For a good 70 years from its founding moment in 1901 Australia *was* White Australia. There was no other Australia going.

Australia's effort to restrict Chinese immigration was distinguished by a number of features but above all by its association with nation building. The two decades of constitutional consultation and debate that preceded federation coincided with a period of anti-Chinese sentiment around the Pacific Rim that gave the Commonwealth an identity defined by the principle of racial purity. This principle found legislative expression in the Immigration Restriction Act of 1901, the first substantial piece of legislation passed by the Commonwealth parliament. Canada and the United States introduced comparable legislation and a range of discriminatory practices that at times exceeded in their intolerance anything practised in Australia.[6] In Australia an ideal of racial purity converged with a triumphalist rhetoric of self-conscious nation building to yield a particular vision of a brand new country able to demonstrate its independence by shutting its gates to all but whites. The White Australia Policy embodied a driving vision of the Australian nation that no amount of discriminatory legislation could capture in full. Deleting the word 'white' from current immigration policies has gone only part way in dispelling the legacy of White Australia.

White Australia continues to cast a long shadow over histories of Chinese in Australia, as well. In some cases the White Australia Policy has been the explicit focus of study.[7] Other works have drawn attention to the social, economic, cultural and political factors leading to the introduction of the White Australia immigration policy.[8] Until fairly recent times few studies have been closely concerned with the social history of Chinese-Australian communities themselves or with consulting Chinese-Australian individuals or families to learn what they thought of White Australia.[9] Up to the 1980s, as Jennifer Cushman pointed out in 1985, 'writing on the Australian Chinese community' was 'less concerned with the community on its own terms and more with Australian attitudes towards Chinese'.[10]

At the time Cushman penned these words little attention was being paid to signs of local adaptation and internal differentiation among Chinese Australians, or to evidence of their intercommunity and international networking. Since then a number of important local community studies have succeeded in tracing the adaptive strategies developed by Chinese Australians to cope with the conditions in which they found themselves from one place to another and from one period to the next. From these studies it has emerged that Chinese Australians survived White Australia more robustly than earlier observers generally assumed, and that they survived with identities shaped by the differences they drew among themselves no less than by the identities that White Australia invented on their behalf.[11]

Few of these recent social studies have directly broached the larger national issues that characterised earlier studies of the White Australia policy, including issues touching on national values, such as egalitarianism and mateship, on the alleged 'culture clash' between Australians of European and Chinese descent, and on the vexing problem of Australian national identity itself. Being chiefly concerned to redress an imbalance in the Australian historical record, the work of social history is done when Chinese are restored to their rightful place in local and regional histories. With few exceptions, the broader implications of these social studies for the history of Australia have yet to be explored.[12]

Studies of Chinese Australia have yet to draw as well on the rich vein of comparative work in Chinese overseas studies. Important insights into the comparative ethnography of Chinese settlers in different colonial settings have been largely overlooked, as has the role of regional and national networks in linking Chinese residents of Australia to Chinese in Oceania, East Asia and North America. And despite abundant Chinese-language newspapers published in Australia and extant Chinese-language archives bearing on the life and times of Chinese Australia, little attempt has been made to fathom the intellectual and cultural history of Chinese-Australian communities through their own eyes.

The present work seeks to extend the range of recent social histories in all of these directions by linking them directly to the debate on Australian national values, by focusing on comparisons with other sites of Chinese settlement beyond white-settler communities, by drawing attention to Chinese-language materials that illustrate the intellectual currents at work in China and Australia in the late 19th and early 20th centuries and by highlighting the role of Chinese-Australian social networks and civic organisations in Australian history and in Australia's relations with other communities in the Asia–Pacific region.

Australian identity, Chinese exclusion

Foremost among the issues touched on here is Australian identity itself. The shift that Cushman anticipated 20 years ago towards chronicling Chinese-Australian communities on their own terms has certainly taken place in recent years. Yet even today the implications of this work for the historical claims of Chinese immigrants to be counted Australian are barely apparent. Indeed, when she classified the problem at hand as one involving 'Australian' attitudes towards 'Chinese', Cushman herself echoed a lingering rhetorical strategy of the White Australia era. She was not alone in implying that the Chinese about whom Australians held attitudes were not themselves Australian. Despite the brouhaha surrounding multiculturalism many whites still reserve the word 'Australian' for themselves and many Chinese Australians refer to whites as 'Australians' and to themselves as 'Chinese'. The cultural legacy of White Australia is powerful and persistent.

The discriminatory practices of White Australia involved multiple exclusions, including cultural and administrative ones. The racially exclusive immigration administration introduced by the Commonwealth government was reinforced in everyday life and language by a limiting assumption about the application of the category 'Australian' to non-European subjects and citizens. The reward for historians who take up Cushman's challenge is to recover a keener sense of social organisation and networking among Chinese Australians 'on their own terms', as she suggested. A further challenge is to embed Chinese-Australian stories in Australian history to the point of demonstrating that Chinese Australians were so unequivocally Australian that so-called anti-Chinese attitudes were not anti-Chinese at all but anti-Australian, even in White Australia.

The approach to Chinese-Australian history and identity adopted here can constructively be contrasted with historian Keith Windschuttle's *The White Australia Policy* (2004). Windschuttle comes to the defence of the White Australia policy by arguing that colonial and Commonwealth restrictions on Asian immigration need to be understood as reasoned administrative responses to community tensions in the Australian colonies, as an effective resolution to a regrettable clash of cultures. Attending to the explicit motives of white Australian legislators and bureaucrats, he overlooks the many voices of the Chinese Australians whose lives and livelihoods were adversely affected by administrative practices of racial exclusion. Few, if any, Chinese Australians are mentioned by name in his dense and closely argued book, compelling the conclusion that for the author they hardly counted as Australians.

Windschuttle's approach is hardly exceptional in the longer run of studies of White Australia. Before the 1990s Australians paid little regard to Chinese experiences of living under White Australia, or about the part they played in Australian history. It was not until the 1960s and 1970s that historians begin to probe some of the racist underpinnings and implications of White Australian attitudes and practices.[13] Before then mainstream studies of White Australia focused on the clash of cultures between white and Chinese Australians to demonstrate the rationality of colonial and national policies of racial exclusion. Correspondingly, Windschuttle draws attention to earlier generations of historians who cleared the path before him, beginning with Myra Willard in the 1920s and reaching to Charles Price in the 1970s.

In her *History of the White Australia Policy* (1923), Willard acknowledged that Commonwealth immigration policies excluded people of Asian background from entry to Australia but she was not prepared to concede that this amounted to racial exclusion. By her account the style of national culture that the founding fathers sought to cultivate was incompatible with the cultural predispositions of people from China. Chinese had to be excluded for reasons of value and culture. Further, she declined to concede that similar discrimination was at work in domestic policy areas. Historian Paul Jones estimates that Willard overlooked at least 60 Commonwealth and state laws and statutes curtailing the rights of non-European residents after federation when she claimed that exclusion applied exclusively to immigration policy. Willard's *History of the White Australia Policy*, in Jones' judgment, 'presents an apologia for the mono-cultural ideology it sought to describe'.[14]

Charles Price's *Great White Walls are Built* (1974) could not be described in such terms. It is certainly not an apologia for White Australia. In his comparative study of the historical background to immigration restrictions in Australia and North America, Price shows little patience for racist arguments and racist advocates. He resorts nevertheless to a style of argument reminiscent of Willard's in characterising immigrants from China as tradition-bound scions of an 'ancient, oriental, and basically very stable civilization' that imprinted timeless values and loyalties on those who came to the Australian colonies, in contrast to the 'restless, inquisitive, acquisitive' spirit of European immigrants who were animated by the promethean ethos of the Industrial Revolution and eager to build a New World in the Antipodean penumbra of the Old. In Price's judgment it was inevitable these two contrasting cultures would clash. 'No wonder the conflict,' Price concludes, 'and no wonder the outcome, despite the efforts of liberal-humanists to avert it.'[15]

In deferring to earlier studies by Willard and Price, Windschuttle taps a deep and rich vein in White Australia's cultural heritage that is still far from exhausted. Since the earliest studies of White Australia appeared in print 80 years ago, historians have resorted to a style of argument that historian Andrew Markus refers to as 'culturalism'.[16] This argument holds that Chinese needed to be excluded not because of who they were (their race) but because they were incapable of appreciating Australian values (their culture). A crude case for the culturalist style of argument can certainly be mounted from the contemporary evidence. Labour, business, political and religious leaders of colonial Australia frequently characterised Chinese immigrants as indentured slaves or servants of Mammon who could not be expected to appreciate the hearty individualism, egalitarianism and spiritual values of New Britannia.[17] Cited without scrutiny, these sources do more to illustrate the problem than to explain it. Neither the historical background to their circulation nor their European ethnographic foundations have been subject to close critical scrutiny in Australia.

Windschuttle repeats the claim that Chinese in Australia lived and worked like slaves, but carries the argument further by tracing their allegedly slavish behaviour to their cultural roots in China. He takes other historians to task for failing to point out that their national culture may have predisposed Chinese immigrants to slip into slavish modes of behaviour on arrival in the Australian colonies. Windschuttle's own account of 19th century Chinese history justifies the caution shown by others. Conflating Maoist totalitarianism with the monastic slavery of an earlier millennium, he arrives at the startling observation that slavery was the norm in China's modern history. Mid-19th century China was, by his account, a land of abject slaves subject to the power of an absolutist state.[18] Windschuttle concludes with an eloquent statement of the ethnographic assumptions underlying the culturalist position:

> *There is no doubt that mid-nineteenth century Australia was the site of an encounter between two quite incompatible cultures. On the one hand was a Chinese culture produced by a society where absolute state power had been the norm for thousands of years, where individual rights counted for nothing, and where the lower orders had been totally dependent on the powerful for the privilege of living. On the other hand stood a burgeoning Australian culture, fresh from a successful campaign against the threat of indentured labour, inheritor of a centuries-old tradition of the 'free-born Englishman' ... A community freeing itself from the hereditary status and privilege of Old Europe met a community steeped in the servility of oriental despotism.*[19]

The ethnographic account of Chinese culture that underlies these claims is as fanciful as a literary hoax. Chinese miners on the Australian goldfields were not indentured and they were not slaves. They came as members of fraternal brotherhoods of the labouring poor and, given time, they set about organising labour unions of their own. Eric Rolls has drawn attention to the case of Chinese cabinet makers in Victoria who formed a union in 1885 to agitate for higher pay and reduced working hours and went on strike in 1893 to protest attempts to reduce their wages in the face of the general depression affecting the colony.[20] Such evidence of Chinese labour militancy did little to encourage Australian workers to lift their bans on Chinese union membership; nor did it stop manufacturers from securing legislation to distinguish Chinese-produced furniture from products made with European labour.

Similarly, the oft-cited workers' claim that 'We want no slave class amongst us' was tactically astute but wrong-headed in implying that Chinese made up a slave caste in the 19th century.[21] They did not. To be sure, a system of large-scale indentured coolie labour developed over the century as a result of European colonisation, but the coolie trade was in no sense a meaningful reflection of popular Chinese customs or values. Chinese labourers were enslaved not by their customs or traditions but by the colonial coolie trade. In any case, indentured coolie labourers – chiefly cooks and shepherds – accounted for a small fraction of Chinese immigrants to Australia in the 19th century.

Nor was China itself a slave society at the time. There were no slave-labour plantations in China as there were in British colonial possessions into the 1830s or as there were in the United States until the conclusion of the Civil War. There was no land-owning aristocracy or hereditary nobility on the scale of contemporary Britain, no lords or serfs on the continental European model. Agricultural land was held in private ownership, farming families generally owned at least part of the land they tilled and the imperial family was not a class of people but a dynastic line of descent.

Neither was late imperial China an absolutist state exercising absolute state power. It was an old-world empire in which 400 million subjects were governed by some 40 000 imperial officials, or roughly one government official for every 10 000 subjects (compared to one official for every 50 people in communist China). The emperor was certainly an important figure of authority but he presided over a largely self-governing society in which local communities enjoyed a similar level of autonomy to that of towns and hamlets in colonial Australia. Even Windschuttle's 'lower orders', as we shall see, were more than capable of looking after themselves.[22]

Invocations of slavery

The attribution of slavery to late imperial Chinese society and culture reflects more the language of modern social and political conflict than the actual state of the Chinese empire or the status of people in China. Actual slavery was certainly an important issue at the time of the founding of the Australian colonies. There were slaves in European colonial territories in Africa and the Americas when the *Endeavour* anchored in Botany Bay in 1770, and the emancipation movement was at its height in Britain when the First Fleet raised its anchors and set sail for Sydney cove in 1787. But in the intervening 17 years, the struggle against actual slavery was joined by a battle over metaphorical slavery waged by Britain's American colonists.

Visiting England in 1770, Benjamin Franklin extended the meaning of slavery to include any class of people who were not masters of their own destinies. He took stern exception to well-meaning British critics of American slave plantations who failed to recognise that the working poor of the English slums were little more than slaves themselves. In America meanwhile petitions against actual slavery were being presented to the British governor of Massachusetts at the very time that wealthy and respectable Bostonians – some of them slave owners in their own right – were casting themselves as slaves in their petitions to the British crown over tea and taxes. Their claims were debated in the English parliament in a similar spirit. Urging the repeal of stamp taxes in the American colonies, William Pitt responded to an opponent on the opposite bench: 'The gentleman asks when were the American colonies liberated? I ask, when were they made slaves?'[23] They were enslaved not by Britain but by the language in which they articulated their demands, a distinctively modern rhetoric of slavery.

This rhetoric was flourishing in the English-speaking world at the very moment white colonisation got under way in Australia. Local colonists came to master the new language of slavery and to apply it selectively to themselves and to others. True to their British heritage, the children of convicts and working-class immigrants to the Australian colonies struggled to escape the taint of convict servitude, to shrug off the stuffy social conventions of England and to earn status and preferment in their native land in the name of freedom and equality. Thus the pioneer poet Charles Harpur: 'Shall the Monarchists condemn us / Into slavery and shame?'[24] Early assertions of a distinctively Australian identity by Harpur and other members of the native-born *literati* took the form of shrugging off 'slavish' adherence to British colonial policies and practices.

At the heart of this new language of slavery and shame, wherever it surfaced, lay an ideal of human dignity. Modern emancipation movements are pulled along by a desire for recognition of equality and at the same time pushed along by the shame that people feel when they are not treated equally. This style of thinking has characterised every movement of its kind in the modern era. As Isaiah Berlin once observed: 'The poor wish to be recognised as human beings – as equals – by the rich, Jews by Christians, the dark-skinned by the fair, women by men, the weak by the strong.' Out of this struggle for recognition emerged the political vocabulary of the modern era, 'the whole terminology of exploitation, degradation, humiliation, dehumanization', which enabled people to distance themselves from what they imagined to be the sources of their slavery and shame. Imperialists and capitalists became slave masters, bosses slave drivers and workers, slaves. It was a language intended to inspire emancipation.[25]

Australia housed a lively emancipation movement in the 19th century. The children of convicts struggled to escape the taint of servitude and to earn recognition and preferment in their native land. White-Australian nativists drew on the political vocabulary of their time to brand Chinese as slaves, irrespective of the merits of the claim. In time, Chinese elites came to brand their own enemies in China as masters and slaves as well, and to characterise the old imperial system as a form of entrenched slavery. The merits of these claims bore little relation to the powerful emancipation struggles they inspired. Indeed, the Chinese communists mastered the vocabulary of humiliation and oppression and profited immensely from its popularisation in the 20th century. Their choice of national anthem for China – one that grows more familiar to the world with every new Olympic victory – begins 'Arise all ye people who do not want to be slaves'. In fact the Chinese struggle against metaphorical slavery gave the Chinese people Mao Zedong just as the struggle against metaphorical slavery gave Australians White Australia. Mao's China and White Australia were each products of what Berlin has called 'the desire for recognition'.

There were, to be sure, as Windschuttle suggests, two major immigrant cultures in mid-19th century Australia, one of them European, the other from China. What distinguished the two was not that one was slavishly beholden to absolute state power while the other cherished the traditions of the free-born Englishman; the question of conflicting values was a second-order issue consequent on more immediate differences that presented themselves to the senses. The bulk of published sources from 19th century Australia indicate that white Australians distinguished Chinese from themselves through sensory impressions arising from contact with a different material culture. It was their physical appearance, bearing, gait, speech, dress, style of cooking and eating, and their manner of building, working and worshipping that chiefly marked Chinese out for comment and caricature. The culturalist argument that racial conflict in Australia represented a clash of civilisations, in which one set of values was pitted against another, diverts evidence of popular racism to the service of a higher cause. Although purporting to explain popular racism, arguments for a clash of values elevate popular racism to a matter of high principle.[26]

The White Australia Policy, the argument goes, was introduced to preserve a fragile Australian way of life from a potentially hostile Chinese way of life. The most substantial histories of the period reject monocausal explanations such as racism in favour of multiple causes embracing a variety of economic, social, cultural and racial factors in play at different points in time.[27] Some conclude all the same that there was an inevitable, perhaps even regrettable, clash of cultures between white and Chinese settlers in colonial Australia that required stern administrative intervention to limit Chinese entry to the colonies in the interests of peace and good order. Something certainly needed to be done to reduce white threats against Chinese residents and to prevent their intermittent trashing of Chinese settlements. Exclusion was the simplest and most readily available administrative option. Historians such as Myra Willard and Keith Windschuttle who trace this administrative decision to irreducible differences in values and beliefs imply that the hostility shown by whites towards Chinese was sanctioned by a commitment to certain values that only white Australians could profess. The case for an historical clash of cultures rests on the assumption that Chinese Australians were, for some reason, less able than white Australians to appreciate 'Australian' values. This assumption has never been seriously tested.

Australians in China

For some reason, Chinese Australians are left out of the national story, even in Australia's dealings with China. In recalling prominent figures who fostered relations between Australia and China over the late 19th or early 20th centuries Australians generally refer in the first instance to George Ernest Morrison and William Henry Donald. Morrison and Donald each worked for major national and international newspapers and served as advisers to presidents or first ladies in the Chinese Republic. They are perhaps not as well known today as their achievements merit but each has attracted at least one formal biography.[28] Morrison is the more famous of the two. As well as a number of books about him, his correspondence has been published in several volumes edited by Lo Hui-min and his contributions to Sino–Australian relations are commemorated annually in the Morrison Lecture series, which has convened almost without interruption in Canberra since 1931.[29] The lecture series has also yielded independent publications that bear his name. For all these reasons the name of George Ernest Morrison is familiar to many in Australia and abroad.

In contrast, the names of prominent figures among Morrison's Chinese-Australian contemporaries are hardly known, even among historians of Australia. Two of them, William Liu and William Ah Ket, did more than any other Australian to commemorate Morrison's memory by initiating and endowing the Morrison Lecture series. Little attempt has been made to commemorate either of his benefactors or the many other Chinese Australians who moved and worked constantly between China and Australia, many of them no less active than Morrison in promoting international trade, bilateral diplomacy and cultural exchange between China and Australia. To date only one Chinese-Australian personality, the flamboyant Sydney tea merchant Quong Tart, has merited a full-length biography in English.[30]

At this point we need to pause and take account of two distinctive features of Chinese-Australian community life over the period in question. One was the scale and frequency with which Chinese Australians moved between China and Australia in Morrison's day; the other, the gendered character of residence and movement. Around 100 000 people entered Australia from China between the 1840s and federation in 1901.[31] At the time of federation 30 000 Chinese immigrants and their descendents were entitled by right of abode to travel to and from China, albeit with discriminatory certification. Over the first two decades of the 20th century some 28 000 registered Chinese departures and arrivals are recorded for New South Wales alone, overshadowing by three to four times the total registered Chinese population of the state.[32] Some of these travellers doubtless journeyed overland from other states to Sydney to board their ships for China. Paul Jones estimates that over the four decades from 1901 to 1939, Chinese Australians made 80 000 journeys to or from Australia.[33] At the close of this period there were no more than 15 000 Chinese-Australian residents on the continent. Some may have been returning home to live out their final years but most were simply travelling to and from Australia.

Most of these people were men. Even allowing that goldrush settlements were made up overwhelmingly of men, the gender ratio of Chinese immigrants was exceptional. In 1861 no more than eight women were recorded among the 24 732 people of Chinese descent (0.03 per cent) who entered the colony of Victoria. The proportion of women increased marginally over the following decade, to 31 of a total of 17 826 Chinese residents in 1871 (0.17 per cent), and to 164 of 11 950 Chinese residents in 1881 (1.37 per cent). In Australia as a whole, the Chinese-Australian population of 29 627 at the time of federation included just 474 women (1.6 per cent).[34]

By this time, some 1500 boys and a similar number of girls were registered as offspring of Chinese men and women or of Chinese men and women of European or Aboriginal descent.[35] Further intermarriages and second-generation marriages between female offspring and Chinese-Australian males pushed the gender ratio towards a more natural balance over time. The proportion of females among Australians of Chinese descent increased to around 14 per cent by 1921. By the late 1920s and 1930s, Jones has estimated, females with one or two parents of Chinese descent made up close to one-quarter of the Chinese-Australian community.[36] Much can be made of these figures. Historians generally assume that the absence of accompanying females signalled the intention of Chinese male immigrants to return home to China. This assumption is not, as we shall see, well founded. In light of the gendered demographics of Chinese settlement in Australia over the 19th and early 20th centuries, the present study is concerned chiefly, albeit not exclusively, with Chinese-Australian men.[37]

The great majority of voyages between China and Australia over this period were undertaken by Chinese-Australian men travelling on business and family matters, the benefactors of the Morrison Lectures among them. William Ah Ket was one of 'seven little Australians' born to court interpreter and businessman Mah Ket in the 1870s and 1880s. After graduating in law from the University of Melbourne, William was invited in 1904 to join the Bar as the first barrister of Chinese descent in that city. He was one of several Chinese-Australian community leaders to enjoy a national profile in the early years of federation.[38] Much of his public life was devoted to the battle against discriminatory restrictions affecting Chinese immigration and industry, and to prohibiting the importation of opium, which was legally traded throughout the British empire to the particular detriment of Chinese communities. He was a founding member and Grand Master of the East Caulfield Masonic Lodge No. 123. His interests carried him several times to China, at one point in 1912 as an Australian representative to China's inaugural Republican National Convention.

William Liu was also a frequent traveller to China on family and business matters. Born in Sydney in 1893 of a Chinese father and English mother, Liu was sent to his father's home district of Toishan at the age of seven after his mother fell grievously ill. Eight years later he was recalled to Sydney to complete his education and, in 1912, he moved to the federal capital of Melbourne to work for the Republican Chinese Consulate. When Morrison met him in Sydney in 1917, Liu had not long been appointed founding director of the Australia–China Mail Steamship Line, a position he held until 1924. This was a substantial position. Morrison recorded after their meeting that Liu had recently purchased the steamship, *SS Gabo*, for £20 500, one of several ships owned or chartered by the Line, including *SS Victoria* and *SS Hwah Ping*.[39] In later years William Liu worked closely with the NSW Chinese Chamber of Commerce. He also helped to found the NSW branch of the Australia–China Chamber of Commerce and Industry on which he served as the inaugural governor of chamber. From the 1920s to 1940s Liu moved frequently between China and Australia, advising the Australian trade commission in Shanghai and the four great Australian department store chains that opened for business in Hong Kong, Canton and Shanghai over that period. When he died in 1983, Liu's passing was commemorated with the publication of a beautifully illustrated booklet containing a brief pictorial tribute, one of the few biographical records in English of an Australian of Chinese descent.[40]

Many other Chinese Australians played seminal roles in the establishment of Chinese-Australian commercial, social, cultural and political ties from the goldrush period to the close of the Second World War. They bore names such as Liu and Kwok and Lee and Mouy and Chan and Choy, names little known in Australia relative to China Morrison and other white Australians of their day, but widely recognised outside of Australia for their contributions to bilateral relations. Some sought to honour the name of Morrison by endowing an annual lecture in his name. This book is intended to honour some of them in turn.

Among the more prominent Chinese Australians who appear in the following pages are the legendary figure Loong Hung Pung who led the underground Yee Hing (triad) network on the goldfields of western New South Wales in the late 19th century, and his heirs and successors who built up the network's links with revolutionary cells in China. Among the latter was the revolutionary James See, from Grafton in northern New South Wales, whose father worked alongside Loong

Hung Pung before returning to China with his family and establishing an underground revolutionary network to bring down the Manchu empire. The young James See created China's first revolutionary party in partnership with Sun Yatsen in 1895, and helped found Hong Kong's pre-eminent English-language newspaper, the *South China Morning Post*. Among his contemporaries were John Moy Sing and James Chuey who between them transformed the underground Yee Hing network into the Chinese Masonic Society and consolidated a national base for the organisation in Sydney from around the turn of the century. Equally significant are the founders and members of the NSW Chinese Chamber of Commerce, the oldest Chinese chamber in the world after that in Hong Kong, and the Ma, Gock, Lee, Liew and Choy families, who built China's finest and grandest department stores in Shanghai on the model of Anthony Horderns in Sydney. Members of another Chinese organisation in Sydney, the Society to Protect the Emperor (*Baohuanghui*), invited the political reformer and leading intellectual of the day, Liang Qichao, to tour Australian cities and towns at the time of federation. The founders and members of the many Chinese home-district clubs (or native-place associations) in Australia vied with these public associations for influence in the community. And the archive of the immensely powerful Australasian Kuo Min Tang (KMT), recently opened, reveals the names and addresses of the chefs and market gardeners who kept Australia's towns and cities going by day, and those of the gamblers, musicians, dancers and debutantes who livened up the cities at night.

The hoax of John Chinaman

I do not recall hearing anything about these Australians and their organisations when I studied Australian history at school in the 1960s or attended university lectures in the 1970s. The one Chinese-Australian source that enjoyed wide currency in my university days was a translated selection of letters written by Hwuy Ung from Melbourne to a brother in China sometime towards the end of the 19th century and published in 1927 under the title *A Chinaman's Opinion of Us and of His Own Country*. The English sinologist JA Makepeace was credited with finding and translating the letters.[41] In the 1960s, selections of Makepeace's translations began to circulate widely through the Francophone and Anglophone worlds following the publication of selected extracts in Roger Pelissier's popular annotated collection of historical documents *Chine entre en scene* (1963); the book appeared four years later in English under the title *The Awakening of China*.[42] Pelissier's extracts from Hwuy Ung's letters were widely used in Chinese history classes from the 1960s to the 1980s.

To read Hwuy Ung's letters is to appreciate their effortless appeal. They carry extensive comments on the habits and customs of White Australia as seen by a casual visitor from the Orient unfamiliar with the British way of life. On current fashions in male dress, for example, Hwuy Ung complained to his brother:

> *Their garments are tight-fitting, and very uncomfortable in hot weather … Around the neck they wear a hard band which took me a long time to endure; it is most unpleasant in this hot weather, for it is like a small cangue. Other articles worn around the wrists like manacles are also of linen, hardened with gum, and very shiny. Why they should punish themselves with wearing these things I do not know, unless it may be as a penance for their sins, as is the practice of some of our Buddhist monks … Their movements, nevertheless, are quick and abrupt; what they would do without the restraint of their garments, I do not fancy; perhaps these cramping clothes are a necessary check to their fury, instituted by their sages.*[43]

Hwuy Ung also wrote home about the local passion for spectator sports. *Kli-kei* he described as a game where 'players struck fiercely with heavy flat club at a hard ball, and sometimes hit. Then ran past each other between sticks stuck in the earth, as if hunted by ox-headed tormentors'. Another game, *Foo-poh*, was 'same as a battle; two groups of men in struggling contention … Men on one side try to kick goose-egg pattern ball between two poles that represent a gate or entrance … knock each other down running in pursuit of the ball to send it through the enemy's pole'. Australian women merit particular mention. 'You my venerable brother know how we measure a woman: that she must neither be seen nor mentioned by strangers.' In Melbourne, however, 'women are freeing themselves from the rule of men and, like liberated slaves, become tyrants'.[44]

The tortured English of the translations should early have roused suspicions about the provenance of the letters. Forty years after their publication Arthur Huck showed that they were nothing more than a fanciful product of Makepeace's imagination, a complete hoax.[45] In fact, they did not come close to representing local Chinese impressions of colonial Australia. Nor did they capture the flavour of Chinese-Australian life at the time. Residents of metropolitan Melbourne, Sydney, Hobart, Brisbane, Adelaide or Perth, and many regional towns between, would have observed Chinese comfortably attired in Western dress in the 1890s and early 1900s, perhaps taking picnics and bathing at the seaside, showing off their photographs, riding the latest bicycles, reading English as well as Chinese-language newspapers, and playing Australian football in their local leagues.[46] Few visitors from China would have had to wait until setting foot in Australia before catching their first sight of Western dress, manners or the everyday artefacts of Western material culture. The entrepots and treaty ports from which émigrés embarked along the China coast were modernising at a pace to match Melbourne and Sydney, if not London and New York.

Makepeace's Chinaman was an ethnographic hoax, an artful representation of an archaic voice reflecting upon the changing morals and manners of Western modernity as seen from another place and, as it were, from another time. At the heart of Makepeace's invention lay an assumption about the cultural ambience of time itself. For Makepeace, China was not just an alien place, but an ancient time, or rather a place caught in time in a way that the progressive West was not. He fabricated his story within an established literary genre of timeless Oriental travellers who imparted words of wisdom on the clash of cultures between a dynamic and progressive West on the one side and a timeless and unchanging Orient on the other. Although transported to Marvellous Melbourne, Hwuy Ung was trapped in the same time warp that marked out China as a cultural space. He was a derivative sample of the popular ethnographic portrait of John Chinaman that circulated in Western art and letters from the 18th century and that still has its place in the Australian historical imagination.

The fictional genre of Chinese travellers' tales is customarily dated to Oliver Goldsmith's *The Citizen of the World: Or, Letters from a Chinese*

Philosopher Residing in London to his Friends in the East, which was presented
to the English reading public under Chinese authorship in 1762.[47]
The genre was revived early in the 20th century with the publication
in 1903 of *Letters from a Chinese Official, Being an Eastern View of Western
Civilization* written by the English philosopher G Lowes Dickinson.[48]
Adopting the tone of a Chinese mandarin, Dickinson wrote of China
as a timeless and stable civilisation that was anchored to an unchanging
moral order in contrast to the dynamic but rootless West, which was
being driven to 'economic chaos' by its obsession with progress. Many
of his contemporaries were fooled by Dickinson's invention, including
US Democratic Party candidate William Jennings Bryan, who penned a
rebuttal entitled *Letters to a Chinese Official* (1906) after taking offence at
the Chinese official's dim views of Western morality and progress.[49] The
public conversation between Dickinson and Bryan, which contrasted
the embedded values of a timeless China and the peripatetic ways of a
modernising West, embraced the differences separating a conservative
Cambridge don from a progressive Illinois Democrat. Their literary
conversation took place half a world away from China.

White Australian commentaries on China and the Chinese in the
19th and early 20th centuries adopted a similarly derivative style of
popular ethnography that bore equally little relation to China. There
is little surviving evidence of literary fraud among White Australian
writings on China. Nevertheless, virtual or surrogate versions of Hwuy
Ung are everywhere to be found in White Australian historical writings
on Chinese Australians. The comic figure of John Chinaman that was
frequently portrayed in the popular Australian press of the day bore a
close resemblance to the timeless and occasionally shiftless Oriental who
passed through the pages of Goldsmith's, Dickinson's and Makepeace's
inventions. Indeed, John Chinaman was no more authentic than Hwuy
Ung. His ubiquitous image derived from a style of popular ethnography
common to the Anglophone world of the 19th century.

Similarly, derivative conventions were at work in China over the
same period, some based on indigenous traditions of travellers' tales,
others drawing explicitly on recent Western travel fantasies. Early in
the 20th century fictional Occidentals started showing up in China
where they spoke (in Chinese) as authoritative Westerners on the

subject of Oriental customs and habits.[50] Shen Congwen selected Lewis Carroll's *Alice in Wonderland* as a model for reflecting on Chinese use of Western ways of writing about the Chinese. In *Alice in China* (1928), he confounded Alice's innocent transferral into the Chinese idiom by ensuring that she was fully acquainted with the established European ethnography of the Chinaman before she set foot in China.[51] Alice prepares for her voyage by reading an English *Guidebook to China* written by an eminent sinologist. On her arrival in China she sets about testing the book's quaint stereotypes against the actual people she encounters, in the company of the White Rabbit. In this case Alice is converted into a device for Chinese exploration of the ways in which the Chinese have come to be represented by Europeans and for ironic reflection on the fact that a modern Chinese author's explorations of Chinese characteristics should have to take serious account of the impressions of a fictional English girl and her pet rabbit.

Chinese observers were burdened with an insight lacking in the Anglophone ethnographic tradition. The China they knew was just as dynamic as the West. Significantly, what sparks Alice's interest in visiting China is the alarming prospect that the timeless Chinaman of the European imagination is on the verge of extinction. In his place was emerging a new genus of modern Chinese people who closely resemble Europeans. In the opening scene of *Alice in China*, Alice is advised to hasten to China before the timeless wonderland disappears under the assault of the modern. Go quickly, she is told, for very soon 'all the most curious customs will disappear and all of the people will be turned into Modern People'. These 'Modern People,' Alice is informed, 'are much the same as Europeans. Their clothes are made of the same coarse wool and their collars are stiff and white'. She might well have been citing the fabulous Hwuy Ung. Alice hastily packed her bags and took the next boat bound for China.

While there were doubtless serious aspects to each of their writings, the fantasy novels of Shen Congwen and other Chinese travel fabulists were written in good fun, in much the same spirit as the hoaxes perpetrated by Goldsmith and Makepeace. More seriously, the outlines of the Chinese character described in these fictional conversations on John Chinaman were reproduced without irony in newspapers, cartoons and public petitions in white-settler communities around the Pacific Rim. In the popular and pictorial press of Australia's federation period, for example, Chinese were widely pictured as slaves to manners and morals that had not changed for a millennium, not unlike the Chinamen found in Alice's *Guidebook to China*. This popular Anglophone portrait of the Chinese continues to be reproduced in histories of 19th and early 20th century Australia. Even Makepeace's fraudulent work is counted among the few 'authentic' Chinese-Australian sources still in global circulation.[52]

This book takes its cue from this resilient tradition of popular Anglophone ethnography. Its subject is not racism but something bigger still. That is to say, the subject of this book is not the 'White' in White Australia, but the foundational premise of Australia itself that universal values are the special preserve of a particular people and that they remain culturally alien to other kinds of people. This premise may or may not be racist. Classical racism holds that the characteristics of a group of people, including their behaviour, are biologically determined: the norms and conduct peculiar to a people are passed down from generation to generation in the same way that physical characteristics such as skin colour, eyes and hair are inherited. This biological style of racism does not seem to have played as prominent part in the White Australian story as it has in the American one. Nevertheless the idea that Australia is characterised by a unique set of values that have been articulated though an historical clash of cultures with Asian or Chinese values remains a foundational premise of Australian nationalism to this day.

In Australia, the clash-of-cultures thesis rests on a model of cultural inheritance that is functionally equivalent to classical racism. In this case a distinctive set of cultural traits is transmitted from generation to generation by the force of culture, language and tradition. Either way, people are first classified according to type and then attributed certain values peculiar to their kind. To be Chinese is to look Chinese and at the same time think and behave in ways that authoritative sinological voices identify as distinctively Chinese. If the imputed Chinese style of thinking and behaving appears inconsistent with the values and beliefs of others (white Australians, for example) then simply looking Chinese is inconsistent with being Australian. For Chinese caught up in this style of argument there is no escaping its circuitous logic. Any profession of belief in Australian values merely indicates they are not authentic Chinamen. This style of culturalism requires explanation on its own account.

The tenacity of the culturalist argument in Australian history can be traced to a premise of Australian nationalism that Australia is an egalitarian, progressive and tolerant society in contrast to class-ridden Britain and the hierarchical societies to Australia's north. In the Australian national imaginary, the imagined clash between Western liberalism and 'Oriental despotism' – or, more parochially, between Australian values and Chinese values – cannot easily be separated from the residual conflict between ideals of social, cultural and material progress on the one hand and the spectre of resistant social and cultural traditions on the other. Chinese are inducted into this conflict on the side of immobile tradition whether they like it or not.

Chinese Australians certainly did not like it in the colonial and White Australia periods. They may not have cared greatly whether the treatment meted out to them was driven by racism, culturalism or simple ignorance, but they did want a fair go and to receive due recognition of their rights as equal subjects before the law. They challenged the culturalist style of argument from the earliest years of colonial settlement. In 1855, for example, the Chinese interpreter Howqua informed a Victorian colonial inquiry that China was not only capable of adapting to modern times but was also in fact changing as he spoke. 'The Chinese now are all Freemasons, and form one brotherhood,' he insisted in his imperfect English. 'The new emperor intends to carry out all one brotherhood.'[53] As a cross-cultural translator Howqua could not have failed to observe the value placed upon popular government and fraternal mateship in colonial Victoria. His insistence that China had already come under the sway of an egalitarian brotherhood of Chinese Freemasons led by the Taiping pretender to the throne (in 1855) was an interpreter's attempt to demonstrate the appeal of egalitarian and fraternal values to people who happened to come from China. As we shall see, similar experiments with fraternal mateship and democratic governance were under way among Chinese émigrés in the Dutch East Indies, where they carved out independent democratic republics of gold miners (to the consternation of Dutch colonial authorities) in the 1850s.

Many an interpreter then and since has pointed out in broken English that China is as dynamic a society as any other, that Chinese culture is as vital and adaptable as any other culture and that people from China are as happy to embrace the egalitarian vision of the modern republic as any other people. Their claims have generally fallen on deaf ears. Few Chinese immigrants to Australia intended to discard their language on mastering English, to forget their annual festivals when they switched to the Gregorian calendar, to abandon classical learning when they adopted Christianity or to exchange pork for mutton on their tables. Few imagined that eating pork or speaking Cantonese was an obstacle to being modern, egalitarian or even Australian.[54] But white Australian assumptions about the timeless character of China and the Chinese were impervious to periodic challenges from Chinese in Australia proclaiming their common humanity, or pointing to the dynamism of China itself. The persistent deafness of white Australia was a necessary condition for the persistent exclusion of Chinese from Australia and from their claim to being counted as Australians.

The characteristics ascribed to the Chinese in Australian history can be traced to popular ethnographic accounts that were shaped by the conditions under which men from China lived and worked in colonial and federation Australia. These conditions were designed to make John Chinamen of them. The values proclaimed by white Australia, including its egalitarian spirit and its ethos of mateship, effectively limited the scope for Chinese participation in public and private life. On their arrival in Australia Chinese found a predominantly white settler community that espoused a popular ethic of egalitarian solidarity governed under the firm hand of British rule of law. They were regarded by this community as hierarchical, separatist and lawless. They entered a society that competed for opportunities to acquire wealth and respectability through industry, agriculture and trade, and that supported a progressive organised labour movement. They were subject to commercial boycotts and not welcomed into the organised labour movement. They entered communities that valued the wholesome and self-reliant family but were not permitted to invite their own families to accompany them to Australia without suffering impossible financial penalties levied through discriminatory poll taxes. From the turn of the century Chinese residents could not leave the country and return without undergoing intrusive and humiliating finger-printing and photographing, and securing Certificates of Exemption from the Dictation Test along with copious letters of reference from upstanding whites. These conditions of life shaped the practice of being Chinese in colonial and early federation Australia and shaped White Australian understanding of John Chinaman.

Where Chinese settlers encountered different circumstances in their host states their patterns of immigrations, adaptation and settlement differed accordingly. In the Dutch East Indies, for example, Chinese miners built democratic and egalitarian communities based on shareholding partnerships in large-scale mining operations. Dutch colonial ethnography differed accordingly. Where Australian ethnography focused on the passivity, slavishness and hierarchical character of John Chinaman, Dutch ethnographic writings on the character of the Chinese focused instead on their sturdy independence, radical egalitarianism and democratic republicanism.[55]

So it was that immigrants from China found the pathetic figure of John Chinaman awaiting them on their arrival in Australia, ready to pick up his carrying pole and follow them wherever they went. Many adapted reasonably well to the challenge. For most, adaptation meant organisation. Chinese Australians were prodigious organisers, forming religious congregations, native-place associations, chambers of commerce, Chinese Masonic lodges, philanthropic societies and political parties that enjoyed links with similar bodies throughout Australia and the Asia–Pacific region. Through membership of these fraternal associations they extended their social networks beyond the range of their immediate families and friends to establish successful business ventures, mount claims for equality of treatment and provide comfort and support for one another.

2
MATESHIP AND MODERNITY

The Coolie Classes have captured the Government in Australia

Japanese statesman, 1904.[1]

In contemporary Australia, membership of the nation is increasingly measured by the values that its citizens profess. In this respect it rather resembles France or the United States of America. But where French citizens swear to uphold 'the rights of man' and Americans declare it to be self-evident 'that all men are created equal', Australians are expected to embrace national values rather than universal human ones. In point of fact there is little to distinguish Australian values from the universal rights of man. *Liberté, egalité* and *fraternité* are translated into Australian dialect as freedom, egalitarianism and mateship. They are nationalised in the act of translation.[2] This chapter explores the wider global setting in which Australian values began to crystallise in the 19th century with a view to grasping what was universal and what was Australian about them.

The argument mounted here is that freedom, egalitarianism and mateship were local Australian idiom for the modern ethical principle that people are born free and equal. This principle was well established in 19th century Europe and America and, as we shall see, by the late 19th century it had come to hold considerable appeal in China and Japan as well. Within Australia, however, the principle that people are born free and equal was not applied universally. What made universal values particularly Australian was their selective application to whites. Historian Charles Price has framed the historical problem well. Australian conservatives, radicals and liberals who held that all men had certain inalienable social and political rights were not, he observed, inclined to include men from China in the category of 'all men'.[3] Chinese were to be excluded from Australia because they were held to be incapable of appreciating the universal values that made some people particularly Australian.

This chapter covers the ethical grounds put forward to exclude Chinese from Australia in the 19th and 20th centuries and some of the major historical arguments on which their historical exclusion rests today. It challenges two strong claims levelled against Chinese in Australian national histories. One is that the great majority of Chinese miners entered Australia as indentured labourers and hence shared few of the values of the 'free-born Englishmen' that shaped Australian nationality and nationalism. The second is that Chinese came to Australia with the intention of making their fortunes and returning to their villages. Their preference for leaving their wives and families at home is said to offer irrefutable evidence that Chinese males had no intention of settling down in Australia. There is some truth to each of these claims but, as we shall see, far more that is misleading.

National values and Chinese exclusion

Historically speaking, the claim that Australian values are uniquely Australian has provided a powerful rhetorical armoury for public officials seeking to exercise administrative discretion over who should and should not be admitted into the country. Launching the national-values framework for Australian schools in 2005, then Education Minister Brendan Nelson warned that 'If people don't want to be Australians and they don't want to live by Australian values and understand them, well, basically, they can clear off'.[4] The bureaucratic edifice of White Australia operated on the same principle: that Australia was a community of values, but with the additional premise that there was an exact fit between race and value. Being white was a necessary and sufficient indicator that someone would understand and live by Australian values. This insistence on the national particularity of Australian values was essential for the effective functioning of administrative regimes set up to manage lawful exclusion from White Australia. There is no longer a simple correspondence between race and value in contemporary Australia but the claim that people should be excluded, not on account of their race or colour but because they cannot appreciate Australian values, is as pervasive today as it was in the era of White Australia.

Discussion of Australian values and the Australian way of life in federation Australia played a comparable role to debates on race in the United States of America in the late 19th and early 20th centuries. In the official manner of speaking peculiar to White Australia, Chinese and other people of colour were excluded from the country because they were culturally predisposed to think and behave in a different kind of way from white Australians on important matters of principle. In an elaborate bureaucratic ruse, White Australian immigration authorities tested intending immigrants for tolerable cultural traits, specifically, by requiring them to pass a written dictation test in a European language in order to gain entry. If they happened to be fluent in English and committed to modern, liberal and egalitarian values, they could be asked to take the test in a language they would be certain to fail.

In October 1908, for example, the Commonwealth Department of External Affairs learnt that China's leading reformer and Enlightenment philosopher, Kang Youwei, intended to visit Australia. Kang was an admirer of the egalitarian modernity of Edward Bellamy and had published influential tracts in his own name on the subject of racial, cultural, gender and national equality. To Australian authorities his profile as an egalitarian reformer made Kang a less, rather than a more, desirable visitor.[5] Believing it highly likely that Kang spoke English, the departmental secretary instructed the collector of customs in Fremantle 'to apply the test say in Spanish or Italian' if necessary to ensure that he could not pass the dictation test.

US immigration policy was different in that it operated on explicitly racial principles. As human beings, Chinese could not possibly fail the test of universal values enshrined in the Constitution of the United States. They were excluded instead on the self-evident ground that they were 'Chinese persons'.[6] Needless to say, the different approaches adopted in Australia and the United States had a similar effect in limiting Chinese entry to a white-settler society. Where American racism was blunt and to the point, Australia's approach was mealy-mouthed. The circuitous logic of official reasoning in Australia ensured that Chinese would not be welcome, however they thought or behaved, because Chinese were understood to embrace a different suite of national values.

The question of whether federal government practices in the White Australia era were racist has generated considerable heat among Australian historians. The ethical and cultural reasoning underlying claims about Australian values, on the other hand, has not been systematically challenged. In the preceding chapter it was noted that an important and persistent trend in Australian historical writing has been the claim that a fundamental clash of cultures between Chinese and Australian values supplied the primary motive and sufficient cause for Chinese exclusion from Australia for the better part of a century from the 1880s to the 1960s. Out of this history has emerged an ethnographic portrait of the Chinese that mirrors and inverts all things Australian. Chinese are hierarchical and not egalitarian, cruel rather than fair, put profit before friendship, demonstrate slavish adherence in place of sturdy independence and prefer Oriental despotism to Australian democracy. The stereotyping of Chinese culture and values around hierarchy and servility was instrumental in the stereotyping of Australian national values around mateship, equality and the fair go.

This chapter introduces evidence for an argument that will be sustained throughout the book – that the ideals that White Australia proclaimed for itself were no less appealing to Chinese Australians than they were to other Australians. Chinese home-town clubs and Masonic fraternities were as egalitarian and democratic as their counterparts in the white labour movement, in Irish Catholic sodalities and in local lodges of colonial and federation Freemasonry. That said, egalitarian brotherhoods of Chinese miners, gardeners and merchants were as

likely to pull rank as bishops in Catholic sodalities and no less inclined
to dress up in hierarchical regalia than colonial Freemasons. There is
more than a little myth in the stories of equality, mateship and the fair
go embellished by white settlers, and more than a little in the stories
that Chinese Australians tell about themselves. The point is that white
and Chinese Australians embraced similar myths about similar values.

Chinese were also among the first Australians to embrace modern
technologies and take up modishly modern lifestyles. In the 1890s they
rode the latest bicycles, in the 1900s they wore sober business suits
and flounced dresses, in the 1910s they picnicked by the seaside, in the
1920s they ran radio repair shops and in wartime they flew Australian
flags.[7] Chinese Australians probably travelled more frequently than
whites and they discovered in their travels that Australia was one of
very few countries where all of the technological and ethical promises
of modernity were on offer. Modern and mobile as they were, however,
Chinese Australians could never qualify as white Australians.

Those who most closely approximated the British-Australian
way of life earned public acclaim as savvy Orientals rather than true-
blue Australians. The Sydney tea merchant Quong Tart married an
Englishwoman, Margaret Scarlett, and raised his family as Christians
on a diet of beef and potatoes in a Victorian mansion in the Sydney
suburb of Ashfield.[8] Quong Tart was a keen cricketer and shooter, fond
of donning a kilt and, when called on to do so, could recite the verses
of Robbie Burns in a lilting Scottish brogue. Quong Tart was widely
respected in Sydney, indeed, was one of the first people of Chinese
descent in the world to be admitted into a Freemason order. Yet to
larrikins lounging about on street corners, to members of the organised
labour movement, to native-born Australian nationalists or to journalists
working for the robustly patriotic popular press, Quong Tart remained
a Chinaman.

This did not worry the man himself. As Sophie Couchman has
noted, Quong Tart wore his kilt and cultivated a Scottish accent and
a fondness for tea and scones to promote the brand recognition of his
Sydney tea shops.[9] Nevertheless, the futility of his efforts to be British
confirmed for other Chinese Australians that immigrants from China
could not become Australian simply by adopting Australian values and

adopting the British-Australian way of life. The colour bar made sure of that. 'No nigger, no Chinaman, no Lascar, no Kanaka, no purveyor of cheap coloured labor,' *The Bulletin* declared in 1887, 'is an Australian.'[10] Other newspapers put other views, sometimes more generous ones. At an official level, however, from the late 19th to the mid-20th century White Australia was really the only Australia on offer.

Australian values and human values

From the earliest days of European settlement white Australians appear to have held a widespread commitment to individualism, equality, fair play and mateship. Historians tell us that the terms 'mateship' and 'fair play' entered into daily conversation as expressions of the everyday values of native-born white Australians in their confrontations with local elites and British colonial authorities.[11] By the late 19th century these terms had become staple expressions in Australian poetry and bush legend. Early in the 20th century they were elevated to national values through family memories of the Great War, and later through public commemorations reinforced by historical re-enactments, played out in books, films, on stage and on television. Prominent historians earned credit for scripting the official version. The ANZAC historian CEW Bean was among the first to codify mateship as an official national creed 'of which the chief article was that a man should at all times and at any cost stand by his mate. That was and is the one law which the good Australian must never break'.[12]

Since Bean's time Australian values have occasionally attracted criticism and derision. A long-standing feminist critique holds that the popular mythology surrounding mateship diminishes the historical contributions of women. In public life it carries implications of cronyism or jobs for the boys. Some critics have pointed out that Indigenous and Asian Australians have rarely been welcomed into the fraternity of white Australian mateship. And egalitarianism, according to its critics, strains again the pursuit of excellence.[13] Quibbles of this order have barely made a dent in the popular status of mateship, fair play and egalitarianism as national values. Any discussion of a nation's fundamental values needs to take them seriously if it is to question their application in public life.

The challenge, as political scientist Judith Brett has put it, lies in telling 'different stories to one's fellow Australians about their past and present and bonds they share'.[14] The stories told in the following chapters illustrate the appeal of values that white Australians called Australian values to people who were not, by their reckoning, white.

The appeal of Australian values should not surprise us. They were local expressions of a revolutionary moral order that was looming into view across Western Europe and the Americas at the time of white Australian settlement. The social imaginary of modernity, as Charles Taylor has dubbed this new moral order, held that individuals were fundamentally equal, that social differentiation was accidental and contingent among fellow nationals, and that the rights, freedoms and benefits associated with membership of a civic community should be shared equally by all.[15] These ideals were articulated in Australian dialect as egalitarianism, fair play and mateship. Australian values were only thinkable insofar as they surfaced among wider intellectual currents flowing through the home countries of immigrants embarking for Australia.

Historically, this modern egalitarian ethic expanded through a sequence of moves from one society to another, progressively overwriting premodern hierarchical relationships of kingship, estates and families. Starting at the outer reaches of the kingdom, the egalitarian ethic challenged the divine right of kings before moving forward to question the social orders that prevailed in medieval estates and villages, eventually striking at the last bastion of the hierarchical order, the family, in the 20th century. Along the way the obscure theses of late-medieval religious heretics and the tendentious hypotheses of Enlightenment philosophers entered into a kind of universal common sense that affirmed the equality of individuals and the right to free association as the only sensible foundations for rational social order.[16]

While the vocabulary of this modern social and political revolution varied from one society to another it preserved a common concern for equality, fraternity and freedom wherever it surfaced. New phrases were invented to characterise old hierarchical regimes as leviathans that made slaves or prisoners of men. Revolutionaries in France proclaimed the principles of liberty, equality and fraternity. Their counterparts in the United States declared that all men were born free and equal.

Britons raised their tankards to the chorus of 'Rule Britannia, Britannia rules the waves / Britons never never never will be slaves'. Later still, cosmopolitan internationalists joined the chorus with 'Arise ye workers from your slumbers / arise ye prisoners of want'. These commonplace references to liberty and equality on the one hand, and to slaves or prisoners on the other, drew on the new ethical vocabulary of modernity to give expression to universal struggles for civic and human equality. In societies around the globe, public expressions of personal, civic and national grievance resorted to a common vocabulary of humiliation and oppression, resistance and liberation, equality and dignity, all of them grounded in the social imaginary of modernity.[17]

The timing of Australian settlement

The establishment of a prison settlement in New South Wales happened to coincide with the rise of this new moral sensibility in England, which was alive to justice, equality, the presumption of innocence, the right to life and the ways in which particular customs and habits (such as adherence to mateship) could bind people together into 'nations of men'. Some of these notions were transported to Australia with convicted felons. One early sign of the new dispensation was the creation of a court of law, in preference to a military tribunal, to serve the first penal settlement. Even convicts, as historian Alan Atkinson has observed, 'were technically to be allowed the status of free men and women when they appeared before the court'.[18] Convicts came to Australia with what would later be termed inalienable human rights.

In an insightful discussion of the legal and ethical dimensions of slavery and servitude at the time convicts were first consigned to New South Wales, Atkinson records the case of *Somerset v. Stewart* (1772) in which Lord Mansfield passed judgment on the relationship between race, slavery and immigration. Mansfield ruled that the Virginian slave James Somerset, who had entered England in the company of his master Charles Stewart, was within his rights in refusing to accompany Stewart to the West Indies as his master instructed. Lawyers in the case argued at length about the common-law implications of customary English variants of slavery, including medieval villeinage, orphaned child apprentices, foot soldiers pressed into her majesty's service and the growing prevalence of labour gangs made up of convicted felons. But never in English law had slavery been applied explicitly to race. 'In all these cases bondage, and even forced transportation, might be imposed without consent,' Lord Mansfield ruled. 'But none of them seemed to apply to labouring men and who happened to be black.'[19] White convicts could be sent to New South Wales under conditions akin to slavery but James Somerset, a black slave, was entitled to enjoy his liberty in England.

A similar sense of what was right and just prevailed in the early Australian settlements, even to the point of retaining Mansfield's sensitivity to race. Nothing more galled native-born white Australians than the prospect that servitude and slavery might be perpetuated in the new south land. Even as Charles Harpur was penning his rhetorical question – 'Shall the Monarchists condemn us / Into slavery and shame?'[20] – an influx of new chums from China was descending on the colonies. Harpur and his peers excoriated the new arrivals not because they 'happened to be' Chinese, as Lord Mansfield might have put it, but because they imagined that Chinese could not appreciate their own historical struggle with monarchy, tyranny and shame.

This self-consciously Australian struggle against servitude, Andrew Markus has pointed out, framed white Australian responses to Chinese immigration in the goldrush era.[21] The arrival of Chinese added an unwelcome complication to the local struggle against British tyranny. So white Australians cannily adapted the verses of *Rule Britannia* to associate the ubiquitous Chinaman with slaves, in place of the more obvious association with their own convict ancestors. Instead of 'Britons never never never will be slaves', they roared 'No more Chinamen allowed in New South Wales'. At the same time, the organised labour movement announced 'We want no slave class amongst us.'[22] Chinese had every reason to resent being branded as slaves, but they had no say in the matter once Chinese slavery became an axiom of Australian nationalism. The servile Chinaman served as an inverted template of the free and equal white man.

The exclusion of Chinese from white-settler society in Australia highlights a paradox of egalitarian modernity itself – its reliance on racial categories. The modern egalitarian ethic operates around mass systems of classification that ascribe particular characteristics to whole categories of people. Earlier hierarchical orders generally classified people by their relative rank order in specific social relationships. Thus a daughter was subordinate to a wife, a wife to a husband, a serf to a lord, a lord to a king.[23] The coinage of modern mass categories such as class, nation, citizen, men and women, enables new ways of thinking about human similarity and difference. Although the ideal of equality was crucial to this new order, the new order did not do away with inequality entirely. Instead, it reclassified the categories around which inequality operated in the modern world. Race was one of these new categories; some races or nations were considered unequal to others. In time the egalitarian ethic came to be associated with policies of racial differentiation and exclusion wherever it appeared.

The underlying tension in Australia between public professions of equality and the unequal treatment of Chinese immigrants was clear to liberal humanitarians of the day. Chinese Australians were systematically excluded from the legendary bonds of mateship that united the organised labour movement, they were actively discriminated against, with little regard for fair play, and they were generally regarded as less than equal on the hierarchy of civilisations and along the Darwinian chain of being.[24] The paradox was clear to those with eyes to see. Historian Charles Price records that William Westgarth, while chairing the Victorian Goldfields Commission in the mid-1850s, asked the fiery anti-Chinese agitator William Campbell Donovan how he could possibly hold that 'all men are born with free and equal rights' when he pushed for discriminatory restrictions on Chinese miners. 'Your universal rights of mankind are knocked on the head immediately.'[25] Donovan's feeble reply did little to uphold the ethical foundations of Australian values.

Equality in China and Japan

Chinese commentaries of the day focused on the same paradox. Liang Qichao, a young intellectual who was touring Australia while in exile from China in 1900 and 1901, argued that the White Australia Policy ran against the course of progressive history because it was founded on indefensible assumptions about racial purity. It made a mockery of

British ethical claims about the equality of humankind by singling out Asians for discriminatory treatment. The only principle Liang could discern in the White Australia Policy was the Darwinian principle that 'the strong prey upon the weak'. Liang's preferred option was for Australians and Chinese to acknowledge the fundamental equality and dignity of all. Failing that, he looked forward to the final outcome of the Darwinian struggle, 'when we yellow people have attained sufficient power to transform White Australia into Yellow Australia'. In time, this racial strain of Chinese nationalism came to dominate the revolutionary republican movement that was associated with Sun Yatsen.[26]

At the time Liang was penning his critique of White Australia, Chinese values were undergoing a revolution no less profound than the ethical revolutions that were shaking the West. As many historians have noted, the Enlightenment, the scientific revolution, the religious Reformation and the ideal of the fundamental dignity of the individual had few direct equivalents in East Asia.[27] Yet the revolutionary principles of human equality and dignity spread with astonishing speed through elite discourse and popular culture in China and Japan. In the 19th and early 20th centuries a modern sensibility regarding human equality was no less evident in the anti-monarchical and anti-colonial movements of Asia than in struggles in its originating sites in Western Europe, North America and Australasia.[28]

Beginning in the late 19th century, China and Japan each underwent a series of egalitarian moves that overwrote their pre-existing social and political orders. In Japan the new ethic of equality undermined the Confucian basis of the feudal state and laid the foundations for a new kind of nationalist polity that shook the world in the mid 20th century.[29] Elite reflections on the principle of equality in China over the same period marked out a field of play for a century of ideological, cultural and political debates about the constitution of the state and the character of the nation. The egalitarian ideal grew in extent and intensity through a series of movements, expressed in the local vernacular, that systematically undermined the foundations of the old hierarchical orders of state and family, and forged a new society that placed equality at the heart of Chinese modernity.[30]

Chinese-language sources of the period indicate that the cluster of values expressed in Australian dialect as fair play, egalitarianism and mateship exercised as powerful a hold on Chinese immigrants to Australia as they did upon Irish and British immigrants and native-born white Australians. Chinese Australians were no less involved in struggles with the hierarchical society of orders that prevailed in their home country than were Irish Australians fighting for home rule in Ireland or Cockneys fighting to forestall the transplantation of the class society of southeast England into southeastern Australia. The stories told in these chapters illustrate the appeal of the modern social imaginary to Chinese Australians by tracing their frustration in seeking recognition as equal members of the Australian nation.

Comparing white settlements with white

The argument that Chinese had to be excluded because they were incapable of appreciating Australian values is reinforced through comparative studies of white settler societies on the Pacific Rim. The best studies of Chinese immigration to white-settler societies highlight similarities and differences in the popular receptions and official responses at various points of settlement. The differences are tangible and significant. As we shall see, however, they pale alongside the differences that emerge from comparisons with non-white societies. Comparing both white settlements with white, and white with non-white, compels us to reframe the point at issue from discussion of primordial Chinese culture to the institutional arrangements of the host communities encountered at different points of settlement.

Among Australian historians Andrew Markus, Charles Price and David Goodman have distinguished Californian and Australian responses to the Chinese Question on a number of fronts.[31] Markus argues that, in contrast to California, the concept of race and notions of racial superiority were barely evident among early white commentaries on Chinese immigration to the Australian colonies. In the 1840s and early 1850s, Chinese were welcomed in Australian communities for their curiosity value. Their dress and travelling paraphernalia, their eating and drinking habits, their private and public entertainments, their religious practices and festivals, all initially stirred more curiosity than controversy. When, over the following decade, the novelty wore off, styles of appearance and conduct that once seemed quaint came to appear threatening. Even so, popular hostility to Chinese was expressed in the late 1850s and 1860s not in the language of race, as in America, but in relation to Chinese conduct and customs. The racialisation of public life came later to Australia than it did to the United States. Responses to the Chinese Question differed accordingly.[32]

Markus takes issue with the argument that white attitudes and conduct towards Indigenous Australians was in any sense parallel or analogous to attitudes to Chinese in Australia. Unlike in California, there was little precedent in the southeastern colonies of Australia for explicitly racial typecasting, and there was little sign of pre-existing racial discourse to ease European settlers comfortably into modern racism. Anti-Chinese sentiment was channelled instead through a particular local concern to distinguish free settlers from convict labourers. Chinese were typecast as members of a servile labour force that was bonded to its masters after the style of convict labour.[33] From the 1870s through to federation, however, the social Darwinist idea that races and nations were locked in a battle for survival began to take root in Australia. By the late 19th century there was little to distinguish the racialised strain of anti-Chinese sentiment in Australia from the racist style of argument circulating in California, not least because white-settler communities across the Pacific were engaged in close and frequent communications on the Chinese Question.[34]

Markus further argues that the Australian colonies were subject to the heavy hand of legal authority to a degree unmatched in the more recently established Anglo settlements of California. This impression appears to be confirmed in comments by Chinese immigrants themselves. Comparing the situation in Australia with that in California one Chinese colonist informed a select committee of the NSW parliament in 1858 that 'Chinese like good law, and in China they say in Sydney very good law, and the people all like to come to this country: no like to go to the other country [America].'[35] Placing their trust in British rule of law, Chinese community leaders pressed legal claims for equality of treatment under British rule of law no less confidently than their counterparts on the west coast of the United States. Community leaders expected colonial authorities to uphold their claims to equal rights and to award compensation when their rights were violated.[36] For their part, white Australians preferred to petition authorities for redress rather than take the law into their own hands. When the force of colonial authority was itself at issue, however, white miners sought redress through militant organised action. Hence, where random acts of violence against Chinese were relatively common in California, large-scale organised violence was more pronounced in Australia.[37]

The distinctive pattern of violence played out on the Australian and Californian fields confirms Goodman's insightful argument that a form of collective ethics prevailed on the Australian fields, marking a striking contrast with Californian individualism. In 19th century Victoria, Goodman argues, gold fever came to be associated with romantic notions of collective solidarity. The golden opportunities of the American West, on the other hand, served to confirm belief in Providence and in individual self-interest guided fortuitously by the invisible hand of the free market.[38] Organised anti-Chinese agitation and collective violence in Australia helped forge solid bonds of mateship.

The extent of Californian influence on anti-Chinese sentiment in colonial Australia has yet to be fully explored. A number of historians have remarked on the selection of the Fourth of July, American Independence Day, for Australia's earliest organised anti-Chinese agitations on the Victorian goldfields. On 4 July 1854, white miners in Bendigo drafted a proposal for a 'general and unanimous uprising ... for the purpose of driving the Chinese population off the Bendigo goldfields'. The plan was foiled by pre-emptive intervention on the part of local authorities and by the timely arrival of colonial troopers. The first successful uprising against Chinese miners occurred three years later to the day at the Buckland River goldfields in Victoria. On 4 July 1857 white rioters rampaged through the Chinese camps, burning, beating and pillaging as they went. Hinting at Californian influence on the timing of the Bendigo and Buckland riots historian Myra Willard noted wryly that 4 July 'seems to have been a favourite date for the disturbances'.[39] Although some miners from California took part in acts of violence against Chinese on the Australian fields, other Americans objected to the selection of that date for anti-Chinese agitation as an 'unsuitable form of celebration' for American Independence Day.[40]

Californian precedents and American ideals were conveyed in person by miners and merchants plying the sea routes linking the Californian and the Victorian goldfields in the 1850s and, as time went on, by postal and telegraphic communications. By the 1870s, white Australians could follow developments in the United States from day to day through the colonial press. In 1877, at a time when Chinese miners had moved from the southern colonies to sluice for gold in the rivers and estuaries of northern Queensland, a US Congressional report on Chinese labour circulated in the colonial press and legislatures. The Queensland postmaster-general highlighted the lessons of the US report for Australia. The United States housed 'a civilised community of the same race as ourselves, possessing similar institutions to our own', he remarked. Like the Australian colonies, the US bore 'the unrestricted invasion of the country by an inferior race'. The Americans had given a lead in legislating to restrict immigration by race. If Chinese were permitted to enter Australia they would stain the spirit and character of a nation that aspired to follow the American path. Australian legislators needed to move quickly if they hoped to pre-empt the arrival of America-bound Chinese who would point their compasses in Australia's direction once their attentions were diverted from California.[41]

American historian Adam McKeown has suggested that the differences often attributed to the Australian and Californian experiences of anti-Chinese sentiment may have more to do with differences among historians than with their sources, more specifically, with the different historiographical traditions bearing on race and values that characterise US and Australian historical scholarship. In all likelihood, he suggests, white Californians talked about culture and values as much as did white Australians.[42] Certainly, the alleged differences in cultural, legal and political settings in California and Australia do little to mitigate two strong conclusions drawn from comparative studies of the white-settler societies. One is that Chinese came with little or no intention to settle, that they intended to cut and run after earning enough to support their families back home in China.'Few Chinese came to Australia as permanent settlers', one local historian wrote. 'Most intended to return to China after trying their fortune in other countries and because of this they left their families at home.'[43] A second argument, common to both, is that Chinese immigrants to California and Australia entered as indentured labourers on terms akin to slavery and hence shared little in common with the values underlying the communities of free settlers into which they happened to stray. 'Of the fervour of Australian nationalism and the social aspirations which had brought Europeans in quest of gold they were ignorant', writes another Australian historian. 'They lacked conspicuously the individualism of westerners.'[44]

These claims make up a shared archive of white accounts of Chinese immigrant experience in the settler societies of the Pacific Rim. The conclusion that flows from them is that popular reactions and legislative restrictions in Australia and California were in every case part of a rational nation-making process that served to identify the kinds of people each needed to exclude in order to remain true to itself. Among those identified for exclusion were allegedly servile, hierarchical, self-interested, uncommitted Chinese immigrants, who held little sympathy for the social and patriotic aspirations of their host communities.

Comparing non-white settlements with white

Judgments about Chinese culture and values made in white-settler societies are not borne out by evidence from other sites of Chinese settlement in Southeast Asia and the South Pacific. The Australian Colonial Sugar Refining Company (CSR), to cite an example close to home, canvassed the merits of large-scale labour contracting of Chinese workers for its sugar plantations in Fiji in the 1880s. On investigation, the governor of the islands and the CSR board formed the view that Chinese contractors 'preferred to be their own masters' and were 'expensive'. The proposal to import workers from China was abandoned on the understanding that they were unlikely to provide the cheap and docile labour force that CSR required for its sugar plantations.[45] Similar judgments on the character of Chinese labourers, farmers and merchants were commonplace among colonial officials governing non-white settlements in Southeast Asia.

To compare white settlements with other white settlements helps to highlight similarities and differences among white-settler societies, but it tells us little about Chinese immigrants themselves. Observable differences between one white-settler society and another, such as the prevalence of collective or individualist ethics and the relative force of the law in each society, pale alongside the common assumptions that confronted Chinese migrants in white settlements generally. Comparing white with non-white settlements invites reconsideration of the most tenacious of these common assumptions, specifically, that Chinese intended to cut and run, that they worked as slaves and that their values threatened the fragile national consensus on Australian values that made Australia Australia rather than merely white.

Adam McKeown mounts a strong case that nation-based comparisons of any kind can be misleading if they fail to make room for the transnational strategies of extended families seeking to maximise their opportunities abroad. Families in China were not restricted to choosing one site of settlement over another, white or non-white. They took advantage of opportunities wherever they arose and they put up with restrictions when they were compelled to do so. In the Australian case, a young man emigrating to Victoria, say, might have a brother in Queensland or New Zealand, uncles and nieces in the Philippines, perhaps an aunt and a family of young cousins in Hawai'i, and more distant relatives living in California or Peru. Movement among these sites was mediated by extended family networks and driven by the opportunities that beckoned from one place to another. On McKeown's calculations, observable fluctuations in the rates of movement among sites abroad correlated more directly with economic opportunities at each site than with immigration restrictions. For Chinese families, coping with restrictions was an art form.[46]

That said, extending the range of comparisons from the Australian colonies to other sites of settlement helps to cast into high relief some of the basic assumptions underlying Australian historical writing about the conduct and expectations of Chinese immigrant labourers. The remainder of this chapter is devoted to different orders of comparison across various sites of settlement, one bearing on the experience of Chinese labourers in the Dutch East Indies, the other on family strategies for managing overseas migration.

CHINESE LABOUR IN THE EAST INDIES

Nineteenth-century Chinese immigration was a world phenomenon, not just an Australian one. Australian authorities often cited precedents from California and the colonial territories of Southeast Asia when they framed their arguments for restricting Chinese immigration.[47] Chinese Australians consulted similar sources in their defence. The Chinese press in Australia was constantly on the alert for signs of anti-Chinese violence and news of restrictive legislation abroad. Legislative restrictions on Chinese entry into the United States and Canada attracted commentary in the Chinese-Australian press over the late 1890s and early 1900s just as they did in the English-language press of the day. Similar interest was shown in the Chinese-Australian press about news from colonial Southeast Asia, including evidence of increasing regulation of Chinese entry into the Philippines and Singapore, and of Chinese actions in defiance of these restrictions.[48]

Among the items of news about Chinese immigrants in Southeast Asia that circulated in colonial Australia were accounts of Chinese anarchy and brutality in British Sarawak and the adjacent Dutch territory of West Kalimantan, both on the island of Borneo. These presented a marked contrast to accounts of meek, docile, servile and hierarchical Chinamen of colonial Australian legend. Nonetheless, an elected representative on the NSW Legislative Assembly supported the passage of a restrictive immigration bill in 1858 by referring to recent disturbances on Borneo. Unless restrained, he argued, Chinese in Australia would take the law into their own hands as they had done in Sarawak, where Chinese miners 'massacred all before them'.[49] In fact, Chinese miners put up very little resistance to white violence on the Australian goldfields. The relative docility of Chinese in Australia was a mark of the respect they held for British rule of law. Where no law prevailed, as in West Kalimantan, Chinese miners legislated for themselves and established remarkably egalitarian and democratic territorial jurisdictions.

Dutch observations of Chinese immigrant behaviour in colonial Borneo differed accordingly from Anglophone commentaries on Chinese morals and manners in Australia. To Dutch colonial officials, the independent micro states of Chinese miners along the coast of Kalimantan appeared remarkably egalitarian, fraternal and democratic, and – regrettably – republican.[50] These contrasting accounts of Chinese immigrant behaviour cannot reasonably be attributed to the different character of the immigrants themselves. The Chinese of West Kalimantan came overwhelmingly from northern Guangdong Province, albeit from a different subethnic group than the Cantonese émigrés to California, Australia and New Zealand.[51] They immigrated to West Kalimantan in search of gold too, in this case a century earlier than Cantonese miners in Australia, California and New Zealand. The difference between Anglophone and Dutch ethnography is best explained by the different local conditions under which immigrant miners adapted to life away from home. In the absence of formal colonial structures in Kalimantan, Chinese miners were at liberty to build autonomous social and political institutions that gave concrete expression to the values they brought with them from China. Further, the Europeans who described their behaviour and captured their values in print were, on the whole, associates of colonial officials in Kalimantan who were keen to bring autonomous Chinese enclaves to heel.

Starting in the late 16th and early 17th centuries Chinese labourers and merchants established settlements in insular Southeast Asia to produce and trade in commodities such as tin, gold, pepper and sugar. Among the earliest of these settlements was the autonomous city-state of Hatien on the coast of Cochinchina (now southern Vietnam), established by the entrepreneurial Cantonese pirate Mac Cuu around 1690. The city was managed as a semi-independent urban republic, not unlike the city-states of mediaeval Italy, although in this case managed through the agency of share-holding partnerships involving Chinese merchants and labourers. Hatien was one of a dozen Chinese émigré commercial entrepots that sprang up around the Chinese 'water frontier' of coastal and island Southeast Asia over the late 17th and 18th centuries.[52]

Every year in the 18th century 4000 to 10 000 Chinese labourers boarded Chinese vessels bound for Chinese entrepots in Southeast Asia.[53] These labouring men were members of egalitarian fraternities that were based in a material sense on share-owning partnerships and founded ritually on the oaths and ceremonies of the secret societies that ran peasant village networks in southern China. They held shares in enterprises financed by merchant capital. Significantly, the disparity between the shares and the profits of head merchants and labourers was measured by their relative contributions to the enterprise rather than by their relative status in a primordial or preordained status hierarchy. As historian Carl Trocki has observed, the share-holding companies and settlements 'espoused egalitarian principles, which were often at odds with conventional Confucian orthodoxy'. When labour conditions deteriorated the share-holding labourers 'could easily strike or simply walk off the job and find another mine'. In the precolonial era Chinese workers in Southeast Asia were known for their militant egalitarianism.[54]

The indentured coolie system found in accounts of early Chinese labour immigration to Australia was an outcome of a later colonial era. The share-owning fraternities were undermined by European colonialism in Southeast Asia, not least because leading Chinese merchants entered into commercial and political alliances with colonial authorities. These alliances broke the back of the old egalitarian labour confederations and effectively undermined the prosperity of the 18th century entrepots. New colonial ports, such as Singapore, arose to take their place, and new kinds of labour contracts were devised for European-style *latifundia* (tax farms) in Southeast Asia and Latin America. The collaborating merchants supplied labour and capital under new contract arrangements, framed in partnership with colonial authorities, that reduced the status of migrant labourers from that of share-owning partners to that of chattels.[55]

By the time Chinese labourers began moving to central and south America and to the Australian colonies in the 1840s, they were entering under contracts that bore little resemblance to the old fraternal agreements. Extant contracts and regulations governing Chinese emigration to Cuba and Peru at this time show that coolies were not shareholders but 'the property of the planters'.[56] Similar conditions applied to the indentured labourers recruited from Singapore to New South Wales and Victoria in the 1840s, to Queensland in the 1850s and to Western Australia later in the century.[57] Trocki has argued that the emergence of Singapore as a British colonial entrepot was the key to the destruction of the independent Chinese labour confederations of Southeast Asia.[58] If this is so, the recruitment of coolie labourers from Singapore to eastern and western Australia was enabled by the same colonial system that brought convicts to the Australian colonies. Unbeknown to themselves, British and Irish convicts in the Australian colonies shared common cause with immigrant labourers from China, who were no less eager than themselves to re-establish more equal relations with their employers and with one another on the egalitarian principles of their male fraternities.

How did the earlier confederations work?

According to historian Mary Somers Heidhues, the earliest cohorts of miners to reach Borneo from Guangdong organised themselves into small share-holding groups known as 'companies' (*Kongsi; gongsi*), not unlike teams of mates operating a small claim on the Victorian fields. They adopted labour practices similar to those found under the Chinese empire. The largest Chinese business enterprises of the late imperial era – including mines, kilns and the imperial mint – were generally held in government hands and staffed not by wage-earning employees but by small teams of workers recruited by individual headmen who held labour contracts with the enterprise management.[59] In Southeast Asia, miners owned shares in the companies they served, retaining a share of proceeds from the sale of the company's gold after the deduction of capital expenses for waterworks, dams, sluices and additional labour costs. Each held a direct share in the collective labour of their workmates.

By the early 19th century many of these share-holding companies had grown into substantial federations embracing numerous companies. Heidhues describes the operations of the four major mining-community federations that operated in West Kalimantan. The egalitarian and democratic ideals of the miners were apparent in the companies' leadership arrangements. Leadership was by election and candidates were elected on the record of their achievements rather than their inherited status. In other respects the mining federations resembled the early craft guilds of Britain that attached themselves to local parish churches and claimed the benefaction of patron saints. Thus the Kalimantan federations were each organised around a community hall that served as a place of common prayer and as a forum for public discussion of issues bearing on federation administration and the election of office holders. In the absence of a functioning state the federations went further to build networks of forts in their territories, station federation officials around their borders, oversee the management of towns and markets in their territories, and levy taxes, charges and duties on commercial markets, passing traders and vessels. In effect they 'conducted themselves as "states"', Heidhues observes. 'Neither the native principalities nor the Dutch colonial power had comparable organisations, infrastructures, or power.'[60]

The democratic character of the federations was widely acknowledged. When Dutch colonial authorities attempted to subdue the Thaikong federation by blockading its ports and settlements and negotiating with elected headman to surrender the company's corporate seal of authority, the residing Dutch governor-general feared that 'ultra-democratic elements' among the miners would undermine the negotiations. His fears were well founded. In December 1852 the miners voted overwhelmingly against the settlement on the ground that they had not been party to the negotiations.[61] The ensuing conflict was seen in colonial Australia as incontrovertible evidence of Chinese cultural predisposition for brutality and lawlessness. In fact, events on Borneo had much in common with the Eureka Stockade.

The Chinese miners who came to Australia were heirs to the legacy of egalitarian secret society networks stretching from Borneo to California. The assembly halls on Kalimantan were not unlike the secret society temples established by male fraternities throughout Australia. As in Australia, native-place associations and society temples housed icons of the patron gods and goddesses of their respective company federations. The local character of these patron deities ensured that membership of a federation was largely restricted to immigrants from the same district or region in China – as with native place associations in Australia – and the rituals undertaken for initiation were similar to those applying to secret fraternal associations in Australia.[62] While the larger federated Kongsi of Kalimantan had no counterpart in Australia, their underlying organisational structure was all but identical to those of the fraternal networks that operated in white settler societies around the Pacific Rim. Male fraternities such as the Yee Hing network were to be found at every mining site and commercial settlement in Australia. They, like the Kalimantan federations and the secret society networks of North America, drew on the institutional template of underground male fraternities found throughout southern China in the Qing Dynasty.

The experience of the federated companies of West Kalimantan exposes the local foundations of white Australian claims that Chinese immigrants were culturally predisposed to aggregate in docile, hierarchical, slave-like gangs of coolie labourers. Neither the normal organisational forms of the federated companies nor the underlying secret society cells to which they reverted under duress revealed an orthodox status hierarchy based on the classical Confucian canon. Nor did they offer any hint of a cultural preference for oriental despotism. The federations of West Kalimantan were egalitarian in their social structure, democratic in their politics, highly entrepreneurial in spirit and tightly disciplined in their organisation and management: they were particular adaptations of community formations found throughout southern China in the late imperial period, modified to take advantage of economic and commercial opportunities in territories lacking formal agencies of government. The same could be said of Chinese community organisation in Australia, in this case adapted to operate under British rule of law. It was not primordial Chinese values that governed the shape that immigrant communities assumed from one site to another but rather the conditions of entry and settlement applying at each site. In other words, Chinese were as egalitarian or hierarchical, democratic or authoritarian, individualistic or communitarian, religious or irreligious, conformist or individually eccentric, as local circumstances permitted.

Sojourners and family emigration strategies

The eminent historian Wang Gung-wu has written extensively about the sojourner pattern of 19th century Chinese emigration and highlighted some of the difficulties this pattern presented for host nations such as Australia.[63] A sojourner is an émigré who takes up temporary residence abroad with the intention of returning home. Needless to say, intentions of this kind do not rest comfortably with states that demand a certain level of commitment from their members. We shall come to the matter of individual immigrant intentions below. At this point we can usefully situate the well-established sojourner pattern of Chinese immigrant labour in relation to long-term family immigration strategies. Individual males travelled to and from Australia as members of extended families. Their short-term sojourning behaviour, as individuals, needs to be understood in light of long-term family immigration strategies.

The appropriate unit of analysis in the history of Chinese immigration is not the individual immigrant sojourner but the extended family. Nineteenth-century patterns of overseas immigration replicated long-established patterns of internal immigration, within China itself, where families spatially deployed their offspring throughout the empire to ensure the survival of the family or to maximise its status and income. The actual movement and settlement of family members to relatively remote sites within China, often over several generations, was accompanied by a nostalgic commemoration of the original site of settlement (the old village, or *guxiang*) as a ritual site of family unity, which gave meaning and purpose to the immigrant endeavour. Substantial sub-branches of families that developed in different sites of settlement in the old empire invariably hankered after the old village even when very few of their number actually returned.[64]

Families in south China deployed similar strategies in relation to overseas immigration in the 19th century. First-generation émigré cohorts overwhelmingly consisted of young men sent abroad to make a living, to send money home in support of other family members and to test the likely reception in the host society to the prospect of permanent settlement by new sub-branches of the family, all the while remaining ritually loyal to their *guxiang*. The strategic thinking underlying this style of immigration can be traced through the gender balance found at different sites of settlement in Southeast Asia, Hawai'i and Australasia.

In Australian history, the well-established preference of Chinese males for leaving their wives and families in their home villages is thought to show that they were determined to return home. There is little doubt that many Chinese immigrants intended to leave the Australian colonies and return to China, if and when they struck it rich. Many certainly retained a sense that their ancestral village would forever remain their home, but, that said, the reluctance of women to accompany emigrating males abroad offers little insight into the intentions of male émigrés. First-generation gender ratios were more or less the same for temporary and permanent settlements overseas. Female and family emigration patterns are indicators not of individual emigrant intentions, but of long-term family strategies for balancing economic opportunities against the relative receptiveness of host communities across different sites of settlement.

The logic underlying family emigration strategies can be garnered from three general observations about the relative numbers of men and women at different sites of settlement overseas. One, already noted, is that first-generation Chinese émigrés were, on the whole, exclusively male wherever they went and whatever their intentions at the point of departure. In the Dutch East Indies, for example, few women accompanied male labourers on their initial voyages to Kalimantan. This did not prevent male immigrants from settling down. Indeed, many of the single adult males who travelled from south China to mine for gold in Kalimantan remained in that district and fathered children with local Malay and Dayak women. Some then sought partners among later cohorts of male immigrants for the female offspring of their local unions. Once the community had become established, women began to emigrate directly from China in greater numbers. In this case the scarcity of wives and women accompanying early miners offered no indication whatever of their intention to stay in Kalimantan or return to their old village in China. Whatever the miners' intentions, actual or ritual, the presence of women was a measure of the stability and security of the overseas community rather than an indicator of male intentions to reside temporarily before returning home.

A second observation is that where gender ratios did achieve balance over time they generally did so through reproduction rather than through large-scale female immigration. McKeown's research on female immigration to Hawai'i and North America indicates that families in China failed to take full advantage of the opportunities for emigration to the United States, restricted as they were in the late 19th and early 20th centuries. Families faced greater difficulty placing a male in San Francisco or Chicago than they did placing a female. They generally opted to place males all the same. Even in Hawai'i, where long-term settlement was the norm, male immigration was the norm. Long-term statistical trends for Hawai'i and the US mainland show gender ratios achieving balance in the mid 20th century as normal sex distributions for locally born Chinese Americans made their way through the generational charts. This happened earlier in Hawai'i than on the mainland due to earlier Chinese settlement in Hawai'i.[65]

A third observation is that immigration restrictions played a part in skewing gender ratios but were not a major factor in every case. The primary impact of immigration restrictions on gender ratios lay in limiting female immigration to the wives and families of wealthy merchants and professionals. The higher proportion of women immigrants in Hawai'i relative to the United States mainland is thought to have reflected the higher proportion of wealthy merchants on the islands.

These three observations about gender ratios and patterns of female immigration apply to the Australian experience, *albeit* with some variation. First, large-scale male immigration could and did precede permanent settlement involving women immigrants when and where it was permitted. Second, the gender balance among Chinese Australians moved towards parity as the locally born population grew relative to the population of ageing male immigrants. Finally, and most significantly, immigration restrictions played a part in skewing the gender balance insofar as fathers raised children in China while living in Australia.

Initially, only the wealthy could bring out their wives. In the 19th century, discriminatory head taxes had the effect of limiting incoming arrivals to wage-earning males who could cover the cost of the tax, which was borne by their families back home. This pattern of male relatives moving to and from Australia persisted beyond the first generation of incoming males through to second and later cohorts of the same families. For women the situation was different. Outside of prostitution there were few trades or professions open to them to pay charges on the scale of colonial head taxes. Nevertheless, many wealthy men who could afford to pay head taxes did invite their wives and families to join them.

After federation wives were prohibited from settling in Australia however wealthy or influential their husbands. This restriction had the further effect of banning even those women whom family immigration strategies would have placed comfortably in Australia before federation. At the same time, it made Chinese-Australian men more than usually mobile, compelling them to commute in ever greater numbers and frequency between Australia and China to marry, raise children and visit their families. The individual sojourning pattern was reinforced as a family strategy for coping with the discriminatory regime of White Australia.

Immigration and repatriation

Intentions at the point of departure are not in any case a fair indication of actual immigrant behaviour. Specialists in immigration studies have long acknowledged that 'most international migrants intend to return to their place of origin sooner or later'.[66] Initial intentions at the point of departure bear little relation to eventual outcomes as many who intend to return change their minds after arrival and others are unable, for one reason or another, to act on their intentions. An initial intention to return home appears to have been commonplace among all immigrant groups in colonial Australia, including British immigrants. According to historian Ken Inglis, a nostalgic yearning to 'go to England when they die' was inscribed all over 19th century English accounts of immigration to the Australian colonies.[67] Some Irish immigrants shared these sentiments. Patrick O'Farrell quotes a Cork woman imploring her husband as they boarded a ship for Australia in 1840 to 'send me home when I'm dead to my own people in Kilcrea – that's my consolation'.[68]

But for most English and Irish immigrants to Australia there was no going back. Australia was a long way from Europe and there was no assisted passage home. As O'Farrell has noted, the distance from Europe encouraged a different outlook among emigrants heading for Australia from those bound for North America regarding the likelihood of their returning home. 'Australia's vast distances from Ireland, dictating little chance of return,' he writes, 'implied two contrasting sets of migrant attitudes.'[69] People could leave Ireland for America knowing there was a good chance they would return home. Australia's remoteness compelled a different approach. 'Above all, the fact of distance and the time patterns of Irish migration suggest that the Irish emigrant to Australia was a thoughtful one … thoughtful in the sense that it represented a forward commitment and investment in life.'[70] European emigrants departing for Australia knew when they set out that there was little chance of their returning alive. Those leaving for America, on the other hand, could set off on a whim.

People could leave China for Australia on a whim. In terms of distance, cost and convenience Canton was to Sydney what Cork or Plymouth were to New York. Comparing the intentions and conduct of Chinese and Irish immigrants to Australia is less productive than comparing Cantonese immigrants to Australia with Irish or British immigrants to New York. The proportion of returnees from America to Britain has been estimated at around 40 per cent.[71] This is not far removed from the most reliable estimates of the Chinese rate of repatriation from Australia.

The actual rate of return immigration from Australia to Europe is difficult to quantify. In all likelihood it fell below the Atlantic ratio of Euro-American remigration. Temporal and spatial variations skew the total picture. Victoria recorded eight times as many immigrants from Britain as departures in the mid 19th century but approximately the same number travelling each way by the turn of the 20th century.[72] Assuming O'Farrell is correct, the relative distances separating the two immigrant destinations from their source countries in Europe depressed the rate of return immigration from Australia relative to the rate between North America and Europe.

The repatriation rate among Chinese immigrants to Australia was certainly higher than that of British or Irish immigrants returning from Australia to Europe, but it was not significantly higher than return immigration from America to Europe. The evidence from Australia fails to support the widely-repeated claim that almost all 19th century Chinese immigrants returned to China.[73] Around half of the 47 000 Chinese who entered Victoria between 1840 and 1865 had left by sea at the end of that period, some heading for their home villages, others moving to Hong Kong and destinations in Southeast Asia and the Pacific Islands. Still, around half of those who left Victoria actually moved to other sites in Australia where opportunities were beckoning.[74] Repatriation needs to be distinguished from mobility. Perhaps half of all immigrants from China left Australia permanently for China by the turn of the century but others simply kept moving.

Chinese repatriation from Australia

Let us try to put a figure on the rate of permanent repatriation to China.[75] The most reliable sources indicate that between 70 000 and 100 000 people emigrated from China to Australia from the mid to late 19th century.[76] In light of institutional incentives for avoiding detection and taxation the higher figure is more likely. Census figures record 32 700 Chinese residents in Australia in 1901 and just half that number in 1939,[77] and yet no more than half of these residents returned to die in China. How do we know?

One native-place association in Melbourne has preserved 8000 memorial tablets honouring natives of the See Yap district who passed away in Victoria the 19th century.[78] Given their many districts of origin apart from See Yap, and the number who emigrated directly to Tasmania, New South Wales, Queensland, Western Australia and South Australia, total Chinese deaths in Australia probably exceed by three to four times the number of See Yap deaths in Victoria. A figure of between 20 000 and 30 000 deaths would not seem unreasonable. Erring on the side of caution, when we add the lower figure for deaths of 20 000 to the census record of 32 700 residents in 1901 it follows that more than 50 000 of the 100 000 arrivals were still on Australian soil at the time of federation. Of the remainder, perhaps 40 000 returned to China and Hong Kong and 5000 to 10 000 settled in New Zealand and the Pacific Islands.

The same pattern was repeated after federation, *albeit* without further prospect of population renewal through immigration in the White Australia era. The number of Chinese people resident in Australia fell by around half over the first four decades of the 20th century from 30 000 to 15 000. Even assuming that all of this shrinkage was accounted for by repatriation – an absurd proposition – no more than half of the resident population at the turn of the century could have returned to China. No doubt many people wanted to return to China, just as many Europeans in America hoped to return to Europe, but on these estimates close to half of all Chinese immigrants to Australia lived out their lives in Australia and the Pacific Islands. The repatriation rate for Chinese from the Australian colonies over the 19th and early 20th centuries was commensurate with return rates of European immigrants from the New World over the same period.

The exceptional feature of Chinese-Australian settlement was not the rate of repatriation but the rate of mobility – the rate of movement between rural and urban settlements, and between different colonies, states and territories in Australia, and international movements to and from Australia and south China and between Australia and British territories in the South Pacific. From personal memoirs and family histories we know that different generational cohorts shifted their lodgings from rural settlements to regional townships in each colony and that they moved as opportunities beckoned from Victoria to northeastern Tasmania and western New South Wales, from western New South Wales to the northeast of the state, from New South Wales to the Northern Territory and Queensland, from one part of Queensland to another, onward perhaps to Thursday Island or Rabaul, perhaps to Broome or Geraldton and, in many cases, to Sydney, which developed from the turn of the century into the largest urban hub for Chinese-Australian networks stretching across the continent and throughout the Pacific Islands.[79]

Permanent repatriation accounts for only a modest proportion of total movements between Australia and China in the prewar period. As has been noted, around 28 000 registered Chinese departures and arrivals are recorded for New South Wales over the first two decades of the 20th century, an interval when the total registered Chinese population of that state declined by less than 3000, from around 10 222 to 7282.[80] They undertook 80 000 journeys to and from Australia from the turn of the century to the outbreak of the Second World War at a time when their total number was but a fraction of their total journeys.[81] Clearly, Chinese Australians were doing more than just going home to die. Chinese Australians packed their swags and moved on many times during the course of their lives. Their rate of domestic mobility and international commuter immigration far outstripped that of permanent repatriation.

Today the style of international commuting that these figures imply is commonplace among European and Asian immigrants to Australia. It was less widespread in the 19th century. International commuting was adopted much earlier by Chinese immigrants due to the particular conditions attached to their settlement in Australia. Take the case of

Evens Leong (*Liang Qiwen*) and her family. Evens was born in northern Queensland to Chinese resident parents in 1883, a time when two-thirds of all farmers in the districts around Cairns, Port Douglas, Innisfail and Atherton were of Chinese immigrant stock. Almost half of all rural residents in the district surrounding Cairns were of Chinese descent, as were one in five residents of Cairns itself, 75 per cent of rural residents around Port Douglas and 40 per cent of the residents of Port Douglas town. The Chinese population of the area fell away over following years with the introduction of discriminatory legislation restricting Chinese access to citizenship, access to ownership and leasing of land, access to participation in local industries such as banana and sugar cane plantations, and access to public goods and services.[82]

Evens Leong was born and raised some distance south of Cairns, in the vicinity of Townsville, where her father operated a banana and sugar cane plantation. She was a feisty and independent young woman who, family legend has it, wanted to attend the University of Queensland after graduating from high school. Her parents prevailed upon her to remain home and manage the paper work for the family firm. In 1905 she married a young man recently arrived from China, Charles Lee (*Li Minzhou*), who emigrated from Shekki in Heungshan County to work on Evens' father's sugar plantation in Queensland. As we shall see in a later chapter, Charles Lee went on to become one of Shanghai's most successful retail entrepreneurs in the Chinese Republic.

Charles Lee's son, Charles Cheng-Che Lee, later wrote of the pride and pleasure that the Chinese community of Queensland took in the marriage of Charles Lee and Evens Leong. For three days the family property was festooned with lanterns and bunting as many in the region – white families included – were invited to a fabulous feast in celebration of a rare Chinese wedding on Australian soil. Why, their son asked, was the wedding such a rarity?

> *Because Chinese had to reside fifteen years in Australia before they could invite their family members in China to join them. This was a clear expression of the White Australia Policy intended to prevent Chinese from setting down roots on Australian soil. So the majority of the older generation of Chinese immigrants had to return home to marry. After one or two years in their home villages they would take*

> *to the sea again and return [to Australia] to make their living. For this reason, second-generation Chinese migrants were born in their parents' ancestral villages.*[83]

Evens urged her husband to take her to visit his family in China. She fell ill and died in his home village on her first trip outside Australia in 1915.

Charles Lee married again in the following year, this time in China, where the author of this passage, Cheng-Che Lee, was born. Prevented by Australian law from taking his new family back with him to Australia, Charles Lee adopted what was to become the standard pattern of the Chinese-Australian male commuter, living and working in Australia but returning occasionally to stay with his wife and family in their village in Shekki. In 1922 he decided to transfer his savings to Shanghai where, with his Chinese-Australian business partners, he built the Sun Sun Department store on Nanking Road.[84] But the family did not sever its links with Australia: in 1949, when restrictions on the movement of wives and children were beginning to relax, Charles Cheng-Che Lee returned with his family. Today over 100 descendents of Charles Lee Snr count themselves as Australian citizens. Charles Lee had to leave and return to Australia many times over to maintain the kind of family and business connections that his descendents can now enjoy in Sydney, as and when they wish.[85]

3

IMMIGRANT LABOUR AND GOLDFIELD FRATERNITIES

The Chinese now are all Freemasons, and form one brotherhood.
The old Emperor and his son are Chinese Tartars, and the new
emperor intends to carry out all one brotherhood.

Howqua, Melbourne 1855.[1]

Legend has it that a Chinese secret-society fraternity, known as the Yee
Hing Company or, alternatively, as the Hung Men brotherhood, came
to Australia in the trail of the Red Turban and Taiping rebellions that
shook southern China in the middle of the 19th century.[2] One fable still
circulating in Melbourne tells of a Taiping leader by the name of Tock
Gee who fled with his followers in a fleet of small boats from South
China to Darwin, in northern Australia, before leading them south to
seek their fortunes on the goldfields of western Victoria. Tock Gee was
known colloquially in Melbourne as the King for Pacifying the South in
the Chinese rebel forces.[3] In the Victorian version of the legend Tock

Gee is remembered as founder of the southern goldfields chapters of the Yee Hing.

Another legend, emanating from New South Wales, tells of an anti-Qing rebel leader by the name of Loong Hung Pung who led hundreds of his comrades to goldfields in the western districts of the colony and there laid the foundations for the NSW lodge of the Yee Hing fellowship. In both legends, everyday tales of large-scale labour emigration from southern Chinese villages are embellished as secret-society sagas of hardship, camaraderie, dedication and the struggle to create a better world for working men in Australia.

Historians are generally sceptical of legend. In the Victorian case there was certainly a man by the name of Tock Gee who passed under the nickname of King for Pacifying the South within the Melbourne Yee Hing organisation, but there is no surviving evidence to support the claim that he led rebel forces in southern China before heading to Australia. In his path-breaking study of Chinese-Australian community history, *New Gold Mountain*, CF Yong is equally sceptical of the legend of Loong Hung Pung in New South Wales. He notes in passing that a certain Loong Hung Pung was rumoured to have headed a group of anti-Manchu revolutionaries to Australia in the 1850s and to have cultivated a band of devoted followers who oversaw the development of the underground NSW network over the second half of the 19th century. There Yong leaves this legend as he found it. Loong Hung Pung rates no further mention in his history of Chinese-Australian communities in the late 19th and early 20th centuries.[4]

Yong's source for the legendary account of Loong Hung Pung was a sensational book, *White China*, written and published many years after the event in 1933 by the Sydney journalist John Sleeman.[5] After weighing up the evidence presented in Sleeman's book, Yong concludes that the reliability of the story 'may be in question'. He settles instead for a more sober account of the history of the Yee Hing that circulated in Australian Chinese-language newspapers of the 20th century. In Yong's view these better documented accounts confirm the pedigree of two other leaders, Moy Sing (*Mei Dongxing*) and James A Chuey (*Huang Zhu*), as founders and organisers of a respectable Yee Hing network in New South Wales that played a marginal role in labour immigration and little part in revolution at any time from the 1850s to the 1920s.[6]

We shall come to Moy Sing and James A Chuey in the following chapter. In this chapter we reopen the story of Loong Hung Pung that CF Yong cast aside in his study of the Yee Hing network in colonial Australia. We explore the place of popular legend in Chinese-Australian history and we put one of these legends to the test by evaluating the merits of its sources. The point at issue is not the existence of the Yee Hing organisation in the Australian colonies of the mid 19th century, which is fully attested elsewhere. In 1855 a Chinese interpreter reported the existence of a widespread Freemason brotherhood on the Victorian goldfields. A secret *Hungmen Handbook*, dating from the same period, has been identified by Nanjing University historian Cai Shaoqing as one of a kind that circulated widely among similar organisations in Southeast Asia in the mid-Qing dynasty. Kok Hu Jin has written a number of papers highlighting Yee Hing designs and inscriptions on Australian colonial gravestones and temples which appear to be based on designs laid out in the *Hungmen Handbook*, which he himself translated.[7]

The purpose in reopening the legend of the Yee Hing is rather to shed light on the role of secret societies in the history of organised labour immigration to the Australian goldfields and to show how this history came to be remembered by later generations of Chinese Australians in a distinctively Australian idiom. Few accounts of Chinese-Australian history fail to make passing reference to the social welfare functions of secret society lodges. Far less is known about the role they played in large-scale organised immigration, about the genealogies of their founders and leaders in the Australian colonies, about their institutional transformation in Australia or about the part played by local Australian lodges in the early history of the Chinese revolution. The legend of Loong Hung Pung touches on all of these little-known elements. By returning to the legend we can begin to understand the operation of working men's fraternities among Chinese immigrants in the 19th century and to appreciate how they came to be remembered early in the 20th century as exemplary moments in the history of Australian values.

Fraternities and organised labour immigration

As it has come down to us, the legend of Loong Hung Pung's role in the founding of the Australian Yee Hing network is a story of organised labour immigration embellished by martial metaphors and revolutionary conspiracies. The most substantial source for the legend is a series of essays penned by a young man from Lismore in northern New South Wales, Vivian Yung (or Vivian Chow). Reflecting back on the role on the Yee Hing network in 1933 Chow wrote:

> *Every Chinese heart must glow with pride to read the wonderful achievements of the Australian Chinese in the gold rushes: of the great expeditions sent out by [Loong Hung Pung] numbering thousands per contingent, and the gathering and marshalling of the entire Chinese population in order to make the offensive irresistible.*[8]

Chow's free use of military metaphors referring to expeditions and offensives reflected his enthusiasm for popular Anzac lore and some of the stories told around the family dinner table. The determination of so many young Australian-born Chinese of his generation to travel to China was driven, he wrote at another point, by 'no other thought but that the ideals that made Anzac should be sown on the fertile soil of Young China'.[9] By Vivian's account young men born in Australia of first- and second-generation Chinese immigrants felt duty bound to return to the land of their forefathers as Australians carrying the Anzac spirit within them. He went so far as to claim that a leading general in the Chinese Nationalist Army had been born in South Australia and served with the Anzacs at Gallipoli before taking on the Japanese in China.[10] One thing that Anzac lore shared with the Yee Hing legend was a respect for the martial values of discipline, sacrifice, patriotism and mateship – and the love of a good yarn.

Elaborating on Loong Hung Pung's expeditions of emigrating workers, Chow observed that the 'offensives' were led by a number of subordinate 'goldfield commanders', including Yeung Lee (whom Chow called the first 'typical Australian Chinese'), Yik Bow, Wai Lee, Kai Koon and the heroic Wai Sun, 'leader of the Victorian Chinese miners' who struggled valiantly in face of the 'tragedy of the race conflict' in the early years of White Australia. Great merchant houses arose among the miners, he claimed, many of them involved in the migrant trade. When proletarian miners came into conflict with powerful Chinese-Australian firms, the legendary figure of Loong Hung Pung would be summoned to mediate their disputes through the Yee Hing fraternity.[11]

Before considering the historical record of Chinese labour immigration to Australia we might pause to reflect on five elements of the legend recounted to this point. One is the spirit of adventure and camaraderie among working men that bound miners together through the Yee Hing fraternity. Another is the association of a distinctively Chinese-Australian legend about Yee Hing camaraderie with wider Australia folklore in the Anzac tradition. A third is the reference to relations between immigrant miners and wealthy businessmen, sometimes conflicting, which were mediated by the Yee Hing leadership. A fourth is the identification by name of able leaders, known as Chinese headmen in formal histories, who oversaw the planning of labour immigration to the Australian colonies and the supervision of workers on their arrival. The fifth is the concern, evident throughout Chow's essays, to establish an orthodox lineage of Yee Hing leadership among a particular group of headmen against possible rival claimants. Many if not all of the people Chow mentions by name came from his family's home district of Doong Goong (*Dongguan*), neighbouring Hong Kong. Doong Goong was not the home county of the majority of labourers who worked the Victorian goldfields, who hailed for the most part from the four counties of the See Yap district, south of the Pearl River. In New South Wales, Doong Goong natives competed for ascendancy with immigrants from Heungshan neighbouring Macao. The claims Vivian Chow put forward on behalf of Loon Hung Pung are contested in other sources mounted by natives of these other counties who told similar stories with different local inflections.

Scale and style of immigration

Either way, the historical record shows that Chinese labour emigration was a large-scale industry in the 19th century. Between 1801 and 1850 an estimated 320 000 people left China for destinations in Southeast

Asia, the Americas and Australasia, 10 000 of them bound for Australia. Around 7 million followed in their trail over the second half of the 19th century of whom between 60 000 and 90 000 made their way to Australia.[12] Consistent with Chinese emigration patterns of the day, large-scale immigration to Australia operated under two kinds of contract, the first involving indentured labour; the second, a system of informal agreements involving the advance of credit to intending émigrés, was known as the credit-ticket system.

The invention of the first of these two systems, indentured labour, followed the abolition of slavery and basically substituted Chinese labourers for African slave labour on plantations in Latin America and the Caribbean. This was a major innovation in Chinese labour practices in response to European and American colonial interventions in Chinese trading networks. Before this time Chinese mining and agricultural labour in Southeast Asia operated as a free market in which émigré labourers could earn up to four times the average income of labourers in their home villages of south China. Under the indentured labour system, however, businesses contracted teams of coolies who were bound to work for a specified employer for a fixed number of years at low rates of pay and to purchase their food and necessities from company stores. This style of coolie labour was largely unknown among Chinese émigré labourers before the modern colonial era.[13]

By the mid-century goldrushes the indentured labour system had largely given way in white-settler societies to the credit-ticket system. Under this system, individuals secured credit for their passage though personal contacts in their local communities or through supportive merchant houses, often against the security of property. Workers repaid their loans with interest from their earnings over time. Use of this system accelerated following the issuing of an ordinance regulating passage brokers in Hong Kong in 1857 and the introduction of legislation in the United States rendering labour contracts signed outside American borders untenable under US law.[14]

Emigration to Australia

Apart from a small number of Chinese craftsmen who accompanied the early convict fleets, the earliest Chinese immigrants to enter New South

Wales were recruited in the 1830s and 1840s as indentured labourers to substitute for the decline in available convict labour. Unlike free settlers, they were bound to work for their masters on limited wages for fixed terms. Supporters and critics of this practice rightly assumed, as Andrew Markus has observed, that 'they would form a subservient class, denied economic, political and social equality'.[15] Opponents of the practice argued that the presence of indentured labourers would inhibit the development of a universal egalitarian social order and the growth of democratic institutions in the Australian colonies. Supporters of indentured labour do not appear to have minded one way or the other. Egalitarianism, fair dealing and mateship were not yet established as orthodox Australian values, but in time, champions of these values came down hard on the notion that Chinese immigrants were, in effect, convict substitutes. They persisted in this claim long after Chinese began entering the colonies as miners and rural labourers on the credit-ticket system. Chinese miners who paid their way or borrowed for their passage found it difficult to escape the accusation that they, too, were in some sense enslaved.

Unlike indentured labourers, the great majority of Chinese immigrants who came on the credit-ticket system were technically free settlers on arriving in Australia. To be sure, the conditions under which Chinese emigrants secured credit for their passage distinguished them from other free settlers who entered Australia from the British Isles, Europe and North America. A little under half of all free immigrants to Australia in the 19th century received government assistance for the journey. Other free settlers from the British Isles paid their own way or were sponsored by relatives, friends, private bodies or prospective employers. Chinese were not eligible for assisted passage and, if the Californian experience offers any guide, no more than 20 per cent could pay their passage to the Australian goldfields without recourse to loans. Some came at the invitation and expense of relatives or friends already settled in the colonies – a style of free immigration captured in a rare goldfields novella that was published serially over 52 issues of the *Chinese-Australian Herald* (*Guangyi huabao*) from 8 June 1909 to 16 December 1910.[16] Others emigrated to Victoria from 1853, to New South Wales after 1859, and to Tasmania, Queensland and Northern Australia in the 1870s by borrowing under the organised credit-ticket system. These were free settlers arriving with debts inscribed in unwritten contracts overseen by fraternal organisations.

Under the credit-ticket system, intending emigrants were sponsored by merchants in Australia and Hong Kong and monitored while they paid off their loans by headmen working in association with fraternal associations such as native-place clubs and secret societies. The initiative often came from Chinese merchants in Australia. As one British observer noted in 1875:

> *A Chinese merchant in Australia, for instance, wants eight hundred or ten hundred coolies for the gold diggings; he sends the order to his merchant-friend in Hong Kong who procures the coolies, charters the steamer, and despatches her with people. The steamer is fitted and provisioned by him in strict accordance with the Act of Parliament and under the eyes of the emigration officers in Hong Kong, and the emigrants are examined and passed by the health officers.*[17]

Although legally free to do as they pleased, labourers arriving under the cedit-ticket system were held in check on arrival by an extensive social network that secured their employment, took care of their needs and ensured that they met their obligations to their creditors.

The operation of the credit-ticket system in the mid-19th century puzzled European authorities in Australia, Canada, California and Hong Kong, who shared a general concern that the system should not replicate the slave-like conditions of the discredited indentured-labour system. In 1857 the Victorian Select Committee on the Subject of Immigration concluded from its investigations that goldfield immigrants from China were not 'coolies' but 'cultivators, traders, merchants, and men from county districts as well as from towns', some of whom paid their own way, while others borrowed on credit from native bankers, village headmen or from relatives and friends. Similarly, the Harbour Master of the Port of Hong Kong reported in 1866 that emigrants to the goldfields of Australia, Vancouver and California were 'unencumbered by any tie' and technically 'free emigrants' under the credit-ticket system. A less favourable report from California found that relations between merchant brokers and migrants under the credit system were based on 'debt bondage'. The system was certainly based on debt but at a level that could be paid off in Australia without great difficulty. One

British observer reported in 1859 that Chinese diggers in Australia were repaying their immigration debts shortly after their arrival and were to be found everywhere working as free agents retaining their earnings.[18]

The experience of Chinese entering under the credit-ticket system was largely determined by the role and character of the civic associations and headmen into whose hands they were cast on arrival in Australian ports. The immigration system was built on networks of trust rather than on legal contracts. Where formal contractual arrangements did apply, for example in relation to arranging debt clearances with the agreement of shipping companies, native-place associations and secret societies undertook the arrangements. The trust that maintained between a headman and his workers was of a different order, based on an elaborate system of oaths, rituals and punishments overseen by secret society networks.

The role of secret societies in the operation of the credit-ticket system, although difficult to pin down, was a source of wonder to outsiders in the 1870s:

> *The whole transaction from beginning to end is arranged by the Chinese in their own peculiar fashion to the mutual profit, no doubt, of both merchant and laborer. Though there is no visible contract on paper, the employer does not hesitate to advance the costs, as he feels confident there will be no evasion or breach of the verbal agreement of the coolie. No people other than the Chinese could manage an extensive migration on such a loose basis. Their excessive clannishness, the secret power of their guilds, and the wonderful social combinations, with which they surround and secure on all sides the repayment of debts, enable them to do this.*[19]

The burden of the credit-ticket systems on individual labourers is difficult to assess without considering the role of the headmen and fraternal societies charged with overseeing their compliance.

Immigrants, clubs and merchants

The two different kinds of civic associations or clubs that worked with headmen in operating the credit-ticket system – native-place associations (also called district clubs) and secret societies – appear to have played a similar role in the Australian colonies to those in California in mediating relations between immigrants and their creditors in China and Hong Kong. New arrivals in California were obliged to register with native-county clubs, which kept extensive records of immigrants and their creditors. None were permitted to return to China until they had repaid their debts at both ends. The system was policed through agreements between the clubs and shipping companies operating on the China line under which the companies would refuse passage to those intending to return to China without written certification from the relevant club that they had cleared their debts. Native-place associations in Australia continued to operate similar agreements with casual arrivals from China into the 1930s. Few Chinese immigrants considered this practice a form of labour bondage. They looked upon native-county associations and secret societies as benevolent agencies devoted to securing their welfare and helping with their repatriation if and when they were called upon to do so. As in California, the role of these societies in overseeing repayment of debts in the Australian colonies was considered a mark of trust rather than of bondage.[20] The moral authority of secret society networks bore little relation to the myths of bondage or slavery by which white Australians characterised them. The dominant Yee Hing brotherhood cultivated an ethic of equality, camaraderie, mutual assistance and independence from the constraints of the hierarchical society of late imperial China.

In practice, merchant houses, native-place associations and secret societies worked closely in overseeing the seamless operation of the credit-contract system, in some cases under the direction of a single individual. Lowe Kung-Meng of Melbourne operated one of the largest credit-ticket networks in the Australian colonies, with immigration services extending beyond Victoria to Perth in Western Australia, Townsville in the north and Wellington and Dunedin in New Zealand.[21] Lowe wore many hats. He was at once a wealthy merchant, a leading member of the Yee Hing secret society network and, remarkably, both a member of the See Yap Native Place association and the chief benefactor of the rival Sam Yap Association. A native of See Yap himself, Lowe sponsored the construction of the Sam Yap association building in Little Bourke Street in Melbourne.

The wealthy Sydney merchant Way Kee played a similar role in New South Wales and Tasmania, and his nephew Way Lee (*Ye Shouhua*) in South Australia and the Northern Territory. Shirley Fitzgerald records that Way Kee was born around 1824 in Doong Goong County and died in Sydney in 1892 at the age of 68. Although he spent his adult years in Australia he maintained close links with his home county community and merchant houses in Hong Kong over four separate visits to China. He first entered Australia in his teens, in the 1850s, and by dint of talent and contacts was appointed to serve as treasurer of the Koong Yee Tong (an association servicing mainly Doong Goong natives) for more than 30 years from the late 1850s to the early 1890s. In the 1880s he leased properties at 164-168 Lower George Street where he built three shops and residential complexes. He also ran stores in Goulburn Street in Sydney and in four rural towns in New South Wales, and maintained business interests in Tasmania. Way Kee regularly represented the Chinese community to white Australian society. He was one of several leading Sydney Chinese businessmen who signed an ornate scarlet address presented to William Lygon, Earl Beauchamp, when the earl assumed office as NSW governor in 1890.[22]

Way Kee also had extensive interests abroad. By his own estimation half of his business was conducted with Hong Kong, the other half presumably with sites in eastern Australia. In 1890 alone he remitted gold to the value of £10–12 000 to Hong Kong, including many small remittances on behalf of Chinese-Australian residents. Shortly before his death he was joined in Sydney by his family, including his wife, his grandson and his grandson's wife. The 1891 Royal Commission into Gambling confirmed his benevolent work in assisting the poor and returning the bodies of the dead to China, for which he was highly regarded within the community. Way Kee's funeral on 4 September 1892 brought 3000 Chinese Australians onto the streets of Sydney. After a Christian funeral service conducted by the Reverend Yong Choy his procession moved along George Street to the town hall, stopping commerce and traffic along the route. The Balmain Premier Brass Band led the way with a rousing rendition of *The Dead March*, and the Naval Volunteer Artillery Brass Band covered the rear of the procession. Way Kee's hearse, drawn by six horses, led three mourning carriages and an estimated 250 Sydney horse-drawn cabs, each laden with mourners, followed by hundreds of sombre pedestrians wearing their finest suits and hats. The procession ended at the harbour where Way Kee's body was taken aboard the *Tsinan* for burial in China. A Chinese ceremony, presided over by Chow Yum, Quen Jah, Mook Sing, Lee Soon and Jar Man, was conducted on the wharf. The eminent tea merchant Quong Tart arranged the ceremony at an estimated cost of £1000.[23]

Way Kee's nephew Way Lee accompanied his body on the *Tsinan* to China. Way Lee was a successful businessman in his own right, with extensive interests in South Australia, the Northern Territory and Queensland as well as New South Wales. He was a prominent Yee Hing member, a master Freemason of the British order and a mandarin of the fourth rank in China's late-imperial honours system. Way Lee used his good offices to lodge petitions with the South Australian parliament to reform immigration legislation and to bring the Yee Hing network under the purview of 'the legislation at present controlling friendly, benefit and other secret societies', which was introduced in South Australia to cover British Freemasonry. In accordance with a common practice among Chinese living abroad, Way Kee and Way Lee were both known and remembered by the names under which their companies traded in Australia: the Way Kee Company and Way Lee Company.[24] Their common surname was Yip (*Ye*). Both were members of a powerful lineage from Doong Goong County, which maintained extensive interests in the British Straits settlements as well as in Hong Kong, China and Australia.

Leading merchants such as Lowe Kung Meng, Way Kee and Way Lee drew on local and international networks of trust to secure their investment in labour immigration. They appointed headmen to assist on the voyage out, to oversee their charges' employment on arrival, and to ensure the timely repayment of money borrowed for the passage. Many if not most of these headmen were drawn from the merchants' and the workers' own lineage systems. Some headmen were influential in their own right, sponsoring and raising young relatives and neighbours to succeed them in their business and immigration networks. Quong Tart, for example, came to Australia as a child of nine in the company of an uncle who acted as headman for a shipload of labourers from the See Yap county of Toishan to the Braidwood goldfields. In all likelihood Quong Tart's uncle was, after the style of the day, selected from among the sponsoring merchants' secret society or local lineage networks and selected his party of workers from among the same Toishan networks.[25]

Individual headmen typically supervised between five and 30 labourers, in exceptional cases supervising 100 or more at a time. Headmen worked with merchant houses and fraternal associations in Hong Kong and Guangdong to recruit the working parties and to pay their passage, maintain order, secure employment on arrival and, as noted, to ensure that the members of their team repaid their passage before they moved on. They were on the whole responsible men, reasonably fluent in English and showed a considerable capacity for leadership. A contemporary British commentator remarked that the appointment of headmen who were respected by their charges and responsible for their employment, conduct and welfare abroad, was a welcome development over the indentured labour system.[26]

Legend and history

The moral economy of Chinese immigrant labour is embedded in the oral traditions of the Yee Hing secret-society network. In the Australian case, it can be traced through the legend of Loong Hung Pung that forms part of Australia's Yee Hing legacy. The Cantonese name Loong Hung Pung, or *Long Xingbang* in Mandarin, can be read to mean 'dragon who founds lodges'.[27] Names of this kind are frequently found in legend but less often in actual life. This particular name could plausibly apply to any lodge-founding dragon who happened to lead the secret brotherhood into uncharted territory; nevertheless, Australian colonial records indicate that the name Loong Hung Pung was attached to an actual historical figure who worked and died on the goldfields of western New South Wales. Legend and history converge in the story of Loong Hung Pung.

Our starting point in exploring the role of the Yee Hing network in Chinese labour emigration to Australia is a series of essays composed in Shanghai by the young Australian journalist Vivian Chow, which circulated among Chinese-Australian communities in the early 1930s through his English-language magazine, *United China*. Chow's Shanghai periodical was the source for Sleeman's account in *White China* of Loong Hung Pung's role in the founding of the Australian Yee Hing network. Chow's account of Loong Hung Pung is best approached, like that of Sleeman, as a later written record of an early oral legend. It is not entirely reliable. It is told, nevertheless, with a passion born of the conviction that the young Chinese-Australian author bore a proud working-man's heritage that could be traced to the time of the headman Loong Hung Pung. As we shall see, Vivian Chow's published essays are bound up with his own family history centred in western and northern New South Wales. The story is animated by the author's own struggle for recognition as a proud Australian of Chinese heritage born in White Australia.

Loong Hung Pung, Chow wrote, was born in China in 1800 and fled to Sydney in 1848 as an outcast and refugee 'with a huge price on his head for his revolutionary activities against the Manchu Dynasty'. By this account Loong died in 1886. Elsewhere Chow described Loong as an 'august scholar ... exiled to foreign parts by the Manchu officials for reform and revolutionary work in the central provinces'. Loong was reported to have travelled to Australia by way of Malaya, where he was trailed by Manchu spies and to have founded the Yee Hing 'Chinese Masonic fraternity' in 1850, a few years after stepping ashore in Australia. Loong 'led the Australian Chinese' until stepping down as Grand Master in 1878. As an exiled scholar and gentleman Loong was reputed to have been on good terms with successive governors of New South Wales and ministers of religion.[28]

Two independent sources confirm Chow's assessment of Loong as a contemporary figure of some note in western New South Wales. At the same time they provide grounds for questioning the dates Chow ascribes to Loong's birth, his arrival in Australia and the year of his death. The first source is a newspaper column dating from 1874. The second is an article that appeared 15 years before Chow put pen to paper, written by a man who had little personal association with Chinese-Australian communities apart from his observations as a child growing up in rural New South Wales.

The first source dates from August 1874 when the *Sydney Morning Herald* ran an article entitled 'Burial of a Chinese Storekeeper', recording unruly scenes that erupted at the burial of a Bathurst storekeeper named Kong Loong. Hundreds of mourners were disturbed when young rascals ran amuck at the funeral.[29] A crowd of 500 or 600 who had 'assembled at the grave which had been prepared for the deceased ... became witnesses of about as disgraceful a scene as perhaps ever occurred in a Christian community'. The account continued:

> *Upon the coffin being removed from the hearse, the six Chinese who were carrying it found their progress toward the grave stopped at the outset. The crowd were asked to stand aside, and allow the coffin to pass; but they refused to budge an inch, and we beheld the melancholy spectacle of a number of Chinamen fighting their way, with a dead comrade, through a body of ruffians who call themselves civilized men.*[30]

The second source was drafted by John Daniel Fitzgerald, a prominent Irish-Australian barrister, Sydney city alderman and Labor member of the NSW parliament. Fitzgerald's memoir of his childhood in rural New South Wales first appeared in 1917 in a book edited by the established literary figure Ethel Turner for distribution among Anzac soldiers and seamen serving abroad during the Great War. He published a similar account a few years later in a children's novel, *The Ring Valley* (1922), that appeared in the year of his death, in which he detailed the life-and-death struggle of able-bodied Irish-Australian youngsters to overcome anti-Chinese racism in rural New South Wales.[31] Both works include episodes recalling the author's childhood encounters with Loong Hung Pung and give an account of Loong's death and funeral in a goldfields town in western New South Wales.[32]

In his reminiscences, Fitzgerald draws attention to a similar scene to the one described above, which he witnessed as a child, in his case embellished by knowledge of the respect in which Loong was held by the people of Bathurst. Fitzgerald wrote,

> *I have seen the funeral of a great King in a European capital since then. But [Loong's funeral] beat it in impressiveness – at any rate to my impressionable mind. Every person of note in the district came to the funeral – families packed in hay wagons, lone horsemen, ladies in carriages, even one rich and haughty squatter in a brougham carriage.*

There they witnessed Loong laid out in a coffin and draped in funeral clothes befitting an emperor or a nobleman:

> *Clothed in some strange dress, new to our vision, [he] had on a*
> *richly ornamented cap, with gold and silk embroideries. With this*
> *splendid robe and the nobility of death upon him, the genuine grief and*
> *exaggerated respect of the Chinese around him seemed meet and fitting.*
> *We boys were overawed and reverential.*

The funeral was marred by a scuffle when local hoodlums broke in and raided the sacrificial meal and burial ceremony:

> *There in the coffin, tipped up slightly, lay Loong Hung Pun, his*
> *noble face only slightly more wax-like than we had known it in*
> *life, a benign smile it seemed on his pale lips, an ineffable peace on*
> *his noble forehead and in the deep-sunk eyes — shaded forever by the*
> *long lids, closing out the light and cares of the world ... Youthful*
> *bands, impatient at their exclusion, tried to fight their way in, while*
> *the Chinese guards struggled to keep them out. Tables were knocked*
> *over, and ducks, fowls, and turkeys, in all their dainty dressing were*
> *strewn about ... And above all this, the calm, peaceful, impressive face*
> *of Loong, in his coffin at the end of the room. It seemed to me that his*
> *noble countenance had assumed an expression of ineffable contempt.*

Fitzgerald was no less shamed by these events than the *Herald* reporter but he placed them in a familiar setting framed by his personal knowledge of Loong Hung Pung. Loong features in his reminiscences as a man of learning who was fluent in English, who enjoyed a vast and loyal following among Chinese miners, labourers and merchants, and who earned the respect of a wide section of European settlers in rural New South Wales.

According to Fitzgerald's account, Loong operated one of two stores in his home town that were engaged in the business of purchasing gold from local fossickers. The second store was run by a European immigrant known as 'The Count'. As a boy, the author and his school friends preferred to take their small weekend gold finds to the Chinese store rather than to the one operated by The Count. 'Looking back now, I can see that the attraction for us was Loong Hung Pung,' he explained. Loong did not serve customers himself. He sat 'on a kind of high chair',

which enabled him to overlook the whole length of the weatherboard
store. He was a man of fine features, pale as wax, with only a light
slanting of the eyes, a high forehead, surmounted by a silk embroidered
cap, from which a long pig-tail escaped down his back over his
embroidered robe, a sparse moustache in which you could count the
hairs, and a long tuft of beard on the chin. The general expression of
his face betokened extreme benevolence; and the boys all found that the
man's nature was written on that face.

Following their small-business transactions, Loong would invite the
boys to the back of the store to taste sweets and dried salted meats and
to engage him in conversation. Speaking in 'perfect and rather precise
English' he would ask the boys about their school work and their sports
activities, and would regale them with stories about the peoples, cultures,
history, myths and legends of imperial China.

Fitzgerald recalls that around 300 Chinese miners were working
at the time on gold tailings in the district, along with several hundred
Europeans who engaged in 'reefing' (working an ore reef) along the
creeks around the town. Among Chinese and Europeans, Loong Hung
Pung evoked similar feelings of respect. To Chinese labourers in the
district Loong 'was a kind of god. They came from far and wide to see
him, and kowtowed to him as if he were a prince'. Local notables of
European descent paid Loong similar respect. The inspector of schools,
the sergeant of the mounted police, the Catholic priest on his monthly
rounds, the Church of England curate, the Wesleyan lay reader, even 'the
man who hawked bibles in the bush on two pack horses', all called by
the store to pay their respects to Loong whenever they passed through
town. The local schoolmaster was a special favourite of Loong's, 'a smart
young Australian then – now a big man in the political world – spent
a lot of his time in the Chinese store, and to him Loong unbent as he
did to no other'. Beyond the district Loong was said to be on familiar
terms with Sydney businessman Robert Macdonald Mackay, with *Sydney
Morning Herald* editor John West and with Sir Robert Torrens of Torrens
Title fame.[33]

A year or so after the funeral, Fitzgerald recalls coming across a
party of mourners conducting a ceremony in the Chinese section of the
cemetery. One of the gold buyers in Loong's store, a man named King

Song, invited the young Fitzgerald to inspect Loong's grave.

> *In the midst of the ordinary graves headed with rough wooden*
> *memorials with strange Chinese characters, was raised a stone vault,*
> *beautifully and strangely carved with Chinese emblems – dragons,*
> *birds and animals – and an inscription in English graven on the side*
> *of the vault:*

> *Sacred to the Memory*

> *Of*

> *LOONG HUNG PUNG*
> *A Friend of the Human Race*
> *Erected by the Chinese Community of NSW.*

Evidently, the gentleman referred to as Koong Loong in the *Sydney Morning Herald* report was known within the Chinese community of New South Wales as Loong Hung Pung. Fitzgerald's childhood reminiscences and the *Herald* story each describe the death and burial of a prominent Chinese Australian named Loong Hung Pung in July 1874 in Bathurst. This is confirmed by the NSW Registry of Births Deaths and Marriages, which records the death of a man surnamed 'Kong Loong' and the given name and initial of 'Hung P' who died in Bathurst in 1874.[34] Handwritten local records preserved in Bathurst confirm the death of 'Kong Loong Hun Pun' on 30 July 1874. The year of death does not match that recorded in Vivian Chow's Shanghai essays, which place his death 12 years later, in 1886, but the details listed on the Bathurst death register concerning Loong's age, arrival, marriage and children, and listing the names of his father ('Chou CHONG, Occupation Merchant') and mother (surnamed Wang) inspire confidence that the man who provided the details of his life and death knew Loong reasonably well. The informant is listed as 'Brother, Sam Yung, who lived at Lower Turon'.[35] The details provided by Loong's contemporary, and possibly close relative, Sam Yung, appear more reliable than those supplied by Chow more than 50 years after the event in Shanghai.

Local registry and newspaper records from Bathurst also supply grounds for querying Chow's estimate of 1800 as Loong Hung Pung's year of birth. Loong's age at death was initially entered on the Bathurst register in 1874 as 37 years. This was subsequently amended in the margins of the register to record his age of death as 43. The death certificate records that Koong Loong was born in Canton, that he married at the age of 20 and that his wife bore two daughters. It notes that Loong spent a total of 16 years in New South Wales. Assuming that Loong was 43 at the time of his death in 1874 he would have been born around 1831. His first daughter Cum Ling seems to have been born around 1855 and his second, Cho Sam, in 1858, making them aged 19 and 16 respectively at the time of his death. Assuming he entered New South Wales 16 years before his death, as noted in the local register, the year of his entry would have been 1858, not 1848 as Vivian Chow claimed. This corresponds closely to later newspaper accounts of the foundation of the NSW Yee Hing in the year 1858, to which we shall return it the following chapter.[36]

Once the dates of Loong Hung Pung's arrival (1858) and death (1874) have been established we can speculate further on the significance of his life and times for the wider history of the Yee Hing fraternity in New South Wales. The founding of the brotherhood in Australia is commonly ascribed to the year 1858 even by those who prefer an alternative leadership genealogy favouring See Yap men rather than natives of Doong Goong County. Loong's place at the head of the Yee Hing fraternity in western New South Wales is nevertheless indicated in the historical sources by the elaborate gown and golden cap in which he was laid to rest, by the respect that his fellow countrymen paid to him in life and in death, and by the Yee Hing emblems of fantastic animalia that adorned his tomb.[37] Vivian Chow may have been incorrect in dating the birth and death of Loong Hung Pung but he was largely accurate in presenting the story of a man who occupied a position at the centre of Chinese-Australian communities on the NSW goldfields from the late 1850s to the early 1870s. Loong Hung Pung was not just a figure of legend but a Yee Hing leader of note who oversaw the local operation of the credit-ticket system on the western goldfields of New South Wales. The legend of headman Loong Hung Pung was important in its own right but more important still in providing an indigenous Chinese-Australian heritage that could be faithfully woven into Anzac lore by patriotic Chinese Australians.

An Australian journalist in nationalist China

Why did the young Vivian Chow go to such lengths to ensure that the legend of Loong Hung Pung did not fade away along with the memories of his father's generation in White Australia? Vivian Chow was heir to a largely forgotten radical lineage of Chinese political activists that can be traced back to the earliest years of the Yee Hing fraternity in Australia. His father was a founding member of one of the earliest political alliances working for a modern democratic form of government in China. According to family lore, this organisation was inspired by the ideas of Loong Hung Pung, and was founded in Australia in the late 1870s or early 1880s under the English title of Revolutionary and Independence Society of Australian Chinese. By the same account, Vivian's mother was the daughter of the second Grand Master of the original Yee Hing lodge who assumed office immediately after Loong Hung Pung died. Vivian's family was also on close terms with the family of James Ah See, known in China as Tse Tsan-Tai, and universally acknowledged as one of the three founders of the Revive China Society (*Xingzhonghui*) in the brief period before Sun Yatsen's faction came to dominate that organisation in Hong Kong. The Revive China Society is remembered as China's first revolutionary political party. Vivian Chow claimed that this party, too, had its origins among the labour fraternities of eastern Australia and that the Chinese revolution was partly inspired by Australian ideals.[38]

The legend of Loong Hung Pung has traceable historical roots in Chow's own family history. Vivian Chow was born in 1906 in the northern NSW town of Lismore to Chow Toong Yung and Jessie Mary King, who married in the nearby town of Casino in 1894. Vivian's father Chow Toong Yung was a native of Chin Mei (*Cunmou*) village in Doong Goong County. Although surnamed Chow (*Zhou*), Toong Yung and his descendents were entered on official records under the surname of Yung after an Australian customs official mistook the father's last name for his surname when he stepped ashore in Australia around 1870. Vivian's own passport was issued under the surname of Yung, after the style of his father, a name by which he is still remembered in his home town of Lismore. Vivian's mother, Jessie Mary King, was the daughter of Stephen King (Jung-Sao, *Zhong Xiu*) and Annie Lavinia Lavett, who married in Grafton in 1877.[39]

It was Jessie's father, Stephen King, whom Vivian extolled as the second Grand Master of the Yee Hing network and a founder of the Revolutionary and Independence Society of Australian Chinese. Vivian recalled meeting his grandfather as a boy in Grafton before King returned to China around the time of the republican revolution in 1911. In Grafton King was known as Sun Hung Kee. This northern NSW city was a focus of Loong Hung Pung's Yee Hing fraternity. Loong was reported to have, for example, been on close terms with Kai Koon, who was 'in charge of goldfields affairs'. Colonial records show that Kai Koon was naturalised as a British subject in Grafton in 1857.[40]

Vivian was a keen observer of life in northern New South Wales. As a child he showed precocious artistic talent, publishing witty cartoons about his teachers and classmates in the biannual school magazine of Lismore High School, *The Lens*. At the age of 15 he was employed as a cartoonist for the *Richmond River Free Press*. His brother Luther, 11 years his senior, worked as a journalist for the *Northern Star*. After graduating from high school Vivian moved to Sydney and wrote home shortly afterwards to Luther indicating that he wanted to visit China, to where their father had earlier suggested that the family should pay a trip. In fact, in 1908 he had advertised a forthcoming sale at the family store in Lismore 'on account of leaving the district'. But their mother insisted that the children remain in Lismore when her husband Toong Yung returned to China.[41]

His father was not on hand in 1925 when Vivian wrote home from Sydney seeking Luther's assistance and his mother's approval to visit China. Concerned that Vivian was prone to asthma, Jessie was reluctant to let him travel alone. Luther was not keen to accompany Vivian as he held a good position at the local newspaper and was serving as a lay preacher with the Church of England in the city. Still Vivian's persistence paid off. In September 1925 the two brothers sailed for China, where Luther went to work as a proofreader with the *North China Daily News* in Shanghai and Vivian travelled through China, Japan and revolutionary Russia, before finally settling down in Shanghai. At the time of his first visit home to Lismore in 1932, Vivian listed his positions as foreign-affairs editor for the Shanghai evening newspaper *Sin Wan Pao* (*Xinwenbao*) and co-editor of the Chinese-Australian journal that he helped to found in Shanghai, *United China Magazine*.[42] Over his term as editor, *United China* came to be known for its anti-Japanese editorials and stubborn opposition to the nationalist government in Nanking. *United China* is one of the few surviving sources for the legend of Loong Hung Pung.

With its twin focus on Chinese-Australian community history and Japanese aggression in China, *United China* stood out from the hundreds of magazines published in Shanghai in the 1930s. The editors of *United China* wrote in glowing terms of the Australian traditions of egalitarianism, fair play and rule of law while regretting that these traditions were not extended under restrictive immigration laws to families of Chinese descent. There were a number of other Australian journalists and media outlets operating in Shanghai in the 1930s and early 1940 but few were as committed to Australian values or as fiercely opposed to Japanese ambitions in the Asia–Pacific as was *United China*.

Other Australian journalists in China

Around the time Vivian Chow moved from Canton to Shanghai another Australian, Alan Raymond, left Melbourne for China. In 1928 Raymond settled in Shanghai where he went to work selling marble, a product in some demand for the construction of the grand Art Deco buildings springing up along the Bund and Nanking Road. Raymond also dabbled in horse racing as a trainer and amateur jockey at the British racetrack abutting Nanking Road. According to historian Bernard Wasserstein, Alan Raymond 'left a trail of dishonoured cheques made out to business associates' when he fled Shanghai for Hong Kong following the Japanese invasion of China in the summer of 1937. He returned to Shanghai in July 1940 after being expelled by the Hong Kong Jockey Club for race fixing.[43]

Rather than flee Shanghai when Japanese imperial forces stormed the International Settlement in December 1941, Alan Raymond remained behind and ingratiated himself with the city's new masters. He made a start publishing articles in the local press supporting Japan's imperial ambitions. Early in the following year he founded an Australian expatriate organisation, the Independent Australia League, with the aim of encouraging Australians to sever their ties with Britain and declare neutrality in the Pacific war. Raymond enrolled a number of white Australian expatriates into the League, including BA Mackenzie, Eyn MacDonald and John Holland. Under the name 'Roy Stewart', Mackenzie ran a shortwave propaganda program directed at Australia on behalf of the Japanese authorities. Eyn MacDonald broadcast a similar program under the title of the *Women's Hour*. John Holland worked as a journalist in Australia before he tried his hand at business in Shanghai and, like Raymond, was better known in Shanghai for his poor credit record than for his business acumen. Raymond himself did a bit of everything: broadcasting Japanese propaganda on shortwave radio to Australia, penning anti-British articles in the Shanghai press and working as an agent of the Japanese naval intelligence department. A number of other white Australian expatriates attended meetings of the League, which attracted 11 people to its first meeting and roughly twice that number to its second.[44]

Australian patriotism

United China appealed to a different tradition of Australian patriotism rooted in Chinese-Australian experience.[45] It strongly opposed Japanese imperial ambitions in China and warned of the dangers that lay ahead if Japan's attacks on China were not repulsed. It also made much of the influence of Australian ideals and values among Chinese Australians in China. For generations, it maintained, young men had been carrying Australian ideals back to China and had there sewn the seeds of a modern commercial and political revolution that was transforming China. 'The Australians', as Vivian Chow called them, had shown everyone in China that they were the most forward looking, unassuming and practical people of Chinese descent the world over.[46] We shall return to these claims, and to Vivian Chow, in a later chapter on Australian business investment in Shanghai. Here we might note that Chow made a special point of insisting that the vision underlying New China was 'inspired by Australia's ideals' that had been held in trust by young Australians such as himself:

> Australians, especially, should know that this trust has not forever been misplaced ... the ideals of fairplay, sportsmanship, and the spirit to 'play the game for the game's sake' are the new ideals of China – New China since the Revolution of 1911 ... In this New China there are spots that shall be forever Australia – the graves of those Australian Chinese lads who have laid down their lives that China might be free; who had no other thought but that the ideals that made Anzac should be sown in the fertile soil of Young China; who cared nothing for the price, but only for the execution of their duty. They shall ennoble Australia for all time.

Vivian Chow typically ended his essays with appeals to white Australians to treat Chinese Australians with the respect that they deserved as Australians:

> The only pleas, therefore, that we make in the name of these our gallant countrymen, is that Australian people shall treat with respect the Chinese who live in Australia; be kindly unto them; lift the color-bar, and other ignoble persecutions that have contributed to making their lot so unhappy and soul-destroying. We ask you to believe they are good Australians. Give them a chance.[47]

At the heart of Chow's claims for Chinese-Australian commitment to the Australian ideals of equality, fair play, mateship and endurance, lay the 19th century legend of the Yee Hing headman, Loong Hung Pung. This legend is framed in *United China* by articles extolling Australian ideals and proclaiming their impact upon the Chinese revolution. Chow largely exaggerated their appeal in China. This mattered little insofar as he imagined that he was writing for an Australian readership. He wanted Australians to embrace the story of Loong Hung Pung as an Australian legend, not a remote and exotic Chinese one.

*Chinese-Australians participate in
Federation, Melbourne, 1901.
Courtesy of Museum of Chinese-Australian
History, Melbourne*

KMT New South Wales and Australasian Branch building in
Sydney 1921. Chen (1935)

Cemetery monument, Melbourne General
Cemetery. Author's photograph

Cemetery monument, Moorina Cemetery,
Tasmania. Author's photograph

KMT Australasian Club in Canton. Chen (1935)

↓ See Yap Temple
(Siyi huiguan), South
Melbourne. Courtesy of
the See Yup Society of
Victoria

↑ KMT Victorian Branch
building with Walter Burley-
Griffin façade in Melbourne,
1921. Chen (1935)

← *Sincere photography department, Shanghai. Sincere (1924)*

↓ *Sincere department store Canton. Sincere (1924)*

← *Wing On building in Nanjing Road Shanghai. Author's photograph (2006)*

← *Contemporary painting of Chinese-Australian department stores on Nanjing Road, Shanghai. Wing On Mansions and the Wing One store are pictured on the left, Sincere, Sun Sun and Dah Sun on the right. Artist unknown*

Sincere Department Store, Nanjing Road, Shanghai.
Sincere (1924)

Sincere famine-relief vessel. Sincere (1924)

Sunday Christian service at Sincere
Hong Kong store. Sincere (1924)

Wing On Mansions, Shanghai.
Xianggang yongan (1932)

William Liu, General
Manager, China–Australia
Mail Steamship Line. Yong
(1977)

Wong Chee (Huang Bingnan),
founder, Kwong Sing and
Co (Glenn Innes), Sincere
(Hong Kong) and Sun Sun
Department Store (Shanghai).
Sincere (1924)

Ma Ying-piu, founder, the
Sincere chain of companies.
Sincere (1924)

Vivian Chow (Yung). From
The Lens, courtesy of the
Richmond River
Historical Society

Vivian Chow (Yung). Self-portrait of the artist as a young
man. From The Lens, courtesy of the Richmond River
Historical Society

*Philip Gockchin (Guo Chuan),
co-founder, Wing On. Xianggang yongan* (1932)

*James Gocklock (Guo Le),
co-founder, Wing On.
Xianggang yongan* (1932)

*Liang Qichao in Sydney,
1901.* Tung Wah Times

*Evens Leong with her father,
Leong Kunhe in 1898.
Lee* (2000)

Committee of Chinese Empire Reform Association of New South Wales, 1901. Courtesy of
Museum of Chinese-Australian History, Melbourne

乙未年中興會要人玉照

1895

Leaders of the HING CHUNG WUI party.

James See (left) of Grafton, NSW, pictured in 1895 alongside two other leaders of the
Revive China Society in Hong Kong, Yeung Ku-wan (centre) and Sun Yatsen (right).
From United China, vol. 1, no. 11 (October 1933)

4

REVOLUTION, RESPECTABILITY AND CHINESE MASONRY

One proud boast the Australian Chinese have, which no other group
dare claim, that they taught the world respect for Chinese and
Orientals in general. The Australian Chinese did.

Samuel Wong, Sydney 1933.[1]

In 1911 the Yee Hing Company opened an impressive building in Mary Street, Sydney, looking west along Campbell Street towards the city markets, where many of its members worked for a living. Over a period of five decades the company had grown in Australia from a loose affiliation of rural clubs into an organised social network with a prominent urban profile. With the opening of its new headquarters in Sydney, the New South Wales organisation put on a respectable public face under the English title impressed upon the building's facade: *Chinese Masonic Society*.

Mounting a respectable public face was a considerable achievement for an organisation whose members many had come to deride as thugs, gamblers and opium addicts. In 1891 a Royal Commission into Alleged Chinese Gambling and Immorality exposed collusion between gambling dens, opium importers, standover gangs and local police. Although the findings of the inquiry targeted corrupt law enforcement officers, much of the testimony brought before the Royal Commission exposed the operation of a nebulous criminal underworld, apparently linked to the triad network of the Yee Hing Company. The same applied in Melbourne. Not long before the Sydney Masonic Hall formally opened it doors, members of the respectable See Yap native-place association established a rival league to do battle with the Yee Hing fraternity. Gangs took to fighting one another in the streets. Sydney, too, had its Tong Wars, but by 1911 these were things of the past. When it went public as the Chinese Masonic Society of New South Wales, the Yee Hing Company became the kind of organisation that respectable men would be proud to join.[2]

The ideal of respectability was one of the most powerful forces working for social transformation among immigrant communities in federation Australia. Drawing on the work of British social historians, historian Janet McCalman has observed that a cluster of social traits associated with the idea of respectability (including self-reliance, independence and self-discipline) were popularised among all classes in the industrial revolution before being transplanted to Australia 'by immigrants hoping for dignity and prosperity in a new land'.[3] The struggle for respectability crossed class, gender and ethnic lines among the inner-urban communities that staffed and ran the factories, utilities, wharves, warehouses and markets of early 20th century Australian cities. Immigrants who did not harbour aspirations for respectability before their arrival were not long acquiring them. Incentives for achieving respectability were particularly strong in societies such as Australia where settlers from England, Scotland and Ireland mixed with one another, as well as with Russians, Germans, Poles, Chinese and other nationalities to a degree unmatched in their countries of origin. Opportunities beckoned not only for prosperity but also for achieving equal recognition for themselves, their families and their particular religious and ethnic communities.

There is no need to turn to China to search out exotic explanations for the behaviour of Chinese secret societies in Australia. When the underground NSW network went public, under the title Chinese Masonic Society, it was responding to forces at work not in China but in Australia. The NSW network sought recognition of the rightful place of a Chinese community organisation in a white-settler country, and sought some acknowledgment that members of the society were decent, law-abiding citizens. By focusing on the distinctive local features of the company in Australia, rather than turning to China for exotic explanations, we can gain some sense of what was Australian about this Chinese-Australian community organisation.

As an Australian story it also carries lessons for China. In standard histories of the Chinese revolution, the political contributions of overseas secret society networks are circumscribed by two limiting assumptions. One is that secret societies were essentially social in their aims, character and activities. The other is that their political aspirations never rose above atavistic notions of imperial restoration. It follows that they needed to be prodded along by Sun Yatsen's modern republican movement before they could become proto-revolutionary allies for the republicans' assault on the Qing empire. Insofar as this standard history is not borne out by the Australian case, the story of the Australian Yee Hing network has important implications for our understanding of Chinese history more broadly.

By reputation the Chinese Masonic Society of New South Wales was a community organisation that provided support for its members, took a patriotic stand on current events in China and occasionally engaged in standover tactics against those who denied its authority. A similar reputation attached to local branches of the Yee Hing Company in North America and Southeast Asia. In the Australian colonies, it seems that members of the company were capable of politicising and depoliticising themselves without help from Sun Yatsen, that they borrowed as freely from white Australian institutional networks as they did from Sun's Chinese nationalist organisation. The local Chinese Masonic Network had an indigenous revolutionary history long before it adopted a respectable public face and well before Sun Yatsen came onto the scene.

When Sun Yatsen's republican nationalists called on Australian lodges to support the Chinese revolution in the opening years of the 20th century, they confronted an organisation that had come to embrace the immigrant ethic of egalitarian respectability. Earlier atavistic notions of imperial restoration had long since dissipated. Indeed, in the process of going public the Australian masonic network was de-radicalised. Evidence for this argument is summoned from two sets of sources. The first is the legend of Loon Hung Pung, introduced in the preceding chapter, and the historical record of his followers in south China in the late 19th century. The second relates to the consolidation of a statewide Chinese Masonic network early in the 20th century, one that enjoyed links to English and Scottish Freemasonry.

Revolution

The legend of Loong Hung Pung carries a strong political message, some of it embellished retrospectively, some confirmed by secondary records of contemporary accounts dating back to the 1880s. In 1933 the serving Grand Master of the NSW Chinese Masonic Lodge, writing under the cryptic title of '19½', published a eulogy for 'The Great Leader' Loong Hung Pung, extolling his role in laying the foundations for China's republican revolution. Loong, he wrote, was the embodiment of the literary and artistic genius of his race, whose writings and speeches were 'faithful to the noblest traditions of the ancients' and at the same time innovative and modern. Loong Hung Pung said and did 'many new things' that made a lasting contribution 'towards the creation of a New China in the New World'.[4]

Reference to Loong's writings touches on a legendary treatise associated with his name entitled 'The Reconstruction of China as a Modern State', which is reported to have circulated internationally among anti-Manchu activists in the 19th century, and to have reached Sun Yatsen some time before Sun penned his famous *Three Principles of the People*. The text, assuming it ever existed, appears to be no longer extant. Vivian Chow made it a subject of controversy by slandering Sun Yatsen with the claim that he plagiarised Loong's work in drafting his own Three Principles: 'Sun Yatsen procured a copy of Loong's great masterpiece ... and started to copy and transpose it. He was unlucky to lose his copy in a fire, and could not procure another, though he tried hard.' As Chow would have it, Sun tried to pass off as his own what he recalled of Loong's work from memory. 'Thus we have the pot-pourri of the Great Leader, Loong Hung Pung, advanced under the name of Sun Yatsen, "The Three Principles of the People".'[5]

Although self-serving and tendentious, Chow's claim finds some indirect support in Sun Yatsen's own writings. Sun complained at one point that he could not access his collection of books and manuscripts when he drafted the *Three Principles of the People* in 1924 because his library had been recently destroyed in a fire. Further, Sun included in his famous manuscript a curious story about a land speculator who made his fortune by bidding for property at auction in Melbourne while gesturing aimlessly in a drunken stupor. The moral of this Australian tale was that the state should capture increases in property values because land speculation was an immoral source of wealth. To this day, the source for the Melbourne episode in Sun's *Three Principles* remains a mystery. Still, the key claim that Sun passed off Loong's writings as his own is unverifiable.[6]

Loong's organisation extended to members in China to whom it remitted funds from the goldfields to support anti-Manchu activities. Some time after his death, their contacts in China let the Australian organisers down. The corruption of the network in China was exposed through an official inquiry undertaken over the period following Loong's death — Vivian Chow dates it to 1889 — that transformed the attitudes of the NSW Yee Hing leadership. They concluded that 'only the intervention of the Overseas Chinese (*huaqiao*) themselves could promote the revolution'. The results of this inquiry led to a decision to cease remitting funds to China and to encourage instead direct intervention by Chinese Australians in the anti-Manchu revolution in China. Loong Hung Pung's successors were directed to leave Australia and carry their ideals to China.[7]

The decision to commit people rather than funds to the cause in China perhaps explains the decision taken by one activist, John See, to return to China around this time. It also accounts for the involvement of his children James See (Tse Tsan Tai) and Thomas See (Tse Tsi Shau) in the avant-garde reform and revolutionary movements that emerged in

Hong Kong in the early 1890s. John, who was born in Hoiping County in Guangdong Province in 1831, arrived in Australia in the late 1850s or 1860s. On arriving in Sydney he established a business at 39 Sussex Street called the Tai Yick (*Taiyi*) Firm. He later moved with his family to northern New South Wales where he opened the Tse & Co. general store in Grafton before finally settling in Tingha, a tin-mining town not far from Inverell. On the northern tablelands of New South Wales the family passed under the surname Ah See. With his wife Que Sam, John had six children over the decade beginning in 1870. All six children were raised as Christians. The young James See, along with his elder sister Sarah and younger brothers Thomas and Samuel, was baptised by Anglican Bishop Greenway on 1 November 1879 in Grafton's Christ Church Cathedral. In 1887 John See moved with his family to Hong Kong, where he remained until his death in 1903.[8]

According to Vivian Chow, John See was a prominent 'secret sect member' and 'Chinese freemason' in Australia before retiring to Hong Kong. He was a co-leader of the Revolutionary and Independence Association of Australian Chinese with Vivian Chow's father, Chow Toong Yung. These claims are supported in a book published by John's son James See in Hong Kong, two decades after the death of his father. In *The Chinese Republic: Secret History of the Revolution*, James painted a graphic picture of the involvement of his father's generation in a secret revolutionary organisation in Australia dating back to the 1870s that continued to maintain links with defeated leaders of the Taiping Rebellion in China well into the 1890s.[9]

In time the young James eclipsed his father in fame, influence and fortune. James See came into the world in Sydney on 16 May 1872 at a time when Loong Hoong Pung was still entertaining visitors at his store in Bathurst. Loong belonged to the generation of James' father. Better known to historians of China under the name Tse Tsan Tai, James played a role in founding the first revolutionary organisation in Hong Kong. Alongside Sun Yatsen he co-founded the first revolutionary party, and helped to establish Hong Kong's pre-eminent English-language newspaper, the *South China Morning Post*. His own published record of these events indicates that the Australian Yee Hing network was on intimate terms with Taiping rebels in China and with a variety of post-

Taiping secret society organisations based in Hong Kong and Canton from the middle to the end of the 19th century. James also acknowledges in passing that his father led an Australian revolutionary party that he called the Chinese Independence Party of Australia – his name for the group that Vivian Chow called the Revolutionary and Independence Society of Australian Chinese.[10]

The See family became involved in insurrectionist movements against the Manchu imperial government shortly after they stepped ashore in Hong Kong. As a lad of 17, James joined a group of like-minded young men to plan the overthrow of the Qing Dynasty. With Yeung Ku Wan (*Yang Quyun*) in 1891 he formed the earliest revolutionary organisation in China, the Foo Yan Man Ser Kwong Fook Hui (*Furen wenshe guangfuhui* – Furen Cultural Society Restoration Association).[11] It was this association that later merged with Sun Yatsen's Hawai'ian faction to form the Hong Kong chapter of the Revive China Society. Yeung was the inaugural leader of the Hong Kong Revive China Society but within a short time surrendered the position to Sun Yatsen. James See followed Yeung in preference to Sun and refrained from joining Sun Yatsen's later organisation, the Revolutionary Alliance (*Tongmenghui*), as a sign of his loyalty to Yeung.

James See maintained his Australian connections and encouraged his patron to consider visiting Australia. Yeung consented. In a letter dated 26 May 1900, Yeung Ku-wan informed James that he planned to visit Australia over the coming year. The visit was possibly prompted by news that Liang Qichao, a leader of the rival Society to Protect the Emperor (*Baohuanghui*), was intending to visit Australia around the same time. Liang visited Australia from October 1900 to May 1901. Yeung never made it here: on 10 January 1901 a gang of hired assassins broke into the schoolroom where he was taking classes and murdered him. The assassins fled to sanctuary in imperial Canton.[12]

James also maintained his father's links with secret society organisations and Taiping rebels through the old Australian Yee Hing fraternity. On one occasion, James recalled, a nephew of the Taiping Christian King, Hong Xiuquan, called by to speak with his father at their home in Hong Kong. The nephew, who travelled under a variety of names, including Hung Chuen-fook (*Hong Chunfu*) and Hung Wu, was said to have trained and fought in Taiping armies in the 1850s and 1860s. On this occasion Hung called by to seek strategic advice from the elderly John See regarding plans to mount an anti-imperial uprising in Canton. John See was too frail to take part in the uprising himself and encouraged his 27 year old son to step forward in his place. James and Thomas then set to work with the nephew of the Taiping leader in plotting an armed uprising under the guidance of the aging leader of the Revolutionary and Independence Association of Australian Chinese.

The aim of the uprising was to overthrow the imperial system and establish a modern democratic form of government in China. They certainly did not propose to 'restore the Ming' but, significantly, nor did they propose to establish a republic. James See described the 1902 putsch as a 'commonwealth' uprising in contrast to the republican uprisings intermittently mounted by Sun Yatsen. He explained the difference:

> *I decided to plan and organize another attempt to capture Canton and establish [a] Commonwealth Government under a 'Protector', as I was of the opinion that the 'Republican' form of government was too advanced for China and the Chinese.*

Before the uprising took place, James expressed the view that the new commonwealth should be set up under 'able Christian leadership.'[13] It is not difficult to detect his Australian experience in James' revolutionary proposal to establish a commonwealth (on the model of the Commonwealth government of Australia founded the preceding year) in which the Chinese people were placed under the care of able Christian protectors.

From January 1900 to December 1902 James acted as chief strategic planner for the uprising. Hung Chuen-fook was assigned responsibility for recruiting and organising martial forces. Dr Yung Wing, who led the first delegation of young Chinese students to study in the USA, was nominated president-in-waiting of the provisional commonwealth government; Thomas See was appointed deputy. In January 1903 Thomas and Hung Chuen-fook set off for Macao to 'direct the operations for the capture of Canton'. The plot was exposed when Hong Kong police raided Hung's headquarters on D'Aguilar Street. Hung and Thomas See narrowly escaped with their lives. Struck by anxiety over the safety of his two sons and disappointment over the betrayal of the revolution, John See fell ill and died within six weeks. Thomas went on to become a successful shipping agent and businessman. From 1925–31 he acted as Chinese secretary to the Canadian Trade Commissioner in Shanghai, where he set up a popular Cantonese social centre known as the Kok Loo Club. He also developed a series of patent medicines (including See's Magic Ointment) that were marketed under the name of the Man Ning (*Wanneng*) Patent Medicine Co. Ltd and sold through the Australian department stores on Nanjing Road. After the communists took Shanghai, Man Ning developed into the ubiquitous Mannings pharmacies of Hong Kong. Thomas died in 1933.[14] After the uprising, James See settled for a life of journalism, fine-art collection and business in Hong Kong. He played an active role in Hong Kong cultural and commercial life until his death in April 1937.

Respectability

Today the Chinese Masonic Hall shows few traces of this revolutionary heritage. A number of old images pinned to the walls still bear messages conveying the spirit of solidarity, justice, patriotism, masculinity and egalitarian defiance that characterised the Chinese masonic network from its earliest days in Australia. But there is no trace of the legendary Loong Hung Pung or the revolutionary James See. Its politics are strictly respectable and patriotic.

To the right of the reception hall hangs a framed photograph of General Cai Tingkai who defied Generalissimo Chiang Kai-shek and confronted battalions of Japanese military invaders in 1931 before founding an independent People's Government in Fujian in 1934. The Australian Masonic Society invited General Cai to tour Australia in March 1935 and meet with Chinese Australians who shared his contempt for Chiang Kai-shek's strategy of fighting Communists in preference to resisting Japanese invaders. The photograph on the wall bears a signed message from General Cai thanking the Sydney Masonic headquarters for its assistance in arranging his visit.

To the left hangs a large framed watercolour of the legendary outlaws of the Liangshan marshes, one of the fabulous sources to which Chinese lodges trace their eclectic liturgy of beliefs and rituals. Legend has it that seven centuries ago this band of outlaws professed principles of loyalty and justice while upholding an ideal of universal brotherhood, expressed in the saying 'All men are brothers', to borrow the title of Pearl Buck's popular translation of the legend.[15] The 108 outlaws swore oaths of loyalty to one another to struggle for justice in the face of corrupt authority. They robbed from the rich and gave to the poor, according to popular legend, and had a rollicking time with local monks and magistrates.

Like their outlaw heroes, members of the Chinese masonic network were partial to the trappings of higher orders, although in Australia these were domesticated into ritual hierarchies of honour and loyalty to which any member could aspire. They also practised collective discipline. A member found guilty of breaking the code of conduct was liable to receive 108 beatings with a cane, a form of punishment that was possibly more familiar to colonial readers of court columns in 19th century Australian newspapers than it is to kung-fu movie fans today. In 1896, for example, Victorian newspapers closely followed a case involving 108 beatings that came before the local bench in Bendigo after a certain Lee Fook gave evidence for the prosecution in a criminal case against a sworn brother. For this violation of the code Lee was allegedly summoned before a meeting of 200 brothers and sentenced to a punishment of 108 lashes.[16] Similar punishment was possibly inflicted in ritual spaces on the third floor of the Sydney headquarters. The painting of 108 heroes of Liangshan hanging prominently on the ground floor serves as a reminder to members of the egalitarian and heterodox values that bound them together and of the punishments that awaited them if they violated the code.

On the far wall facing the entrance hangs a set of framed scrolls boldly scripted in large characters. Two vertical scrolls hang left and right, the one on the right reading 'Exert effort for the Hung League [Yee Hing] through commitment to loyalty and justice,' and the one on the left, 'Sacrifice personal interests for the common good in working for the Lodge'. Between the two vertical scrolls hangs a large horizontal work of calligraphy framed behind glass. It reads:

Our history can be traced to the two Grand Lodges
Our prestige reaches out forever through branches overseas
Hung League [Yee Hing] brothers are all loyal and just
With one heart protecting the Chinese Masonic Lodge
[Zhigongtang][17]

Tracing the history of the Australian Chinese Masonic network to the 'Two Grand Lodges' in China leaves unanswered many of the questions we might want to ask about the arrival, expansion, institutionalisation, politicisation and, indeed, the depoliticisation of the network in colonial and federation Australia. For these we need to consult local Australian historical records.

The founding of the consolidated NSW grand lodge is customarily attributed to John Moy Sing and James A Chuey, two community leaders who brought the underground rural network into the open in Sydney and built the grand Masonic hall in Mary Street over the first decade of the 20th century.

Around the turn of the century the NSW masonic network went under the name of the *Hongshuntang* (Hung Obedience Hall), derived from the title of the Cantonese Lodge in China. Within a decade it ventured into the wider English-speaking arena as the Chinese Masonic Society.

In June 1916, the Chinese title was changed from *Hongshuntang* to *Zhonghua minguo gonghui* (Chinese Republican Association) to keep pace with a similar change of name on the part of the organisation's general headquarters in Hong Kong. Three years later, the Sydney office adopted yet another Chinese name, the Chee Kong Tong (*Zhigongtang*, lit. 'Exert Public Benefit Lodge') in keeping with the title adopted some years earlier by the North American regional office based in San Francisco.

Despite these changes to its formal Chinese designation, the organisation retained its informal titles of Yee Hing Company and Hung Men League in colloquial Chinese; it has retained its formal English title of Chinese Masonic Society to the present day.[18]

These changes in the English and formal Chinese titles of the masonic network coincided with the leadership transition involving Moy

Sing and James Chuey, who between them oversaw the transformation of the network from a loose rural affiliation of secret-society lodges into a tightly focused urban institution with a prominent public profile. Moy Sing is credited with founding the parent organisation around the mid-19th century. Historian CF Yong regards Moy Sing as the founder of the company from its establishment in 1858 to his retirement in 1913 when James Chuey is assumed to have succeeded him in office. This account of the leadership transition is important in another respect. In Singapore and the Straits settlements, Trocki has written, the charismatic military and political leaders of the early Yee Hing organisation made way in the late 19th century for successful urban merchants who enjoyed close ties with European businessmen and colonial authorities. The same appears to have occurred in Australia. The leadership transition to the wealthy businessman James Chuey marked the Masonic Society's entry into public life.[19]

In an earlier chapter we questioned the claim that Moy Sing was the sole founder of the NSW Chinese masonic network and considered the rival claim of the legendary figure of Loong Hung Pung. In fact, a number of loosely-related lodges representing immigrants from different counties were founded at various goldfield sites and tin mines from the middle of the nineteenth century, most of them associated with the credit-ticket system of labour migration, some of them organised under charismatic leaders, and all of them generating their own legends of bonhomie and camaraderie. Moy Sing appears to have played a key role in consolidating these rural lodges into a statewide network based at his Sydney headquarters over the federation period. At one point he based the lodge at his private home for a spell pending completion of the Mary Street headquarters.[20]

The transformation of this loose network of lodges into a consolidated federation based in Sydney followed the pattern of triad consolidation under way in North America, where the San Francisco Chee Kong Tong came to exercise increasing influence over lodges in California and other parts of North America through a loosely federated Chee Kong Tong network. Many of the factors at work in the United States in the 1880s and 1890s also operated in Australia, including immigration restrictions, immigration rackets and the preponderance of unskilled male labourers among Chinese migrants. Of special significance in Australia was the internal immigration of Chinese-Australian labourers from rural farms to towns, from towns to provincial cities and, in significant number, to the two capital cities, Sydney and Melbourne. In the 19th century the most active Yee Hing lodges were based in rural settlements and regional townships where 90 per cent of Chinese labourers and merchants lived and worked. The early history of the Chinese Masonic network was bound up with the experience of these rural community networks. This history was soon overshadowed as the network shifted from a rural to an urban base in Australia.[21]

Archival and family records support the outline of legendary accounts of Chinese life on the western goldfields and northern tin mines of New South Wales in the mid-19th century. The same sources help us to trace the extension of Loong Hung Pung's network into a republican brotherhood based in northeastern New South Wales later in the century, and to observe its further elaboration into a modern revolutionary organisation centred in Hong Kong and Canton at the turn of the 20th century. This network survived in attenuated form through the efforts of Vivian Chow and his comrades in Hong Kong, Canton and Shanghai into the 1920s and 1930s. By this time, however, the Chinese masonic network on the eastern Australian seaboard was moving in quite a different direction, indicated among other things by the English title Chinese Masonic Society impressed on the facade of its new headquarters in Mary Street. The Australian network was becoming urban and respectable.

Chinese Masons and Freemasonry

In one sense the adoption of the term 'Masonic Society' was a straightforward cross-cultural translation. Chinese secret societies were often likened to European Freemasonry in early British and European accounts. Commenting on their elaborate rituals and traditions in 1925, JSM Ward and WG Stirling observed that, 'like Freemasons in the West, the Hung or Triad Society seems justly entitled to claim that it is a lineal descendant of the Ancient Mysteries'. Gustav Schlegel made a similar observation four decades earlier: 'Every person who has read anything of the secret societies in China must have been struck with the resemblance between them and the Society of Freemasons.' Earlier still, in 1855, the interpreter Howqua engaged in cross-cultural translation when he told the Victorian goldfields commission that the rebels who were known to Chinese miners as Yee Hing or Taiping rebels were 'Freemasons'.[22]

In another sense, the Yee Hing Company's adoption of the title Chinese Masonic Society was not merely an act of translation.[23] Chinese Masons were linked with white Freemasons through a variety of personal and business networks. The reorganisation of the Yee Hing Company in the 1890s and early 1900s followed closely on the consolidation of European Freemasonry as an urban-based network in Sydney, in 1888, when scattered rural and urban lodges of European Freemasonry merged to form the NSW United Grand Lodge. The Chinese brotherhood followed suit, first moving towards colony-wide consolidation in the 1890s before funding and building impressive offices for its state headquarters in Mary Street over the following decade, and finally proclaiming itself the headquarters of the Chinese Masonic Society of New South Wales.

This analogous sequence of masonic consolidations involving the Chinese Masonic Society and the United Freemasons could be regarded as fortuitous were it not for a number of identifiable connections linking the two fraternal networks. Chinese Australians were among the first people of Chinese descent in the world to gain entry to the international order of Freemasons. Some time before the successful consolidation of colonial Freemasonry, Sydney tea merchant and teashop entrepreneur Quong Tart (*Mei Guangda*) was admitted into the Order of Oddfellows under the English constitution. On 8 October 1885 he was initiated into the Lodge of Tranquility which convened at Bondi in the neighbourhood of his early residence in Waverley in the eastern suburbs of Sydney. Quong rose to the second degree on 11 March 1886 and was elevated to the status of Master Mason on 12 July 1886. He does not appear to have been a member of the Yee Hing when he joined the Freemasons but he was certainly on close terms with a number of Chinese masonic leaders and remained an active Freemason until his death in 1903, when forty members of the fraternity accompanied his funeral procession in full regalia processing behind an oak coffin draped with his Master Mason's apron.[24]

By one account Quong Tart was the third Freemason of Chinese descent to be admitted to an order anywhere in the world. By the time of his death in 1903, however, he was one of a number of important Chinese-Australian business leaders who had followed him into the Freemasons. Chinese-language newspapers of the day reported that 'Chinese and Western' Freemasons marched side by side in Quong Tart's funeral cortege. Some of the business leaders admitted into the order between Quong Tart's initiation in 1885 and his death in 1903 include Sun Johnson, WRG Lee and his son William Lee, in New South Wales, and Way Lee in South Australia. Unlike Quong Tart these men were prominent Yee Hing member who played a role in translating its idioms and rituals for the wider English-speaking community.[25]

Sun Johnson and William Lee acted as English secretaries for the Chinese Masonic Society during James Chuey's term as director. Way Lee petitioned the provincial parliament of South Australia in 1891 to bring Chinese secret societies under the purview of the law on the same terms as Freemasonry. He petitioned that the Secret Societies Suppression Bill before the House should

> *be so amended as to extend its operation to all dangerous and*
> *unlawful societies, and so as to enable it to suppress all gambling*
> *dens in the Northern Territory as well as throughout the province,*
> *and that the societies specified in the Bill should be brought within the*
> *influence of the legislation at present controlling friendly, benefit and*
> *other secret societies.*[26]

At the time his petition was presented in Adelaide, Way Lee's uncle, the wealthy Sydney businessman Way Kee, was under investigation before a Royal Commission in Sydney for alleged involvement in illegal immigration rackets and gambling. In conforming to legislation governing British Freemasonry and establishing indirect contacts with Freemason lodges, the Yee Hing Company was cleaning up its act.

Not all Freemason lodges embraced Chinese Australians by any means. Indeed, relatively few Chinese names are recorded on Australian membership rolls before the mid-20th century. Where extant minute books make reference to Chinese nominees they are as likely to record black-ball attempts at exclusion as new initiations. Records of the inner-Sydney Wentworth Lodge record a case in 1903 when a Chinese nominee was withdrawn before his name came up for voting:

> *In September [1903] a Chinese merchant was proposed, but before*
> *his separate ballot was reached his name was withdrawn, and his*
> *proposer and seconder called off, together with three other members.*
> *The interruption to the smooth working of the Lodge, which was very*
> *unpleasant, however, proved only temporary.*[27]

Although some lodges discriminated against nominees on racial grounds other lodges accommodated minorities. The invitation issued to Quong Tart in 1884 was issued by a Jewish lodge founded with an exclusively Jewish membership in June 1875. Three years elapsed before the first non-Jewish member was admitted (in May 1878) and no more than a dozen non-Jewish members were admitted to the brotherhood in any one year when Quong was initiated in the 1880s.[28]

Despite occasional restrictions on membership, invitations to join Freemason lodges were issued to some of Australia's most prominent Yee Hing members in the 1890s and early 1900s. These members ensured that the transformation of the Yee Hing Company into the Chinese Masonic Society over the first decade of the 20th century mirrored that of the NSW United Grand Lodge of Freemasons through the late 1880s and early 1890s. European Freemason lodges came together to form the NSW United Grand Lodge in the third year of Quong Tart's membership of the fraternity. Under the leadership of Moy Sing and James Chuey, rural Yee Hing lodges converged to form the NSW Chinese Masonic Society and refocused their energy from the political emphasis that had characterised rural lodges associated with Loong Hung Pung towards social, economic and domestic political priorities related to their members' immediate concerns in colonial and federation Australia. Its leaders built a statewide organisation on a substantial urban base to mobilise support for reform of Australian laws and regulations governing Chinese immigration, for the promotion of business ties between Chinese and White Australians, and for the expansion of Australian imports and exports with colonial Hong Kong and Malaya and the treaty ports of imperial and republican China.

They also took advantage of the resources of the consolidated European network. As early as January 1896 Chinese-Australian community leaders were convening public meetings in the Sydney Freemasons' Hall. In 1901 they gathered in the Masonic Hall to celebrate Emperor Guangxu's birthday. Chinese Masons also made use of the hall. In November 1911, Chinese Masonic Grand Master James Chuey, together with Sydney merchant George Bew, convened a meeting of the Young China League in the United Freemasons' Hall.[29] Prominent Chinese Masons, such as James Chuey, continued to hold partisan political views and to participate in reformist and revolutionary organisations, including the Young China League and, at a later date, the Chinese nationalist movement. From the turn of the century, however, the Chinese Masonic network no longer sponsored its own political party. It worked instead to forge links with other community organisations including, white Australian institutions and Chinese-Australian ones.

These institutional innovations were grafted onto the early foundations of rural Yee Hing networks then operating in New South Wales. The politics of the early lodges established new kinds of regional Australian networks that existed in parallel with ties of kin and native place that were rooted in China. The year of Loong Hung Pung's death falls into the earliest period for which we can find written records of pan-Chinese associations based on Australian soil. As we have seen, Loong himself was laid to rest under a tombstone that recorded the gratitude of the 'Chinese Community of New South Wales' to their departed leader in 1874. If true, this was a significant gesture. Historians are accustomed to thinking of Chinese immigrants as organising themselves along lines of Chinese native-place or kinship associations for mutual aid and social advancement. To be sure, many of the consolidated organisations that appeared around the Pacific Rim from the mid-19th century were loose confederations of native-place and surname associations that referred in their naming practices to China.[30] As early as the 1870s, however, Chinese institutions in Australia were organising regional colonial networks that were only indirectly linked to native-place or kinship ties in China and were more specifically related to their place of domicile in Australia. Those who mourned the death of Loong Hung Pung in 1874 did so through the agency of a pan-Chinese community of an Australian colony – with the organisational locus of New South Wales – and an appeal to friends of the human race.

Revolution and respectability in death

Between the 1870s and early 1900s a number of cemetery monuments bearing Chinese-language inscriptions were erected in Victoria and Tasmania. Their distinctive inscriptions warrant mention here. The early Victorian monuments convey a modern sense of China as a national state, while the later Tasmanian ones invoke a new kind of Confucian national community. The erection of these two different styles of monument from one period to the next parallels, monumentally, the transformation from the 1870s to the early 1900s of the Australian Yee Hing organisation from revolution to respectability .

Beginning in the early 1870s in colonial Victoria, monumental stele began to appear bearing Chinese-language inscriptions commemorating the deaths of elders from all provinces who were laid to rest on Australian soil. One of the earliest of these steles was erected in the Melbourne General Cemetery in 1873. The central column reads 'Graves of Honorable Elders from all Provinces of China (*zhonghuaguo*)'. The column on the left reads 'A common offering from native villagers of the two Guangdong prefectures of Guangzhou and Zhaoqing'. The right column reads 'Erected on an auspicious day in the spring of 1873 (*Tongzhi guiyounian*)'. Similar steles were erected in Ballarat, Bendigo and Beechworth cemeteries over the following decade. Their choice of words reflects the development of a style of pan-Chinese nationalism focusing on a new state called 'China' among Chinese social networks in Victoria. This 'China' had no counterpart in China itself, where the country was properly known as Great Qing State (*Daqingguo*).

The earliest steles refer to the immigrants' country of origin, not by the then current Chinese term Great Qing State, but by the neologism 'Chinese State' or 'China' (*Zhonghuaguo*). These are among the earliest recorded references to China as a modern political state to be found on Chinese-language monuments anywhere. They are possibly secret-society monuments. A Yee Hing banner, preserved among holdings of 19th century artefacts in the Bendigo Golden Dragon Museum, bears the same inscription for China (*Zhonghuaguo*), indicating that the term circulated throughout the rural Yee Hing network at the time the Victorian memorials were erected.[31]

By the turn of the 20th century, this modern term for China was no longer inscribed on Australian cemetery monuments. Steles erected in the early 1900s in cemeteries across northeastern Tasmania refer to the 'Great Qing State' in preference to the 'Chinese State'. Unlike the earlier monuments in Victoria they make reference to the teachings of Confucius. One stele erected alongside a ceremonial oven in Moorina Cemetery in 1906, for example, bears inscriptions in Chinese and English. The Chinese reads, 'Great Qing State, Graves of honourable elders, 32nd year of [Emperor] Guangxu'. The accompanying English inscription reads, 'This stone has been erected by the Chinese of Garibaldi, Argus and Moorina as a place of worship of Confusias [*sic*] religion to the departed Chinese in the Moorina Cemetery'. An almost identical memorial, erected in nearby Weldborough Cemetery in 1909, begins with the Chinese expression 'Great Qing State' and ends with the English dedication: 'This stone has been erected by the Chinese as a place of worship of Confusias religion to the departed Chinese and those connected with the Chinese in the Weldborough Cemetery.'[32]

References to the Great Qing State or Confucianism are nowhere to be found among earlier cemetery monuments in rural Victoria. The differences may indicate varying political orientations on the part of Chinese-Australian communities in Victoria from those of colonial Tasmania, though given the close association between Tasmanian and Victorian Chinese communities, this seems unlikely. It is tempting to speculate instead that the replacement of the modern term for China, carved onto memorials in the 1870s, by explicit references to the Great Qing State on later monuments reflects a new style of community politics that was emerging around the turn of the 20th century. This was a politics of urban respectability that was consistent with the conservative leadership of Yee Hing elders Moy Sing and James Chuey in Sydney, and supported by their counterparts around Australia at federation.

The arrival of this new politics of respectability left a deradicalised space into which Sun Yatsen and his republican revolutionaries could introduce to Australia their particular style of nationalism and their own political party, the Kuo Min Tang. Veteran members of the Yee Hing brotherhood could well conclude, with Vivian Chow, that 'the advent of Sun Yatsen was really a mild diversion in the great record of the Chinese revolution'.[33]

5
CHINESE AUSTRALIA AT FEDERATION

*The year 1904 will be remembered by the workers of the world
and should be commemorated throughout the whole world … The
government that has been set up in Australia this year marks an
historical breakthrough.*

Liang Qichao 1904.[1]

Tasmanian Chinese community leaders were in one sense pioneers
when they erected monuments commemorating the Confucian heritage
of people laid to rest in Moorina and Weldborough cemeteries. No
family in China had yet thought to remember its dead by invoking
the Confucian religion on a cemetery memorial. Confucius was widely
revered in China but honoured more as a moral philosopher and
political strategist than as a religious prophet. By the turn of the 20th
century, however, Chinese in Australia were starting to imagine their
Confucian heritage in ways that made new sense to themselves and a
familiar kind of sense to the predominantly white communities in which

they lived and worked. One of the axioms of Australian nationalism was that national peoples – British or Germans, for example – were endowed with distinctive national cultures and values that united them as a people. Another was that national peoples were driven by religious convictions that inspired them to lay down their lives for their countries. People from China ran the risk of not being taken seriously if they could not show that they too came to Australia with a national cultural and religious heritage. Chinese Australians needed Confucius in ways they had never needed him before: to serve as an emblem of China's national culture and as a prophet of China's national religion.

In a broader sense the Tasmanians were more imitators than pioneers. Few people in China may have thought of inscribing references to the Confucian religion on cemetery monuments but Confucianism was nevertheless undergoing a metamorphosis in China. For a brief moment around the turn of the 20th century the venerable philosopher was resurrected as a new kind of religious figure who could convert China's vast and varied civilisational heritage into a uniform national culture of the modern European kind. To elite reformers in China the novel idea of a Confucian culture and religion promised to make Chinese nationals out of everyone who happened to be born of Chinese parentage, whatever their ethnicity and wherever they happened to live or die, even in Tasmania, and to mobilise patriotic sentiment around national symbols and religious convictions. It did not matter that mention of a Confucian religion was better appreciated by foreigners than by people in China. The new prophet, Confucius, bore little relation to the Confucius of old China, but China was no longer the China of old.

The Confucian ethical tradition was being renovated on two fronts. On one side it was being recast as an ethical system that embraced the ideal of universal equality. Kang Youwei, a leader of the reform faction in China, was at this moment mounting a Confucian case for egalitarianism and fraternity in a vocabulary and syntax that would have been familiar to any Chinese scholar preparing to sit for the imperial examinations. Challenging the place of social hierarchy in Confucian thought, Kang merged the Confucian principle of human-heartedness with concepts drawn from China's Buddhist tradition to promote egalitarian ideals in the language of Confucianism itself. Kang Youwei did as much as any scholar of his time to introduce traditional debates on ethics and statecraft to the egalitarian ethics of modernity and to the emerging world of nation states.[2]

On a second front Confucianism was being reorganised as a religious system in the style of reformed Japanese Shintoism and modern Western Christianity. Early in the 20th century, champions of the new Confucian religion proposed to reset the Chinese calendar to commence with the birth of Confucius, just as the Gregorian calendar began with the birth of Christ, and to convene weekly ceremonies on the model of the Sabbath to commemorate Confucius' newly-ascribed divinity. The Tasmanian monuments were linked to the Confucian religious movement in China through political connections linking leaders of the Australian-Chinese community with the Confucian reform party in China.

The efforts made by Kang Youwei and his fellow reformers to recast Confucius as a national saviour were part of a wider strategy to reclaim momentum from a rival party associated with Sun Yatsen. Sun was a republican who wanted to overthrow the imperial system altogether. The reformers hoped to retain the emperor system while refashioning China into a modern national and constitutional state that preserved its social, ethical, ritual and political foundations. They called for reform of the traditional Confucian education system, for deeper government involvement in commercial and industrial development, for reform of government administration and for greater participation by Chinese subjects in political decision making and affairs of state. Their opportunity came in 1898 when Emperor Guangxu invited the reform party to implement its program at court.[3] But within months of this invitation the reformers, along with the emperor, were cast aside in a conservative coup engineered by the Empress Dowager Ci Xi. Some of the reformers were executed, others, including Kang Youwei and his student Liang Qichao, fled abroad; the emperor himself was placed under house arrest within the palace complex in Peking.

In 1900 Kang Youwei sent Liang Qichao to Australia to raise support for the political organisation he had founded in exile, the Society to Protect the Emperor. On arriving in Australia Liang summoned Tang Caizhi, brother of the martyred reformer Tang Caichang, to join him and edit the leading reform newspaper of the day in Sydney, the *Tung Wah News*. By the time Liang Qichao set foot on Australian soil in

Fremantle, in October 1900, an Australian network of the Society to Protect the Emperor had been established around the country. Liang toured Australia for six months to May 1901, drawing on local members of the society to serve as his guides and interpreters along the way. At every point of call from Fremantle to Sydney he gave public lectures on the place of equality in the making of modern nations.

Liang's speeches and writings over the course of his visit focused on an issue that was to be of some importance in China and Australia over the following century – the question of equality. The writings he published at the end of his tour in one sense confirmed white Australian perceptions of the hierarchical mentality of the subjects of the Chinese empire; nevertheless, his arguments undermined the culturalist foundations of the case for Chinese exclusion. In vulgar white-Australian nationalism Chinese were characterised as racially inferior to whites. In elite circles such crude racism was eschewed in favour of the more powerful claim that Chinese were culturally incapable of understanding what it meant to be equal and hence unable to appreciate the value that white Australians placed upon equality. To NSW Colonial Secretary Henry Parkes, for example, Chinese did not merit equality of treatment as they failed to comprehend the egalitarian ethics of White Australia. In 1880 Parkes rebuked a group of angry anti-Chinese petitioners for suggesting that Chinese were a race of 'semi-savages'. They were, he insisted, 'a very intelligent people'. Parkes declared that he himself had never classified the Chinese people among 'the inferior races' (who remained unnamed) and had formed a view that their superior diligence and intelligence threatened white society.[4] Superior or inferior, Chinese were to be denied equal entitlement to citizenship and Christian salvation because they were culturally predisposed to value hierarchy and propriety. Liang Qichao would have none of this. China's hierarchical system had political and historical roots, and his agenda for political reform would make 'New People' (*xinmin*) out of the people of China.

As far as Chinese Australians were concerned, Liang timed his visit well. His arrival coincided with federation. To appreciate the enthusiasm with which Chinese Australians welcomed Liang Qichao and the Confucian reform party in Australia we need to appreciate how closely they were engaged with the remaking of their own traditions in an effort to make sense of their lives in Australia at the time of federation. Some of these concerns they brought to bear on Australian federation itself. Others were focused more directly on the value of equality and their entitlement to equality of treatment with white Australians. This chapter explores the intellectual history of the Chinese-Australian community over the federation era, paying particular attention to the value of equality and the act of federation.

Federation

Australian federation was not an event of great moment in China. It surfaced now and again in Chinese newspaper commentaries on developments in the British empire and in abstract debates on the finer points of constitutional reform. In almost every case the point of the argument was that Australian federation offered proof of the wisdom of Britain's *laissez-faire* policies towards its colonies. This line of argument also found favour among Chinese Australians.

Australian federation, reported one paper in China, was a tactical move in Britain's long-term strategic plan to consolidate the empire following the loss of the American colonies. 'British colonies are scattered all over the world,' it began, 'but until now there has been no way to keep them united.' The move to Australian federation was thought to have followed a phase of relatively lenient British imperial policy designed to prevent a recurrence of the American War of Independence by conceding autonomy to the remaining colonies. More recently, the Boer War had ushered in renewed demands for unification, resulting in approval by the queen and parliament for a federal constitution for the Australian colonies. The Australian Constitution demonstrated the benefits of relative autonomy and central consolidation – at once uniting the Australian colonies and conferring greater autonomy on them as a federated union.[5]

Over the decades that followed, Chinese constitutional reformers occasionally referred to the Australian federal model in their experiments with local federalism. Constitutional draughtsman Huang Yi consulted the Australian Constitution in drafting the 1921 provisional provincial constitution for Guangdong Province. Sun Yatsen himself kept a copy of BR Wise's *The Making of the Australian Commonwealth 1889–1900* in the library of his home in the Shanghai French Concession, where he penned some of his most influential essays over the period of 1916 to 1922. On the whole, though, interest in the Australian federal Constitution in China failed to match the level of interest shown by Chinese-language newspapers in Australia.[6]

The Chinese-language press treated federation in much the same fashion as did the English-language press of the day. To be sure, restrictions on movement in and out of the Australia after federation happened to affect Chinese residents more than others, and the papers pursued news of Australian restrictions with special rigour. They also printed accounts of immigration restrictions in the Philippines, Hawai'i, New Zealand, North America and Europe. Their coverage of federation was not limited to immigration issues. The *Tung Wah News*, for example, took an active interest in day-to-day developments surrounding the act of federation and shared in the general euphoria associated with the birth of the Australian Commonwealth in the belief that local Chinese had a part to play in the new Australia ushered in by federation. For all Australians federation was a good in itself.[7]

From 1898 into the early years of federation the *Tung Wah News* reported regularly on federation conferences and referenda, disputes and differences among states, debates over the siting of the national capital, the role of the British crown and, in general terms, the meaning of federation for the future of the country.[8] Australia's natural endowment and economic potential attracted particular comment. The *Tung Wah News* reported that federation would benefit all Australians by unifying, enlarging and strengthening the country: economically, it would simplify communications, politically, it would unify territorial jurisdictions; on the military front it would ensure more effective continental defence. Federation conferred practical benefits on all Australians.[9]

Federation also offered a new model for public participation in civic life. In September 1899, the *Tung Wah News* warmly applauded a reader's suggestion that Australian Chinese should come together to promote their common interests as other Australians were doing. Everyone seemed to be organising themselves into parties and clubs for their mutual benefit. It was time that Chinese in Australia overcame their local differences, struggled for unity and contributed their energy, ideas and wealth to public life in the new Australia. The convergence of the six separate colonies into a united Australian commonwealth provided a model of co-operation for each of the communities that made up the Commonwealth.[10]

When the day of federation arrived, Luke Chong, editor of the *Tung Wah News*, published a series of articles and editorials indicating that he was carried away by the event. He was exhilarated, he wrote, by 'the unity of this country and its people'. When a crowd of 250 000 people took to the streets of Sydney to celebrate the act of federation, he reported, there was not a whisper of bad language, not a sign of pushing or shoving, not a single report of injury. Chong was equally impressed by the progress the country had made since colonisation, including the vast acreage of land that had been brought under cultivation, the rail lines under construction to link distant points of the continent, the hospitals catering for the sick and injured, and social welfare provisions for the elderly and disabled. Even the national census was conducted on a scale that China had not been able to match, by Chong's reckoning, since the Zhou era 2500 years earlier. Australia was a country to be proud of.[11]

The issue of federation was taken up again by the Chinese-Australian press a decade later, in 1912, when the Chinese emperor was toppled in the Republican Revolution. This time the press focused explicitly on the prospects for China as a centralised or federated state.[12] 'Many changes have taken place in the world political system over the past four or five hundred years', one article in the *Tung Wah News* began. 'Among these, one of the most obvious developments in the public realm has been the tendency for smaller countries to come together to form larger ones.' There was a time when Europe was a world of feudal division: mediaeval England, France, Austria and Poland were made up of many small estates, or fiefdoms, where 'the reach of central authority did not extend beyond the metropolitan capital'. The English were the first to consolidate their central authority, which occurred at the turn of the sixteenth and seventeenth centuries; other states followed its lead. Others again, such as Switzerland, Germany and Italy, found federal systems more appropriate to their situations. Which of these systems was best suited to China?

The newspaper introduced to its Australian readership a number of arguments mounted by reformers in China on the implications of current global trends for China's future as a centralised or federated state. Some of them have a contemporary ring:

> *There is a political group in China that maintains that the underlying reason for China's weakness is that its territory is too large and hence ungovernable. They propose that the land should be divided up into a number of small states (xiao guo), each of them self-governing, and that these states should come together to form a federation ... Competition, they say, is the mother of progress, and China has been slow to progress because it pursues unification at the expense of everything else. Each province should be allowed to compete, independently, and the authority of the centre should be no more than sufficient [for its allocated responsibilities].*

Editorial comments pointed to the US Constitution as the outstanding contemporary model of a free and democratic state operating under a federal republican constitution. 'In America, people generally place great emphasis on freedom and equality and, not surprisingly, find centralised authority distasteful.' Still, faced with the consolidationist trends of world history, even the Americans felt compelled to make concessions to state unity. Thus 'a number of independent towns and cities came together to form states and the majority of independent states came together to form a country'.

Compared with the US Constitution, the Australian model offered little guidance on questions driving republican debates in China – how, for example, a president might be elected in a federal republic – but it offered useful pointers for an old imperial state trying to negotiate the transition from a unified empire to a federated republic. Britain's conferral of sovereign status on federated Australia was interpreted as a sign of a metropolitan power granting autonomy to peripheral states within a federated British empire. In this sense the 'customs union and the various parliaments of the dominions' could be regarded as a illustrating a federated model of Greater British Empire that could offer lessons for China. Australian federation was only incidentally a case of self-governing states coming together to form a sovereign and united territorial state. Its world significance lay in its demonstration of the willingness of a great empire to concede autonomy to a remote territory (Australia) within a quasi-federal imperial union (the empire). The emergence of Australia from within the empire was the greatest lesson of Australian federation.

Among Chinese Australians, understanding federation as part of a British imperial project was preferable to considering it a purely national event. Australian nationalism offered Chinese little cause for celebration. They celebrated federation because its constitution (an act of the British parliament), its sovereign (the queen), and its local pageants (including Chinese lion dances) were grounded in the British imperial ideal. Community leaders were, on the whole, champions of the imperial ideal because the treaties binding the British and Chinese empires were their last line of defence against the Australian nationalist leagues calling for their removal. Many Chinese Australians found refuge from White Australian nationalism in the ideal of Australian national confederation within the greater British empire.

Equality and empires

Despite the casual comparisons drawn in the Chinese-Australian press, the Chinese empire and the British empire were very different entities. China was an old-world empire with a political centre that overwhelmed the suzereinty of its neighbours. And yet China's sovereignty progressively diminished over the distances separating the capital from the empire's porous borders. Britain was a modern nation-state with parliamentary institutions driving its imperial ambitions. The social, political and diplomatic arrangements of the Chinese empire were grounded in Confucian notions of hierarchy and propriety. Britain, for all its social hierarchy, professed the equality of subjects before the law and the equality of sovereign nations. Britain was a new kind of beast, an equal and independent nation, sanctioned by a revolutionary law that Swiss philosopher Emmerich de Vattel called the *Law of Nations* (1758). Vattel observed that 'Nature has established a perfect equality of rights between independent nations.' At the time these words were written the Chinese empire certainly did not recognise the perfect equality of rights that governed its relations with its neighbours. Nor did the old world empires of Europe.[13]

For the sake of argument, the hierarchical ethics of old-world empires and the egalitarian ethics of modern nations can be imagined as two quite distinct ethical systems. At one level they are incommensurable. To the hierarchically minded equality is base; to egalitarians hierarchy is unequal. Neither claim makes sense to the other. As great historical movements go, however, hierarchy can be characterised as the orthodox ethic of old-world empires and equality as that of national states and the international state system. Common sense tells us today that all citizens should be equal before the law and that all states should enjoy equal sovereignty. This was not always the case in Europe or in China. Vattel's *Law of Nations* signalled a revolution in relations among the states of Europe that was to have profound implications for the Chinese empire.

In practice, of course, things are rarely this simple. The formal hierarchies of monarchies and empires coexist alongside greenwood ethics of brotherly camaraderie, and claims of the formal equality of citizens often ring hollow alongside the inequalities between rich and poor.[14] Nevertheless, the historical encounter between the two great ethical systems can be traced through the struggles between empires and nations that culminated in the victory of the modern nation-state. Nationalism overturned old-world empires not just by force of arms but more fundamentally by overturning social hierarchies inherited at birth and replacing them with new ones based on force of arms, the acquisition of wealth, the practice of professions and personal achievements. These encounters involved massive social, cultural and political revolutions from which no monarchy or empire in Europe or in Asia was exempted.

China was not spared. In 1840 the British government resorted to war to force the Chinese empire to open its ports to trade in opium. In Europe, British victory in the Opium Wars was widely celebrated as enforcing the principle of international law that China was a national state just like any other. In China, the idea that states should be counted formally equal by virtue of their equal sovereignty was still not well understood when Queen Victoria and the Emperor Daoguang signed the first of China's 'unequal treaties' in 1842. Fifty years before the 1842 treaty was signed Emperor Qianlong famously required a visiting British delegation to kowtow in his presence to signify Britain's subordination to the Chinese emperor. Lord McCartney, equally famously, is said to have declined.[15]

Recognition of the formal equality of states came gradually to China over the closing decades of the 19th century, in part through reports of the day-to-day practice of diplomatic relations submitted by representatives of the Chinese empire attached to the courts and councils of Europe, Japan and the United States. By the turn of the 20th century it was an axiom of Chinese statecraft that relations between countries should be based on the principle of equality. At this time Chinese nationalists coined the phrase 'unequal treaties' to characterise the terms on which the Chinese empire had been forced to sign treaties with Britain and other countries following its defeat in the Opium Wars. Invocation of the word 'unequal' at the turn of the 20th century indicated growing recognition that states should enter into formal negotiations on equal terms, that is, growing recognition within the Chinese political elite of the nominal equality of sovereign states.[16]

The idea of racial equality, as distinct from the idea of the equality of sovereign states, came into currency over much the same period in China because, paradoxically, racial equality was encoded in the unequal treaties themselves.[17] China's 19th century treaties with Britain indirectly established the equality of peoples in reciprocal provisions, which allowed freedom of movement throughout the British empire. Chinese émigrés transiting through Hong Kong or the aptly-named Treaty Ports in China were entitled to move as freely as native Englanders through India, Canada, Australasia and the British colonial settlements of Southeast Asia. These treaty entitlements to equal rights of movement and abode made no provision for discrimination on the grounds of race. The imperial treaties implied the equality of peoples.

Racial equality was not a difficult idea to comprehend. In the British and Chinese empires, hierarchical orders were generally based on class or caste and only secondarily on ethnicity.[18] Nevertheless, in China notions of racial hierarchy, racial honour and racial degradation were widely conveyed through popular epithets in the late Ming and early Qing dynasties in China. In the mid-19th century, the Taiping Rebellion gave these epithets added currency when rebel propagandists mocked their Manchu rulers as alien 'slaves' and, in Pamela Crossley's words, portrayed China 'as being in a condition of enslavement by slaves, a conceit that would become a fairly ubiquitous feature of nationalist rhetoric at the turn of the century'.[19] Levelling accusations of slavery against one's opponents was as commonplace in 19th century China as it was in 19th century Australia. Nevertheless, racial identities in China were largely framed in hierarchical terms. The principle of racial equality seems to have come to official attention through the court's dealings with Chinese living abroad.

The emergence of racial equality as an idea and an ideal can be traced through the recorded voices of Chinese-Australian communities. Through Britain's 19th century treaties with China they became familiar with the idea of the equality of sovereign states. In 1879, for example, the three prominent Melbourne businessmen Lowe Kong Meng, Cheok Hong Cheong and Louis Ah Mouy published a pamphlet, *The Chinese Question In Australia*, in which they drew their readers' attention to the claims for state equality set out in *Law of Nations*.[20] This pamphlet, as we shall see below, also pressed claims for the equality of peoples. The idea of equality among national peoples turned not on the notion that states were nominally equal, but on the claim that national peoples were entitled by natural or divine right to be judged equals of one another. Like sovereign-state equality, the ideal of national equality can be traced through Chinese-Australian voices in 19th century Australia.

In May 1887 the Melbourne *Argus* ran an editorial welcoming an official visit by two imperial commissioners from China. Actually, the editorial made only fleeting mention of General Wong Yung Ho (*Wang Ronghe*) and Commissioner U Tsing (*Yu Qiong*), who had come to tour the colonies to inspect and report on the conditions under which Chinese were living in Australia. The editor's attention was chiefly devoted to the appearance of a 'remarkable' article by China's minister to London, the Marquis Tseng, which had not long come to public notice in Australia (insofar as China's relations with the Australian colonies were handled through the Colonial Office in London, the marquis' standing in the Court of St James made him China's effective ambassador to the Australasian colonies). The remarkable feature of the marquis' article was his forceful and reasoned argument for equal treatment for China and the Chinese people. The visiting commissioners, the editor maintained, had merely come to do the marquis' bidding. The editors of *The Argus* were persuaded that the Marquis had mounted a strong case for the commissioners' right to investigate the treatment of Chinese in Australia in order to ensure their equality of treatment.[21]

In the article to which *The Argus* referred, the Marquis highlighted three areas in which the Chinese empire sought recognition of equality in the 1880s: equality of national sovereignty, equality of peoples and recognition that China enjoyed its own regional sphere of influence equal to that of the Great Powers (a principle not entirely consistent with the first). In regard to the equality of peoples the marquis asserted that the empire would ensure that China's subjects abroad were treated with the respect accorded to other immigrants in the colonies and settler societies of Asia and the Pacific. One of the marquis' strongest claims for equality of treatment with the Great Powers extended to what he called the 'outrageous' mistreatment of Chinese living outside of China.[22]

As an official of the Chinese foreign ministry (the *Zongli Yamen*) the marquis was in a position to appreciate the outrage.[23] Chinese in Australia were at this time petitioning the ministry in Peking over their unequal treatment at the hands of colonial authorities. The petitioners referred explicitly to clauses of the treaties signed in Peking and Tianjin that established equal rights of movement for Chinese embarking from British treaty ports in China with those that Britons enjoyed embarking from their home ports in Great Britain and Ireland. The Australian complaints had diplomatic repercussions.

Among the petitions drafted by Chinese Australians at this time was one presented to the imperial commissioners for forwarding to Sir Henry Loch, governor of Victoria, in June 1887. This was a representative petition bearing 47 signatures and drafted by Lowe Kong Meng, Cheok Hong Cheong and Louis Ah Muoy, whose *The Chinese Question In Australia* had been published eight years earlier. Their petition presented two basic grievances: first, it complained that a special tax of £10 per head had been imposed upon Chinese and Chinese alone, and second, that special restrictions applied to Chinese wishing to travel from one Australian colony to another in contravention of the treaties.

The ground for each complaint was that the restrictions were 'in direct violation of all international law and usage, and in contravention of the Treaty engagements entered into by the Governments of the two Empires'.[24]

Similar complaints were made in the following year. In June 1888, a group of Sydney businessmen led by Quong Tart and representing 'Chinese residents in Australasia and New Zealand', petitioned the intercolonial conference in Sydney. The petition led with an assertion of the legal foundation for equality of treatment contained in the treaties, pointing out that

> *by Article Five of the Treaty of Pekin, made on the twenty-fifth day of October, One thousand eight hundred and sixty, between Her Majesty the Queen of Great Britain and Ireland and His Imperial Majesty the Emperor of China, it was amongst other things, provided that the Chinese, in choosing to take service in the British Colonies or other parts beyond the seas, were to be at perfect liberty to enter into engagements with British subjects for that purpose, and to ship themselves and their families in British vessels at the open ports of China.*[25]

Based on the provisions of the Treaty of Peking, the petitioners sought redress for restrictions on their freedom to travel to and from China and argued for the repeal of restrictions on movement between the Australian colonies.

One of the striking features of the negotiations that followed presentation of the petitions is the way in which, on the one hand, the ideal of equality moved between a legal notion of obligations under contract and, on the other, a sense of fair play grounded in natural justice and divine providence. Government representatives on each side negotiated around legal terms and precedents. Protests lodged by the Chinese court typically referred to Britain's obligations under the Anglo–Chinese treaties; British negotiators did likewise in responding to claims by Chinese and Australian government representatives.[26] In light of the Colonial Office's reluctance to confront Australian demands for self-determination, however, Chinese community leaders came to realise that the case for equality of treatment could not rest on appeals to treaties alone.

Treaties could be revised to enshrine inequality. Under the Angell Treaty, signed by the United States and China in November 1880, Peking conceded the right of 'the Government of the United States [to] regulate, limit, or suspend' the entry or residence of Chinese in the United States.[27] The Angell Treaty demonstrated to Chinese communities the world over that legal treaties offered little defence against discriminatory regulation. Chinese community leaders in Australia then began to appeal to ideals of fair play, over and above Britain's treaty obligations. The sense of natural justice evoked in their petitions and publications was based not only on reciprocal rights and obligations under treaties but to broader recognition of the equality of Chinese and Europeans as fellow human beings.

Documents held in the Qing imperial archives in Peking record their complaints. 'We are also human beings, living in this world, and we expect to be treated with justice', argued one Australian-Chinese petition sent to the Chinese foreign ministry in 1889. 'Why should people in Australia act in this unfair and harsh way, unprecedented in history?' Chinese were mistreated on the sole ground that 'the colour of their skin is different from that of Europeans'. Why, the petitioners asked, were Chinese alone denied the universal rights otherwise bestowed on immigrants?[28] Another petition in the Qing Archives, presented by around 50 Chinese merchants in Australia in 1889, referred to the 'humiliation' and 'insults' heaped upon China and its people by the Australian colonies. 'Why are Chinese people looked down upon and treated differently?', they asked.[29] A further petition, bearing around 40 signatures, linked its appeal to fair play to China's national claims for equal recognition. Local authorities in Australia, it reported, 'tolerate everyone except Chinese ... Their prejudice, harshness and contempt are starkly obvious'.[30] These pleas from the Australian colonies were read by clerks and higher officials of the Chinese foreign ministry in the 1880s, forwarded to the Chinese mission in London with recommendations for action and, on failing to secure a satisfactory outcome from British colonial authorities, were filed away in the ministry's growing archive of national grievances in Peking.

The same questions had been addressed to white Australians some years beforehand. In 1879, Lowe Kong Meng, Cheok Hong Cheong and Louis Ah Mouy assembled a range of arguments for equality of treatment in their passionately argued pamphlet. They appealed to contracts and treaties and highlighted the reciprocal obligations imposed on the Australian colonies to allow freedom of movement under the treaties signed between the British throne and the Chinese empire. Significantly, they appealed as well to the universal ethical claims set out in the American Declaration of Independence – 'We hold these truths to be self-evident: that all men are created equal' – and they wondered why a profession of equality endowed by Providence did not appear to apply even in the United States. They also appealed to universal human nature in responding to claims that Chinese labourers depressed general wages by their willingness to work for little reward. 'Human nature is human nature all the world over; and the Chinaman is just as fond of money, and just as eager to earn as much as he can, as the most grasping of his competitors.' Finally, they appealed to the moral precepts laid down in the canons of Christianity and Confucianism. The moral, intellectual and social lives of the common people of China, they argued, left nothing to be desired when compared with any national people in Europe. 'You do not endeavour to exclude Germans, or Frenchmen, or Italians, or Danes, or Swedes. There are men of all these nationalities here. Why then are Chinese colonists to be placed under a ban?'[31]

Paradoxically, the question of equality lay at the heart of White Australia's rejection of Chinese residents' appeals for equality of treatment. In May 1888, just as Chinese community leaders were drafting their petitions for equality of treatment, NSW Premier Henry Parkes prohibited Chinese from disembarking from *The Afghan*, then moored in Sydney Harbour, on the ground that he 'did not want to see any race here who were not entitled to all immunities, privileges and rights of citizenship – of *equal* marriage, *equal* salvation, with the best and truest of any of the races here already.'[32] No matter how eloquently they framed their case for equal treatment, how closely they read Britain's imperial treaties, how forcefully they asserted their equal status as human beings, Chinese residents were to be denied the equal bounty that only a free and equal people could enjoy because, it was assumed, they were culturally predisposed to be hierarchical. As far as Parkes was concerned this was not a matter of racial equality or inequality. He had long ago dismissed the complaints of vulgar anti-Chinese agitators that Chinese were members of an inferior race.[33] They were nothing of the kind, Parkes insisted. They were to be denied equal access to Australian citizenship on the ethnographic claims of distinguished sinologists that they could not appreciate equality if it were offered to them on a platter. And so it was that the eloquent appeals and petitions of Chinese residents to be treated as equals alongside white Australians fell on deaf ears.

Equality and nations

By the 1890s, philosophers and reformers in China were taking up these claims for equality of treatment and extolling what they termed a new 'theory of equality' (*pingdeng lun*) that would help transform imperial China into a modern civic democracy. The writings of Tang Caichang, brother of Sydney newspaper editor Tang Caizhi, illustrate the connection, linking ideas of racial and sovereign equality in the international order and ideas of equality in China, including the equality of citizens, social classes, and men and women.

Around the time of the 1898 reforms at the imperial court, Tang and a number of friends in Hunan founded the Society for the Study of Public Law in the provincial capital of Changsha. In announcing the society's foundation, Tang applauded Japanese officials for citing the principles of international law in their formal approaches to the British and US governments to renegotiate their treaties. In consequence, Tang recorded, 'over the last few years each of the Great Powers has revised its treaty [with Japan], to convert it to a statute of equality'.[34] Again in 1898, his group addressed the problem of human equality in one of the earliest writings on the subject to be penned by members of the modernising elite, rather than by pious monks or popular rebels, an extended essay entitled 'Egalitarianism' (*Pingdengshuo*).

The essay began with an explicit reference to the problem of classification in egalitarian and hierarchical ethics: 'Egalitarianism means establishing equality in accordance with heaven's endowed classifications.' The natural order, the essay argued, offered no ground for hierarchical classification. The standard Confucian categories of rulers, ministers, husbands, wives, elder brothers and younger brothers were falsely based on analogies with nature. Heaven established hierarchies in nature but it did not preordain hierarchical relations in human society. The human species was an irreducible classification: the single category endorsed by nature was the universal category of 'people'.[35]

'Egalitarianism' was one of a number of tracts that drew on elements of the Chinese canon to mount a case for universal equality sanctioned by classical learning. In the 1890s, arguments for equality were presented as exegeses on the classical canon. As we have seen, Kang Youwei presented his case for human equality in the language of Confucianism. In a similar work on the Confucian principle of human heartedness (*ren*) another scholar, Tan Sitong, fused the Confucian *Book of Rites* with Edward Bellamy's recently published *Looking Backward* into a utopian vision of a world with 'no boundaries, wars, suspicion, jealousy, power-struggles, or distinction between the self and others; then equality would finally emerge'. Kang and Tan pushed the limits of classical learning by reconfiguring key concepts of the Confucian canon, stripping them of their hierarchical implications and re-presenting them as claims for a modern egalitarian ethic.[36]

The theory of equality began to take root outside Confucian debates on statecraft around the turn of the 20th century. Australia was an important site for this discussion. In mid-1901, Tang Caizhi came to Australia to edit the *Tung Wah News*. More importantly, as we have seen, Kang Youwei's disciple Liang Qichao, after he had been in Australia over the preceding six months, presented a series of weekly lectures in the upstairs reading rooms of the *Tung Wah News* building in downtown Sydney in which he dealt with the problems presented by Confucian notions of hierarchy and the current imperative to recast person-to-person relations and China's system of territorial government around the principle of equality. A revised version of the talks was later published in Japan under the title *Tracing the Source of China's Weakness*. These published lectures are among the earliest writings in which egalitarianism was discussed without reference to canonical Chinese works on philosophy and religion. In his Sydney lectures, Liang selected instead the Taiping rebels' motif of a people enslaved by slaves, a motif he developed into a critique of the systemic problems that made China 'weak'.[37]

Liang Qichao was a remarkable young man. He was the founder of China's first easy-reading journals, an acerbic commentator on public affairs, a pioneer of clear written expression, a writer who popularised the ideal of the critical citizen and, in his spare time, a poet and novelist. During his Australian tour he proved himself a brilliant champion of civic equality, gender equality, class equality, racial equality and national equality. As it happens, his visit took place at an extraordinary turning point in Australian history. When Liang stepped ashore on the Fremantle docks towards the end of October 1900, he set foot on the western edge of a continent that was divided into discrete self-governing territories. When he embarked from Sydney six months later, 2000 miles to the east, he left behind a national state that had become united and sovereign, the Commonwealth of Australia. In between he visited Perth, Geraldton, Adelaide, Melbourne, Ballarat, Bendigo and the New England district of New South Wales.

Liang was too preoccupied with events in China to be anything more than an observer of the events surrounding federation. His visit followed closely on the suppression of the imperial reform movement of 1898 and a failed revolutionary uprising in the following year, and coincided with the suppression of the Boxer Uprising that threatened foreign communities and privileges over the months preceding his visit. His intention was to raise funds for the reform movement and to publicise its cause. His method was to present public lectures on the importance of equality in the modern world order. His talks on 'the sources of China's weakness' focused on strengthening the country by extolling the virtues of egalitarianism and individual autonomy.

Wherever he went in Australia, Liang was accorded the honours customarily reserved for visiting dignitaries. Coming as it did so soon after the suppression of the Boxer Uprising in north China, his arrival was timely. Australian colonial forces had not long since been despatched to China to assist in the suppression of the uprising. As an outspoken critic of the Boxers, Liang was greeted by colonial governors and welcomed by local mayors and members of parliament at several ports of call. He was invited to speak in temperance halls and churches and was taken on tours of the premises by chairmen of hospital boards, governors of museums, newspaper proprietors and directors of botanical gardens from Perth to Sydney. On 12 January he was invited to a function at the Sydney Town Hall to celebrate federation in the company of Australia's first prime minister, Edmund Barton. Two days later he called in person on the governor to wish him well and discuss political reform in China. Lord Hopetoun expressed his earnest wishes for the success of the reform party in China.[38]

Over the months surrounding federation, Liang had occasion to observe anti-Chinese sentiment in Australia; by the end of his visit, later in the same year, the Immigration Restriction Act was passed. He reconciled the contradiction between pro- and anti-Chinese sentiment in Australia by concluding that the hostility he witnessed was grounded not in particularistic racism, but in the universal struggle between 'traditional' and 'modern' ways of living. The contradiction as he saw it was not a clash of civilisations between East and West but a conflict between traditional and modern ways of being human. Shortly after leaving Australia he began writing his seminal work, *The New People;* he also founded a pioneering journal of the same name.[39]

Liang was a fierce critic of imperial China. Indeed, his attacks on the flaws and faults of the Chinese people echoed anti-Chinese pamphlets circulating in Australia at the time of his visit.[40] The people of China were faulted in Liang's eyes not for being Chinese but for being insufficiently enlightened citizens of the world and insufficiently patriotic citizens of China. On his Australian tour he railed against China's superstition, dissimulation, superciliousness and backwardness. The mainstream English-language press covered his movements and activities with interest, publishing a number of interviews expounding his views on China's current situation. English-language journalists introduced Liang as a reformer who had devoted his life to improving the lot of his country. He was particularly commended for introducing 'Western ideas of civilisation into China'. Progressive fractions of the local Chinese community were redeemed on the same account. As one English-language journalist reported:

> *The mission is one of great importance and the members of the Chinese reform party sincerely believe that an expression of opinion from the Chinese resident outside the limits of the empire will materially assist them in their efforts to release their country from its present condition of unrest and to establish a progressive form of government.*

Liang summoned respect through what he had to say. He accommodated local enthusiasm for free trade and spoke in favour of official tolerance towards Christian missionaries in China. 'We desire to open up China to free commerce between all nations,' he announced in an interview with the English-language press, 'to establish trade, to do away with the old laws and form a government in Western principles.' On Western educational and missionary endeavours in China he said:

> We wish to establish educational reforms and to wipe away
> superstition and distrust of the foreigner. [Our] party has no desire to
> disturb the religious beliefs of the Chinese. That is a question we would
> leave entirely in the hands of the people. No, we have no objection
> to the Christian missionaries. They have been and are doing good
> work in the translation of English books into Chinese. By this means
> Western ideas have been disseminated, the books are being read, and so
> our aims have been forwarded ... [Educated Chinese] are opposed to
> the Boxer movement.[41]

Chinese communities up and down the country also greeted his arrival with enthusiasm. Natives of the See Yap counties hailed Liang as a fellow native who had bestowed fame on their home districts in Guangdong and conferred honour on Australia by visiting New Gold Mountain. The Kong Chew Society attempted to claim him for themselves (Liang was a native of Sunwai County, which housed the prefectural capital of the ancient district of Kong Chew) and local representatives of his own Leong (*Liang*) clan came out in force to welcome him. He crafted a pair of parallel scrolls for the Kong Chew Society Hall in Melbourne, on display to this day, and he drafted a commercial sign for the Hoong Cheong Company owned by the Leong family of Melbourne. In Sydney and Melbourne, natives of Heungshan County (now *Zhongshan*) and from the three counties represented by the Nam Poon Shoong Society (*Nanhai Panyu Shunde*) set aside their parochial differences with the See Yap community to welcome Liang into their clubs and homes. Civic associations in cities and towns along his route competed to host him at banquets, and they turned out in their hundreds to hear his lectures in churches, community halls and business premises. Local Chinese newspapers with links to the Society to Protect the Emperor devoted space in every issue published over the course of his visit.

When Luke Chong introduced Liang Qichao to Australian readers of the *Tung Wah News* he framed the visit by pointing to the unequal treatment of Chinese in Australia. He expressed particular regret that equal access to the new Australian Commonwealth was denied to people of Chinese descent, who were, he pointed out, subject to discriminatory immigration regulations and poll taxes, and prone to racist abuse. The position of Chinese sojourners in Australia brought to mind the position of China as an enslaved nation, Chong complained. Those who had arranged a privileged life for themselves in Australia had contrived to carve up China and to treat Chinese in China as slaves, or mules, forever destined to serve their Western masters. How were the Chinese to throw off their shackles and escape their slave status?[42] For Chong, only the reform party of Liang Qichao and his teacher Kang Youwei could help the country escape the fate of slaves:

> *China would prosper in a matter of decades if only its people would unite and sacrifice themselves for the nation, as Messrs Kang Youwei and Liang Qichao suggest, and set out to reform the obsolete system, to cultivate people of talent, promote social morality, encourage progress, construct railways across the twenty-two provinces, exploit the country's natural resources and educate the people. Then who would fear being enslaved by others?*[43]

Liang Qichao himself had less to say about China's enslavement by others than about China's self-enslavement to its inherited social, cultural and political order. He blamed the imperial state for allowing Western encroachment and, although a self-proclaimed patriot, stood firmly on the side of Western modernists in the clash between tradition and modernity.

Over the last months of his Australian visit, Liang composed the first draft of his strongly-worded essay, 'On Tracing the Sources of China's Weakness', in Sydney. After it was revised for publication in Japan the essay reached a far wider audience. It was read not just by members of the Chinese diaspora, but also by generations of political reformers and intellectuals in China, and by later generations of students in the West.[44] 'On China's Weakness' marks an important moment in the history of China's encounter with the modern ethic of equality. Liang invited his Sydney audience to consider the fate of the imperial state back home. Few needed persuading on this point. In China, Liang complained, ordinary people paid little heed to affairs of state. In Australia he could see that local Chinese communities took a keen interest in Chinese affairs in the belief that a strong and united China would earn the respect of foreign powers and deter them from introducing discriminatory legislation.

Throughout the essay Liang developed a consistent argument about the importance of equality in the making of modern nation-states. 'A country is founded on equality,' he declared, 'and love [of country] arises from the way [people] treat one another.' The chief culprit, in Liang's view, was a political one – the imperial court in Peking, which treated its national citizens as its 'personal slaves'. The modern West showed the way forward:

> *Westerners look upon their countries as the common property of*
> *rulers and people. It is just as though fathers, elder brothers, sons and*
> *younger brothers all worked together in managing a family's affairs.*
> *In this case, every single person is a patriot. Not so in China, where*
> *the country belongs to one family and every one else is a slave.*

By contrast, Liang claimed, no person or government in the modern West could humiliate another without inviting resistance founded on the principle of equality. In contrast to China, children in the West, rich and poor, male and female, were taught from an early age to 'govern their own selves'.[45]

It is worth noting here that Liang had little experience of the West before travelling to Australia. The characteristics of youth, vigour, public spiritedness, fairness and equality that he famously attributed to the West in his early writings reflected many of the attributes that Luke Chong of the *Tung Wah News* attributed to Sydney at federation. The same might have been said of Fremantle, Adelaide, Melbourne and many of the cities and towns that punctuated Liang's Australian itinerary. On the back of the gold fever of the mid-19th century Melbourne had developed into the world's fastest-growing city by the 1880s. The extensive rail yards, palatial residences, substantial community halls and churches, banks, zoos, parks and gardens that Liang visited in Melbourne were, in many cases, products of his own lifetime.[46]

He also encountered Chinese communities busy caucusing among themselves over the local implications of the impending federation of the colonies. Some laid claim to civic membership of the federal union, many played prominent roles in celebrations surrounding the opening of the new federal parliament and a number petitioned colonial governments for a fair hearing in negotiations leading to the Immigration Restriction Act. Outside the purview of English-speaking communities, however, many complained bitterly in the Chinese-language press of increasing restrictions placed on their freedom to travel to and from Australia. 'Foreigners can travel to any place they choose in China,' noted one editorial in the *Tung Wah News*, 'but Chinese face numerous restrictions when they travel overseas.'[47] Liang's appeal for funds for the reform party found a receptive response among local Chinese who were willing to donate some of their hard-earned savings to strengthen China in the hope of elevating their own status abroad.

While China remained weak and backward, by this reasoning, people of Chinese descent would be despised wherever they happened to reside. Australian Chinese often remarked at this time that their position had deteriorated after China's defeat by Japan in the war of 1895. Over the few years between that defeat and Liang Qichao's visit, anti-Chinese sentiment, encouraged by members of parliament, had been fanned in the colonial press. This would not have happened, it was felt, had China not suffered such a devastating defeat by Japan.[48] It followed that the lives of Chinese abroad would substantially improve when China had become sufficiently wealthy and powerful to avenge its defeat. 'The strength or weakness of a country,' the *Tung Wah News* concluded, 'has significant bearing on the lives of its people.'[49] Liang was not deaf to this refrain. At a gathering in Melbourne one month into his Australian tour he offered advice that was to prefigure Mao Zedong's claim 50 years later, that the Chinese people would 'never again be humiliated by others' once China had 'stood up'. If only China could educate its people and enrich and strengthen itself, Liang told his friends in Melbourne, 'then those who live within the country and overseas will never again be humiliated by foreigners'.[50]

Liang initially imagined the West (Australia) as a land where humiliation of one person by another would simply not be tolerated. Australians certainly valued equality. South Australia was one of the first electorates in the world to recognise the rights of women as voting citizens. In Sydney and Melbourne he observed a powerful labour movement that protected the rights of workers in their dealings with employers and governments. A few years after leaving Australia he wrote an article celebrating the establishment of the country's first federal Labor cabinet, recommending it to his readers as the first national government of its kind in the world. To Liang's way of thinking this was an epochal event:

> *The year 1904 will be remembered by the workers of the world and should be commemorated throughout the whole world. Why? Because this year witnessed the birth of the first national cabinet organised by a Labor Party ... No leader of a Labor Party has ever held the authority to serve as prime minister or to organise a cabinet. The government that has been set up in Australia this year marks an historical breakthrough.*[51]

And yet Australia presented an anomaly that no person of Chinese descent could ignore, however distinguished their pedigree. Chinese Australians were humiliated by the failure to count them as equal subjects and citizens in Australia – the failure to receive equal recognition. Over the years following federation a portfolio of discriminatory legislation was introduced to prohibit further Chinese immigration, prevent Chinese residents from becoming citizens, ensure that wives could not accompany their husbands and generally ensure that Chinese Australians could neither leave nor return to Australia on the same terms as white Australians. When his West failed to live up to his expectations, Liang published a bitter critique of the White Australia Policy.

The White Australia Policy ran against history, Liang argued, as it was founded on indefensible assumptions about racial purity and difference. It undermined Western ethical claims about the universal equality of humankind. It failed to recognise the struggle that Chinese people were waging in the name of racial, social, political and national equality. In fact, the only principle demonstrated by the White Australia Policy, he concluded, was the Darwinian principle that 'the strong prey upon the weak'. In view of the West's overwhelming power in the current world order, Liang continued, the spectre of the Yellow Peril summoned up to justify the policy, was a fabricated justification for the 'white race' to suppress the peoples of Asia. In dealing with China and the Chinese, the West was unwilling to act upon its most fundamental principle – the ethic of human equality.

For Liang and those who applauded his Sydney lectures there was nothing particularly Chinese about the hierarchical ethics of the Chinese empire. Hierarchical ethics were the ethics of empires. Other countries had shown that a nation could shrug off the effete mannerisms of court by embracing liberty, equality and fraternity; China could do the same. Liang envisaged a new kind of polity that would yield a new kind of people in China. The Chinese would surely be counted the equal of other peoples once they had mastered the ethics of equality.

In fact, white Australians were not prepared to make allowance for egalitarians of Chinese descent. Over the two decades leading to federation, Chinese residents appealed without respite for equality and fair play in petitions to colonial authorities. They insisted that they were equal because they were human. Like Liang Qichao, their commitment to egalitarian values was based on universal principles, not national ones. But it was not sufficient to be modern, egalitarian – or even human – to be the equal of a white Australian.[52]

6

THE AUSTRALASIAN
KUO MIN TANG

*Send a Chinese to America and he tries to become a monopolist
because of the ambitious example set before him. Send him to British
Singapore and he strives to become a contractor with designs on
knighthood … Send a Chinese to Australia, he becomes a labor leader
and a booster 'for the working man's paradise'.*

Vivian Chow, 1932.[1]

Barely a year after Liang Qichao had left Sydney, Luke Chong abandoned
the Society to Protect the Emperor in favour of the fledgling Chinese
republican movement based in Melbourne. It was a sign of things to
come. Chong had done more than any other Chinese newspaper editor
in Sydney to promote Liang's tour of Australia. In 1902, however, he left
the imperial reform faction's *Tung Wah News* and moved to Melbourne,
where he founded a rival newspaper, the *Chinese Times* (*Aiguo bao*), to
promote the republican cause. This was the first of four successive
republican newspapers to appear in Melbourne over the next two

decades, each under a different Chinese title, but all preserving the same English title for the purpose of local registration. When *Aiguo bao* ceased publication after four years another republican newspaper, edited by Wong Yue-kong (*Huang Yougong*) and Lew Goot-chee (*Liu Yuechi*), took its place. This ran for nine years between 1905 and 1914. A third paper followed in 1918, again edited by Wong Yue-kong, and a fourth from 1919 to 1923, when the paper was transferred to Sydney to become the official organ of the Australasian regional headquarters of the republican Kuo Min Tang (KMT).[2]

Luke Chong's departure for Melbourne prefigured a new style of partisan politics among Chinese communities in federation Australia. The visit by Liang Qichao stimulated a flurry of political organisation and publication around the country but at the same time triggered a political fault line down the east coast between Liang's monarchical reformers and local Chinese republicans. Republican sentiment was especially strong in regional and metropolitan Victoria, as Liang discovered for himself in Ballarat when a scuffle broke out during one of his lectures in the old gold-mining town. A section of the audience interrupted his talk and, on being told to keep quiet, began throwing chairs about the room. Police were called in to restore order.[3] On the whole, Melbourne in particular and Victoria in general were republican strongholds while Sydney was the home base for reforming monarchists. After the emperor abdicated in 1912, the imperial reformers lost their *raison d'etre* and Sydney also turned republican. From that time forward the republican movement began to recruit some of the best and brightest republicans from Melbourne and by the mid-1920s had established itself as the national and Oceanic regional headquarters of the republican KMT. Two decades after the start of the century, when Luke Chong had left Sydney to establish the *Chinese Times* in Melbourne, his successors carried the republican presses back to Sydney.

In the 1920s the Sydney KMT headquarters launched a number of initiatives that shed light on Chinese-Australasian networks and identities in the White Australia era. One was the consolidation of the KMT itself as an Australasian organisation. Another was the party's successful effort to build an Australasian party clubhouse in Canton. Despite the self-evident transnational character of these initiatives, they

marked the Australasian network out from other KMT organisations
on the Pacific Rim, including the KMT network in North America.
Its distinctive features included a formidable capacity for organisation
within China, an emphasis on labour politics, respect for rule of law and
Melbourne–Sydney rivalry.

Growth and consolidation of the Australasian KMT

In April 1925 the KMT convened its inaugural Australasian regional
party congress in a three-storey building in Sydney's Haymarket district.
The building, which had opened four years earlier, offered an impressive
demonstration of the party's development and consolidation over the
preceding two decades from a loose affiliation of branches scattered
across major urban centres in Australia, New Zealand and the Pacific
Islands into a hierarchically structured regional system centred on the
new Sydney headquarters. With a facade designed by Walter Burley
Griffin, the Victorian branch in Little Bourke Street in Melbourne,
boasted an equally impressive building, which is still standing today.
From 1925 the Sydney offices came to house not only the NSW state
branch but also the party's new Australasian regional headquarters,
which subsumed the Victorian state branch and other state and local
branches under Sydney's direction and control. The 1925 party congress
marked the culmination of two years of institutional consolidation
that paid homage to the principles of democratic centralism that the
party leadership in Canton had adopted in 1923 on advice from the
Communist International (the Comintern).[4] Sydney was the Comintern's
chief beneficiary in Australia.

The worldwide KMT reorganisation launched in 1923 was a
substantial operation. The Sydney regional office was listed among
13 comparable regional party headquarters overseeing 75 branches
and 430 sub-branches in China and abroad. The Sydney office itself
supervised seven branches in New South Wales, Victoria, Western
Australia, Wellington, Auckland, Fiji and New Guinea, which in turn
supervised 24 sub-branches within their jurisdictions. An additional 11
sub-branches located in Brisbane, Adelaide and Darwin were managed

directly by the regional headquarters in Sydney. Membership of the regional network was around 'six to seven thousand' members.[5]

Sydney's historical claims to regional party leadership were slim. KMT party cells were operating in New Zealand and Victoria for years before the first party branches opened Sydney. Sydney was selected as the regional headquarters in recognition of its contemporary maritime links with Asia and the Pacific Islands. Even the Francophone KMT branch in Tahiti was placed under Sydney's jurisdiction: 'Chinese heading for Tahiti,' explained the official party historian; 'all pass through Sydney en route to their destination'.[6]

In keeping with Melbourne's lower status in the reformed national hierarchy, the party building in Little Bourke Street hosted two branches in 1925, the Victorian state branch and the Melbourne city sub-branch. Both were legacies of the earliest republican organisation in Australia, the New People Awakening Association, which convened weekly lectures and debates in Little Bourke Street in the early 1900s. The association subscribed on its members' behalf to the latest revolutionary books and journals coming out of Hong Kong. In 1909 or 1910 it merged with like-minded groups to form the Young China League, which was relaunched once more in 1912 as a formal branch of the parliamentary Nationalist Party (also known as KMT). The Melbourne branch of the KMT was demoted to a sub-branch in 1923 following a two-year tug of war for supremacy with Sydney. The Victorian state branch was proclaimed in the same year.[7]

Having founded the earliest pro-republican institutions in Australia, Melbourne party members had reason to be proud of their revolutionary heritage. They were also more active than their Sydney counterparts in opening modern Chinese-language schools and in publishing party periodicals. Melbourne republicans ran Chinese schools continuously from 1916 to the late 1920s, catering for between 30 and 50 students at every session. Two comparable attempts to establish Chinese schools in Sydney foundered in 1916 and 1920.[8] Melbourne published a series of republican newspapers before the first appeared in Sydney. Sydney, as noted, poached Melbourne's *Chinese Times* in 1923.

In light of their long-standing republican credentials, members of the Melbourne branch of the KMT did not take kindly to instructions to subordinate themselves to the authority of the 'Sydney Branch', as they preferred to call the reorganised Australasian Kuo Min Tang. In 1921 the Sydney branch convened a constituent assembly with the aim of restyling itself as the Chinese Nationalist Party of Australasia. Under the Sydney office's proposed articles of association – approved by a party delegate from China – the registered office of the Australiawide KMT was to be situated in Sydney, its eight listed subscribers were all merchants based in Sydney, its annual general meetings were to convene without fail in Sydney and, most galling to Melbourne members, a council elected by the Sydney organisation was empowered to exercise sole authority to 'open and manage' party branches 'in any city or town in any of the states of Australia, in New Zealand and in any of the Islands of the Pacific', including the appointment of Melbourne's local branch officers.[9]

The Melbourne branch reacted defiantly by creating new branches on its own initiative in regional Victoria and interstate. The Sydney branch responded forcefully by imposing a rival party branch in Melbourne (called the KMT Liaison Office in Melbourne) under Sydney's direction to circumvent the existing Melbourne branch. The dispute was resolved in 1923 when a visiting delegate from China intervened in favour of the Sydney-based transnational structure. Sun Yatsen issued instructions through his plenipotentiary in Australia, Chan On Yan (*Chen Anren*), for Australian, New Zealand and Pacific Islands branches to place their operations under a general branch headquarters of the Australasian KMT in Sydney. The Melbourne office was compelled to comply. After a struggle lasting two years it was reduced in status to a sub-branch under a new Victorian state branch that was placed under the jurisdiction of the Sydney regional headquarters.[10]

Sydney's Trojan horse in Melbourne, the KMT Liaison Office, then merged with the Melbourne branch to form the Melbourne sub-branch under the Victorian state branch. The Sydney headquarters recognised Melbourne's role in launching branches in Ballarat (founded April 1920) and Adelaide (founded February 1921) by granting Melbourne jurisdiction over them, later adding Darwin (founded May 1924) for good measure. The Darwin sub-branch was recognised for promoting women's rights within the wider KMT movement; it was one of few in the world to appoint women to executive positions. In 1934 a fifth sub-branch, Geelong, was added to the Victorian network. Two leading party figures in Melbourne over this difficult period, Chen Renyi and PH Hoong Nam (*Wu Hongnan*), were later rewarded with posts in China where they managed the Australasian KMT clubhouse in Canton (discussed below).[11]

Although it could not quite match Melbourne's republican pedigree Sydney could claim a revolutionary heritage of a kind. It hosted the most important republican newspaper of the period, the *Chinese Republican News* (*Minguobao*), which was launched in 1914 as a co-operative venture involving republican sympathisers and the more powerful Chinese Masonic Society of New South Wales. *Republican News* circulated widely throughout the region. In time, its penchant for co-operating with the Masonic Society and other Chinese civic associations helped the Sydney republicans make up lost ground in its competition with republican associations in Melbourne. In 1916 they organised their own Nationalist League that, in time, expanded into an informal party network for republican operations in New Zealand and the Pacific Islands. The new organisation held a formal opening ceremony in Sydney on 20 June 1916, and in the Australian spring of the following year convened formal meetings with the Chinese Masonic Society with the aim of establishing a national republican network. Nothing came of the talks. The Sydney branch then initiated moves towards regional consolidation of the KMT in Australasia. In April 1920 it hosted the first local convention of republican organisations in the region.[12] From this time the Wellington branch came under Sydney's jurisdiction and was downgraded from a branch to a sub-branch. The larger Victorian party network, based in Melbourne, declined to follow Wellington's example.

The KMT and the Chinese Masonic Society

KMT relations with the Masonic Society broke down in 1922, precipitating renewed calls from Sydney headquarters for unity within the party. As we have seen, the Chinese Masonic Society was the largest and most powerful Chinese community organisation in Australasia before the establishment of the KMT. At the turn of the century it is

likely that more than half of all Chinese in Australia were members of
Masonic triad lodges. In the 1910s Sydney KMT leaders drew readily on
their Masonic connections to expand the reach of their party network
through various co-operative ventures. Republican party membership
often overlapped with membership of a Chinese lodge. In 1922,
however, relations soured between the two organisations for a number
of reasons, some local and some related to concurrent events in China.
In Sydney, local Masons beat up a KMT propaganda team in April 1922
for distributing misleading information about them.[13] Around the same
time in China the KMT's supreme leader, Sun Yatsen, fell out with his
revolutionary ally, Guangdong Governor Chen Jiongming, who was a
powerful figure in the Yee Hing Masonic order.

Before this time Sun Yatsen and Chen Jiongming held concurrent
membership of both organisations. Sun Yatsen joined the Hawai'ian
lodge of the Yee Hing in 1904 while *en route* to San Franciso where he
planned to mobilise the North American Yee Hing network in support
of his republican revolution. After the republican revolution Chen
Jiongming was a prominent KMT member and Yee Hing Masonic leader.
When the two men came to blows in 1922 Sun banished Chen from the
KMT, and Sun himself was expelled by the San Francisco branch of the
Chinese Masonic Society. Scuffles broke out between the rival networks
in a number of ports around the world, including Sydney.[14]

In the following year Queensland police received a tip-off that
the Yee Hing had taken out a contract on Sun Yatsen's KMT emissary
in Australia, Chan On Yan. Local authorities on Thursday Island made
provision to foil any possible assassination attempt when Chan stopped
over in June 1923 on his way back to China to attend the First Nationalist
Party Congress in Canton. He passed through Thursday Island without
incident. Chan was carrying a formal complaint from the Australasian
KMT branch office in Sydney to the first Party Congress concerning
the behaviour of the NSW Chinese Masonic Society. He placed this on
record in January 1924 in his formal report to the congress.[15]

At the time this dispute broke out, the Sydney KMT office was in a
position to enforce compliance with Sun Yatsen's directives everywhere
but in Melbourne and its affiliated branches. Sydney already boasted
a larger branch network. By 1921 the Sydney network had grown to
encompass 23 sub-branches and four branch cells in Australia and the

Pacific Islands. Shortly after its founding in 1916 the Sydney-based Nationalist League opened branches in Rockhampton, Townsville and Brisbane at the invitation of republican sympathisers in Queensland. All three branches were subsumed under the Sydney KMT headquarters early in the 1920s, and in 1931 were placed under the direct jurisdiction of the Australasian party headquarters in Sydney. Cairns hosted a lively republican network from around 1917 to the 1920s, with subordinate party cells active in Atherton, Mackay, Bowen and Ayr. The reorganised Sydney KMT teamed up with republicans in Western Australia to establish a sub-branch in Broome in 1920 and Perth the following year. Perth was granted full branch status in 1924, with jurisdiction over Broome and a number of party cells based on ships plying between Perth and Singapore. In 1931 the Sydney office created a Western Australian state branch to take control of the Perth and Broome sub-branches and party cells still operating in the merchant marine. Sydney and Melbourne party members travelled intermittently to Tasmania on party business for 15 years before a local branch opened in Hobart in 1932. By the mid-1930s two out of every three members of the Tasmanian executive committee in Hobart were drawn from the leading merchant family in the city, the Chung (*Zhen*) family.[16] Each of these branches was closely tied to Sydney headquarters.

Labour politics

Competition for pre-eminence between the party's offices in Sydney and Melbourne would appear to offer a sufficient indication of the Australian character of the national KMT network – numbingly familiar in Sydney's trumping Melbourne. For the purpose of isolating the national features of the Australian KMT, parochial comparisons between sites in Australia pale alongside comparison with regional party networks based outside Australia. Among the 13 regional KMT headquarters in operation around the world by 1925 the US party organisation offers the best counter-example to the Australasian KMT. The KMT network based in San Francisco was reorganised around the time the Australasian regional headquarters was founded in Sydney. The US experience differed in significant ways from the Australian.

The Australasian regional network was no match for its US counterpart on the scale that really mattered back in Canton — its relative financial contributions to party causes in China. From the outbreak of the Republican Revolution in 1911 to the end of 1922, the US party network, based in San Francisco, raised and remitted over US$2.5 million from party members in the United States. Included among in-kind donations in 1922 was a fleet of 12 warplanes kitted up and ready to go, their pilots trained and their weapons honed for battle. Remittances from the Australasian network in 1922 ranked third after the United States and Canada but totalled no more than one-tenth of US contributions in the same year (see table 1).[17]

Table 6.1   Overseas remittances to KMT Shanghai Party Centre,
             July–December 1922 (in Chinese yuan)

United States (excluding Hawai'i)	405 000
Canada	78 000
Australasia	40 000
Philippines	38 000
Hawai'i	17 000
South Africa	11 000
Other	81 000
Total	**670 000**

Donations from 'Other' sources listed in table 1 appear to disguise contributions from the party's extensive network in the Dutch East Indies, British Malaya and Singapore, territories where the KMT was effectively banned as an open political party. Colonial governors of Malaya and the Straits settlements routinely required social organisations to register with British authorities under a series of Societies Ordinances dating from the 1860s. Between 1912 and 1924, 27 separate KMT branches were registered as independent societies under the ordinance. In 1913 the Societies Ordinance was amended to prohibit registered societies from collecting funds for political purposes, effectively preventing KMT branches from collecting or disbursing funds in their own name and remitting them to party headquarters in China. From 1919 the authorities went further in policing KMT publications and schools and in 1925 outlawed the KMT completely from British colonial territories. These formal restraints do not appear to have prevented the party from organising, recruiting or raising political donations, which were channelled to the party anonymously.[18]

In the wake of the worldwide party reorganisation of 1923 the Australian party network grew in size and importance at a time when the US network fell into decline. In 1923 the US network remitted US$60 000, a substantial sum by Australian standards but well short of the San Francisco headquarters' annual average remittance over the preceding 12 years of US$200 000. Over the following two years the US branch network remitted virtually nothing at all and party membership fell away dramatically. In February 1924 San Francisco reported that only 6000 of 9000 members had renewed their KMT party membership in compliance with party regulations.[19]

The main reason for the precipitate decline in the party's support abroad was a shift in KMT priorities from fundraising activities among Chinese overseas to popular organisation and mobilisation in China arising from the party reorganisation of 1923 and 1924. From 1923 to 1927 the Canton party centre drew on technical and financial support from Soviet Russia to reorient its political programs towards mass mobilisation of organised workers, farmers and soldiers, as well as women and student groups.[20] The shift from cultivating Overseas Chinese patriotism to enforcing radical peasant and labour policies was swift and unanticipated. The key figure in the San Francisco party headquarters, Chen Yaoyuan, interpreted Sun Yatsen's alliance with Soviet Russia and admission of communists into the KMT as a sign that their party was 'turning red'. The majority of members in the US branch network responded by withdrawing their sympathy and financial support.[21]

Significantly, the Sydney headquarters of the Australasian KMT responded warmly to the emergence of 'Red' Canton. By the start of 1926 the party's global overseas branch network shed three-quarters of its membership, falling to under 44 000 members outside of China's borders. The Australasian regional branch expanded over the same period to 6289 certified members, making up almost one-seventh of the party's entire international membership. The Australasian membership in 1925 was higher than the total registered membership of the US network in 1924 and, by mid-1925, second overall among overseas regional party headquarters after French Annam.[22]

The exceptional history of the Australasian KMT can be explained by the enthusiasm with which key figures in Sydney's regional branch headquarters embraced the party's policy reorientation towards labour, peasants, youth and women. One sign of this enthusiasm was its contribution towards aircraft purchases for Sun Yatsen's revolutionary organisation at a time when US aircraft donations froze. Another was its involvement in organised labour. Fired by the example of the Australian labour movement, key figures in the Australasian KMT network worked to create a working man's paradise in Australia and in China.

Aircraft purchase

Over the years following the radical party reorganisation of 1923 and 1924 the party's head office in Canton received few overseas donations for aircraft purchases. No donations comparable to the 12 fighter-planes made by the US branch in 1922 were made by the United States until after Japan's invasion of Manchuria. One notable exception to the pattern of aircraft donations was the presentation of the famous *Guangzhou* aircraft to Sun Yatsen in 1924 with funds raised through the Australasian KMT network.

The man behind this donation was Seeto Kwan (*Situ Guan*), a native of Hoiping County who, as a child of 12, accompanied his elder brother to Australia in 1899. Growing up in Sydney and Rabaul in German New Guinea, Seeto mingled with local republicans and joined a branch of the Revolutionary Alliance (*Tongmenghui*). After spending some time on party work in Rabaul he returned to Canton as the party reorganisation was getting under way in 1923 and there met up with Sun Yatsen, who commissioned him to head a new body known as the Chinese Aircraft Comrades Association (*Zhonghua hangkong tongzhi hui*), which was dedicated to raising funds for aircraft purchases. In 1924 Seeto returned to Australia to solicit donations for the purpose and later in the same year returned to China with the aircraft *Guangzhou*.[23]

In 1925 the party's central executive committee in Canton called again on overseas party members to make substantial donations for the purchase of aircraft. The appeal met with little response in the United States. Among Australian party members, however, Seeto revived his Aircraft Comrades Association and set about raising funds as he had done the year before. He began by soliciting donations from senior Comintern advisers in Canton itself, including Borodin and Rogachev, and from left-wing leaders in the Nationalist movement such as Provincial Governor Liao Zhongkai and the head of the party's women's bureau, He Xiangning. The receipt book of the Aircraft Comrades Association for 1925 and 1926 lists a number of contributions in English pounds – the currency of Australian and New Zealand donors – alongside the names of 32 donors to the aircraft fund. These donors were, in all likelihood, drawn from among Seeto Kwan's connections in Sydney and Rabaul.[24]

Seeto's fundraising efforts could be attributed to the eccentricities of an individual member rather than to a general orientation on the part of the Australasian branch network. A number of individuals from San Francisco favoured the party's new policy orientation, including Guangdong Governor Liao Zhongkai, born and raised in San Francisco, whose signature topped the list in Seeto's aircraft subscription book. But unlike Governor Liao, Seeto retained political sympathisers within his own regional branch network. He acted with the concerted support of the Sydney regional office, which later invited him to sit on the board of the Australasian Comrades Office in Canton (discussed below).[25]

Chinese merchant mariners

Seeto Kwan's sympathy for the radical labour and peasant policies of the reorganised KMT was widely shared in Sydney. Aircraft donations aside, Australian KMT work with Chinese seamen suggests a close affinity between the Sydney KMT and the radical party centre in Canton. At its inaugural regional congress in 1925, the Sydney headquarters resolved to expand its influence and membership through targeted recruitment among seamen and engineers working on vessels plying between Hong Kong, China and Australasian ports, a decision consistent with the pro-labour policy then current in Canton. Within a few years of this decision the Australasian branch network had established 15 sub-branches on mercantile shipping: nine on ships operating out of Sydney, five on ships operating out of Perth and one on a vessel operating from Auckland. These were substantial party units. The nine sub-branches based in the port of Sydney held between 40 and 120 registered members each, inducting in all 630 new party members into the Sydney-based network between 1925 and 1927. Assuming that the six vessels operating from Perth and Auckland recruited new members at a comparable rate, another 400 or so party members would have been recruited on the Perth and Auckland routes. In all, by 1927 around one in six registered Australasian party members were able seamen and ship's engineers. In light of this achievement the official KMT historian listed the recruitment of Chinese seamen as the most important activity undertaken by the Australasian KMT from 1925 to 1927.[26]

Samuel Wong (*Huang Laiwang*), a founding member of the Sydney nationalist organisation, was largely responsible for the party's pro-labour orientation in the 1920s. His persistence served him well. Wong won re-election over successive years to deputy head of the NSW branch of the KMT in addition to a number of other senior positions, including head of the liaison section and head of the propaganda section of the NSW branch. As the party's liaison officer he established close working relations with the wider organised labour movement in Australia, inviting a delegation from the Sydney Trades Hall to attend the inaugural Sydney KMT convention in April 1920 (where they gave speeches on socialism). He also built a pro-labour coalition within the KMT and led the push to enlist working seamen into the Nationalist Party in 1925. At the first regional congress of the Australasian Nationalist Party held in April of that year he was elected one of the four most senior officers in the Australasian regional party network.[27]

Along the way Sam Wong made a number of enemies within the Chinese-Australian merchant elite. In 1919 he was listed as one of several 'republicans' who resisted attempts by the Chinese consul-general in Australia to register 'Chinese' in the country with the support of leading conservatives in the NSW Chinese Chamber of Commerce – including William Gockson (*Guo Shun*) and Ping Nam (*Ye Bingnan*). In the following year, as a member of the board of the China–Australia Mail Steamship Line, he opposed the management style of the young businessman William Liu (*Liu Guangfu*) and his partners on the board.[28]

His propensity for plain speaking eventually cost Sam Wong his place in the regional KMT hierarchy. Until 1927 opposition to his robust political style was muted by party solidarity. In April 1927, however, General Chiang Kai-shek gave comfort to Wong's enemies by unleashing the infamous White Terror against communists and labour organisers in China and launching an international Party Purification Movement to weed out their sympathisers in the Chinese Nationalist Party. Across China up to 100000 people were summarily executed by criminal hit squads, local police chiefs and district military garrison commanders.[29] In Sydney Sam Wong, along with his pro-labour sympathisers, was purged.

The KMT convened its second Australasian regional congress in Sydney in August 1927 to endorse Chiang Kai-shek's command of the party. When the chair tabled an instruction from party headquarters in Nanking to approve Chiang's Party Purification Movement, Wong rose to his feet and declared the document 'unacceptable' to Australian comrades. Over Wong's objections a motion supporting the resolution was passed. Sam Wong opposed a further resolution supporting the new nationalist government in Nanking and upholding Generalissimo Chiang Kai-shek's position as unrivalled party and government leader. When this motion also passed over his objections Wong returned his party badge to the chair, stormed out of the congress and called a meeting of the Investigation Commission of the KMT Australasian regional headquarters to condemn the party congress and its resolutions. The congress responded by overruling the Investigation Commission for exceeding its authority, dissolving the commission and expelling its members form the party. In addition to Sam Wong, five members of the committee were expelled in perpetuity – Seeto Kun (*Situ Kun*), Poon Sum (*Pan Sen*), Leong Wailum (*Liang Weilin*), Wong Loyshing (*Huang Laishun*) and Yee Gatping (*Yu Jiping*).[30]

The ease with which Sam Wong could rally the Investigation Commission to his side points to the level of opposition among Australian members to the anti-labour turn in party affairs. Other Australasian party members voted with their feet. Following the 1927 regional congress, the Sydney headquarters set up a Party Purification Committee for Australasia to scrutinise the beliefs and credentials of local party members, as a result of which membership rapidly fell away. By the end of the Party Purification Movement, party membership stood at around 3500 members or a little under half of the 'six to seven thousand' members reported to party headquarters before the purge began.[31] Writing in the mid-1930s the official historian of the KMT attributed this decline to the effects of the White Australia Policy upon a shrinking pool of eligible party members. But White Australia was not responsible for the decline in party membership: the cause was Chiang Kai-shek's Party Purification Movement.

The 1927 dispute was not the last to disrupt the operations of the Australasian party network over the period of Chiang Kai-shek's rule. In 1934 General Cai Tingkai visited Australia. General Cai was widely acclaimed at the time as a patriot for leading the 19th Route Army against an unprovoked Japanese military attack on Shanghai in January 1932. On that occasion he earned the nationalist government's disapproval for exceeding his authority in taking the attack to Japanese forces. In November of the following year he co-founded a People's Revolutionary Government in Fujian Province in defiance of the nationalist government, which suppressed the rebellion early in 1934. General Cai then set out on an international tour of Chinese communities abroad which brought him to Sydney and Melbourne. His visit was opposed by the Chinese consul-general in Sydney and by the Australasian KMT network, which was by this time acting in consort with Nanking government representatives in Australia. Once the KMT headquarters banned its members from associating with General Cai, his visit was formally hosted by the NSW Chinese Masonic Society.

In Melbourne, leading KMT members worked closely with local Chinese Masons in an umbrella organisation known as the Chung Wah Association. This interparty community association hosted General Cai's visit to Melbourne. Members of the association arranged a reception for General Cai as he alighted from the train at Spencer Street Station. When the KMT's Sydney head office learnt that this reception committee included a number of local KMT members (although not acting in their capacity as KMT members) it issued a directive expelling them from the party. Among those expelled was Leong Goong. Leong objected to his expulsion through the formal KMT appeals system in China and won his case. He chose not renew his party membership.

Canton Australasian Club

One of the boldest initiatives of the inaugural Australasian party congress in 1925 was its decision to found an Australasian residential clubhouse in Canton. The establishment of the Canton clubhouse pointed to an historic reversal in the status of Chinese Australians. In the 19th century Chinese immigrants to Australasia set up native-place clubs and guesthouses to welcome strangers to Sydney, Melbourne, Auckland and elsewhere; the Canton clubhouse welcomed Australian strangers to China. Seen from Australia it was a Chinese institution; seen from China it was an Australian one.

Men visiting their ancestral villages from Australia and New Zealand were commonly derided as 'Gold Mountain Males' (*jinshanding*), a phrase that implied they entered China as aliens with no home to welcome them and no claim to native-county status. Australian visitors often looked in vain for a familiar face. In place of a family member they might be confronted by a corrupt official insisting that they pay an arbitrary levy on the contents of their trunks, or perhaps deceived into parting with their savings by one of the notorious 'local bullies and evil gentry' who ruled in place of the law in republican Guangdong. By the 1920s and 1930s the experience of visiting China was, by one contemporary account, 'a most painful and heart rending experience for returning countrymen'.[32]

A model remedy was close to hand. Emigrés from counties in the Pearl River region were long accustomed to setting up native-place associations (*huiguan*) in urban settlements overseas. These associations served to provide temporary board and lodging, to supervise credit and repayments, to handle procedures and problems associated with immigration and repatriation, to offer advice and security, and to impose sanctions, stage entertainments, mediate disputes among members and assist members in their dealings with bureaucracy and the law. A number of these associations were set up in Melbourne, Sydney and regional mining towns from the 1850s to the 1890s. Some were dissolved early in the following century. By the 1920s and 1930s the most prominent associations in Melbourne were the See Yap Association (for natives of four counties in southeast Guangdong), the Sam Yap Association (three counties surrounding Canton), the Ling Ying Association (Toishan county), the Kong Chew Society (Sunwei county) and the Heungshan Association (Heungshan county). Comparable associations in Sydney included the See Yap Association, the Yum Tak Tong and Bow On Tong (for Heungshan county), the Doongchang Lin Yik Tong (for Doong Goon and Changsheng counties) and the Hong Fook Tong (for Goming and Goyou counties).[33]

By 1925 there was a pressing need for comparable native-place associations in China to cater for visitors from Australia, New Zealand and the Pacific Islands who were in need of personal contacts, temporary lodgings and *ad hoc* assistance in dealing with local bureaucrats, tax agents and the law. Overseas native-place associations in republican China typically took the form of clubs, organised around KMT branch offices and loosely affiliated with the party organisation in China. By 1924 the party's central executive committee in Canton formed a view that the alleged party affiliations of these overseas associations actually serviced visiting émigrés more effectively than they did the Nationalist Party. In April 1924 the central executive committee commanded that overseas native-place clubs should place themselves under direct party control or cease claiming Nationalist Party affiliation.[34]

Just a year later, the Australasian KMT convened its first congress in Sydney and decided to set up its own party clubhouse in Canton. One of the Sydney office's aims in creating the new institution was to assist comrades and their families visiting China in dealing with corrupt bureaucrats, local bullies and evil gentry. The formal aims of the new office included two further aims: encouraging investment in Nationalist China and reporting counter-revolutionary elements to KMT authorities. To visitors from Australia, however, local KMT party and government authorities were part of the problem.

The primary aim of the Australasian Canton office was to assist visiting Australasian members to cope with the arbitrary rule of party and government authorities in China.[35] This problem surfaced again at the fifth Australasian regional KMT congress held in Sydney in 1933. Conference delegates complained that visiting Australian and New Zealand party members were harassed by customs officials as soon as they set foot in China. 'Chinese abroad have made many contributions to the party and the country', complained one party member. 'But no sooner do they return home than they are subjected to kidnapping and extortion by corrupt officials, local bullies, and evil gentry.' Worst of all were customs officials in China. It was humiliating enough to be frisked by colonial customs officers in Hong Kong but the grilling and mistreatment at the hand of customs officials in Guangdong was 'ten times worse'. At every port and wharf encountered on their way returning émigrés were threatened by customs officials who compelled them to pay extortionate 'customs fees' to gain entry. Delegates reminded the Chinese government that it was responsible for protecting visiting Chinese émigrés and could do so by cleaning up corruption among local KMT officials.[36]

The Australia and Oceania Comrades Office (*Aozhou ji nantaipingyang qundao tongzhi zhuyue banshichu*) opened in Canton in 1926. Acting Director Wang Jianhai, despatched to Canton after the close of the first Sydney congress, had rented rooms for the association on the second floor of the Eastern Mansions on Dongheng Street in central Canton. Chen Renyi was appointed its first formal director. In August of the following year, the Second Australasian Party Congress decided to construct a dedicated building for the clubhouse. The congress committed the substantial sum of £6000, which was to be raised through voluntary donations and a compulsory levy on branch membership. One member, Cen Fuyuan, donated £1000 to the project.[37]

In April 1929 the director of the Australasian general headquarters, Peter Yee Wing (*Yu Rong*), visited Canton to oversee the purchase of land and to contract for the design and construction of the new building. The Canton directorship was transferred from Chen Renyi to Chen Yansheng. Once in Canton, Peter Yee Wing and Chen Yansheng settled on a block of land at 84 Hi Ton Road in Canton and convened a meeting of Australasian party members resident in Canton to secure their assistance in overseeing construction of the building. The meeting appointed a construction committee and changed the name of the clubhouse from the Australia and Oceania Comrades Office to the Canton Office of the Australasian KMT Headquarters (*Aozhou zongzhibu zhuyue banshichu*). The Fifth Regional Party Congress meeting in Sydney in 1933 appointed a new director and supervisory council for the Canton office. Liu Xizuan was appointed director and Chen Yansheng his deputy. Seeto Kwan, the aircraft donor, was invited to act as one of three members of a new supervisory committee along with Wu Hongnan and Cheng Zhonghuan. Peter Yee Wing was appointed deputy supervisor on the committee with Gu Jichang.[38]

The 1933 congress also revised the charter of the Canton office. The director was required to welcome returning comrades, assist them in dealing with corrupt local authorities, help the government in apprehending counter-revolutionaries, offer advice on business and investment, carry out instructions from the Sydney party headquarters and act on behalf of local Australasian party branches. Under the charter the position of director was to be filled through indirect elections of the Australasian branch network from among current members of the Australasian branch of the KMT. In addition to the director the office employed two salaried assistants.[39]

The charter was particularly strict in defining and enforcing eligibility requirements for members hoping to avail themselves of Canton clubhouse services. Current members who had paid £1 for a guarantee certificate from their home branch were entitled to use the facility. Those carrying a certificate were entitled to approach the club for assistance free of charge but were liable for any additional expenses incurred in following through on their requests. They could also make use of lodgings on the third floor free of charge for a period not exceeding a month in any given year and to take meals inhouse for 20 cents a sitting. Stays in excess of one month were strongly discouraged but in exceptional circumstances lodgers could reside beyond one month at a cost of Y1 per day. Initially, the clubhouse's operating expenses were covered by the Sydney office. This practice ceased after the Fifth Regional Party Congress when the Australasian headquarters ordered the Canton office to cover its operating expenses from commercial rents on the ground floor of the premises. From this time the Australasian party headquarters decided to retain in Sydney all fees earned through the sale of guarantee certificates to party members intending to visit the Canton office.[40]

The Australasian Nationalist Party office was reported to be the grandest of the KMT national clubs in Canton. Housed in a large, modern, purpose-built, three-storey structure in downtown Canton, the

Australasian office provided a range of services for visiting or returning party members from Australia, New Zealand and the Pacific Islands. It dealt with local party and government agencies on behalf of its members, provided advice on investments, handled immigration procedures for people in transit, provided board and lodging for members passing through Canton on their way to and from Australia and New Zealand, and generally held out a hand of welcome to Australasian visitors. The club was more substantial than any comparable Chinese native-place association to be found in Australia or New Zealand; it appears to have been the largest association in China as well. In the words of an official KMT party historian, the Australasian office was 'beyond doubt the most outstanding of all the overseas party offices in Canton'.[41]

The Canton Club at work

How well did the Australasian Canton office perform its assigned role? The *Guangdong Administrative Weekly* for June 1927 records a particularly interesting case. In mid-1927, while the new office was still housed in rental accommodation in Dongheng Street, Director Chen Renyi registered a complaint with the Guangdong provincial government concerning the behaviour of the county magistrate of Hoiping County, one of the four counties that made up the See Yap district. Chen Renyi had lodged an earlier objection through the party system with the provincial KMT party headquarters, making related charges about the behaviour of the KMT branch office in Hoiping County. Both complaints arose from the mistreatment of a returned Australasian émigré named Xie Yongguang.

The case highlights the persistence with which the Australasian KMT club represented Australian members in their conflicts with local KMT party and state authorities. According to the official complaint, the Australian Xie was unlawfully placed under arrest by KMT County Party Secretary Guan Zutang and his accomplice Xie Liangong, a committee member of the powerful KMT Investigation Commission in Hoiping County. The Australian had become involved in a feud between local party and family factions, which led to a charge that he was a counter-revolutionary element in collusion with a local bully named Xie Danhan. The Australian was bound and dragged before local state authorities at the insistence of the Hoiping County KMT party branch.

The Australasian KMT office was treading on delicate ground in challenging a local party boss. The Hoiping party secretary had technically contravened party regulations in effecting the arrest since only government authorities were authorised to issue arrest warrants, although summary arrests by party officials were commonplace at the time and rarely open to challenge. The Australasian office then appealed to higher authorities at the provincial level. The provincial party branch responded sympathetically to the complaint by demoting Hoiping County Party Secretary Guan Zutang for breaching party rules. The head of the county government subverted this provincial party decision by promoting the demoted party secretary to the position of ward head of Chikan Ward, a prized appointment in the Guan lineage network based in the county seat of Chikan in Hoiping County. To avoid detection, the Hoiping county head promoted Guan under his alternative name of Guan Shuangxia. The Australian comrades' office brought this development to the attention of the provincial government, which referred it on to the Provincial Investigation Commission, which directed it in turn to the provincial government's executive committee for resolution.

Some of the most senior officials in the Guangdong provincial government became involved in the case, including director of the Provincial Department of Civil Affairs Zhu Jiahua, and Lin Yungai, chair of the Canton City Government Commission (known colloquially as the mayor of Canton). The provincial government committee found in favour of the Australian comrades' office, a decision that had serious ramifications for local government officials in Hoiping. County Head Wu Tongsheng was removed from his post and declared ineligible for further appointments for three years. Two leading members of the Hoiping party branch, Guan Zutang and Xie Liangong, were similarly dealt with by the provincial party headquarters. The Australian Xie Yongguang walked free.[42]

In successfully defending Xie Yongguang, the Australasian office in Canton demonstrated to its supporters back home that it was capable of defending returning Australians from the ubiquitous corrupt officials, local bullies and evil gentry who made life difficult for visitors to China. The office was not afraid of dealing with bullies and bureaucrats even when they included the most senior KMT party and government officials within a county jurisdiction. Its evident success in dealing with senior provincial party and government agencies highlighted the advantages for all concerned of organising an Australasian native-place association in the form of a national KMT party agency rather than merely a national or regional native-place association. The Canton office provided board and lodging and offered advice and contacts to members who passed through its doors. Above all, it offered protection from the arbitrary rule of KMT party and government agencies in China.

In later years the Australasian Canton office continued to cultivate key people and institutions among party and government networks in China. When Peter Yee Wing and Chen Yansheng visited China in 1929 they paid their respects to party headquarters in Nanking before heading south to Canton and selecting their piece of real estate for the new club building. In May 1931, Office Director Chen Renyi attended the National Citizens Conference (*Guomin huiyi*) in Peking to speak on behalf of the Australasian party network. In December he was selected as one of four Australasian delegates to the Fourth National KMT Congress in Nanking.[43]

Chinese-Australian perspectives on the Australasian KMT

Vivian Chow had not long learnt of Sam Wong's expulsion from the Australian KMT in 1927 when he penned the quotation that begins this chapter. 'Send a Chinese to Australia,' he wrote, 'he becomes a labour leader and a booster for the working man's paradise.'[44] Chow was working as a journalist in China at the time the Sydney party headquarters split over Chiang Kai-shek's rise to power. He was well acquainted with Sam Wong's work with the NSW labour movement and aware of his efforts enlisting Chinese seamen into the KMT in the mid-1920s. But it was not until he boarded a ship for home in August 1932 that Vivian Chow learnt from a fellow passenger that Sam Wong had been purged from the party in the Australian Party Purification Movement of 1927. Chow returned home to Australia to find a KMT that was quite different to the one he had left behind.

Like Sam Wong, Vivian Chow believed that Australian Chinese stood out from their kinfolk around the world on account of their sympathy for the working man and their courage in standing up for their rights. He cited Sam Wong to this effect: 'One proud boast [the] Australian Chinese have which no other group dare claim. They taught the world respect for Chinese and Orientals in general. The Australian Chinese did.' Like Sam Wong, Chow shared equal pride in his Australian working-man's heritage and his Chinese ancestry.[45]

Chow's pride in his Chinese-Australian heritage was not limited to admiration for the Chinese-Australian labour movement. His informant on the ship home was Gilbert Yip Ting Quoy, a successful Sydney businessman with commercial interests in Hong Kong and the Straits settlements. Quoy was a prominent public figure in Sydney – a leading member of the NSW Chinese Chamber of Commerce and the father-in-law of William Liu, the high-profile managing director of the China–Australia Mail Steamship Line in the 1920s. Vivian Chow wrote admiringly of Gilbert Quoy's successes and of his family's achievements.[46]

He was especially proud of the successful Sydney business enterprises that had sprung up in Shanghai over the years he had been working in that city. 'The Australians', as he called them, had shown everyone in China that they were the most forward looking, unassuming and practical people of Chinese descent the world over. This was nowhere more apparent than in their success in modern business and trade:

> The world can see how true this is by a visit to Shanghai. They note the difference between the Australian Chinese department stores and the 'homeside' attempts at business. There is no comparison, the superiority of the Australians is so marked.[47]

Chow was referring to China's best-known department stores in downtown Shanghai, built by Chinese residents of Sydney over the early decades of the Chinese republic. In their design and management style these stores drew on the example of major department stores in Sydney, especially that of Anthony Horderns.[48] In their day they were counted the most modern and prestigious retail stores along China's premier shopping strip on Nanking Road. Today they are preserved as heritage sites commemorating Overseas Chinese enterprise in China (see below, chapter 8).

Business and labour aside Vivian Chow derived special satisfaction from the contribution of the Australians to China's political revolution. To his way of thinking the first wave of Australian revolutionaries had contributed more than their share to the republican cause from the 1880s to the overthrow of the Qing dynasty in 1911. 'Aliens though they were,' he reflected, 'Great Destiny handed to the Australian-Chinese ... the key to the fatherland's heart.' As we have seen in an earlier chapter, Vivian was heir to a Chinese Masonic lineage that dated back to the earliest years of the triad secret-society network in Australia. He carried this tradition with him to China when he travelled to the revolutionary base of Canton, as a young man of 19 or 20 in 1925, and then toured revolutionary Russia before settling down to work as a journalist in Shanghai. In the early 1930s he listed himself as foreign-affairs editor for the Shanghai evening newspaper *Sin Wan Pao* (*Xinwenbao*). As noted above, he was also chief editor of an Australian-Chinese journal published in Shanghai under the title *United China Magazine*.[49]

In August 1932 Chow boarded the P&O steamer *Ranpura* for the journey from Shanghai to Hong Kong before transferring on 2 September to the *SS Tanda* for the final leg to Sydney. He reached Brisbane on 18 September and three days later, when he steamed through Sydney Heads, he inhaled, as he put it, 'the sweet, chill air of my native land, and tingled all over with the freshness of the typical Australian morn'. As well as a fresh appreciation for what it was that made Chinese Australians distinct from others of Chinese descent, Chow discovered that

> among all Chinese the ones who went to [Australia] stood apart
> ... because of great courage and enterprise. They were the leaders of
> Chinese initiative and the instigators of Chinese progress ... They
> were the only Chinese trained and equipped mentally and physically
> for such a task [of rejuvenating China].[50]

When the *SS Tanda* docked at Circular Quay he was approached by a Mr Marr, acting for the collector of customs, who had been alerted by the consular representatives of the KMT nationalist government in Sydney to possible problems arising from his visit. These cast a shadow over his homecoming:

> But Mr. Marr [was] at pains to show me that the portals of my native land were wide open, as they always are, to native born sons, and that in New South Wales I could move and do as I pleased so long as I did not commit any criminal acts or crimes.

As an Australian of Chinese descent he found refuge in Sydney from the forces in China that sought to silence him. But these now extended through the Sydney Chinese community to include the local KMT branch headquarters. Once the KMT came to power in China its Sydney headquarters doubled as a local agency of the nationalist government.

Word preceded Chow to Sydney of the KMT's reaction to a number of newspaper articles he had published in Shanghai that were highly critical of the nationalist government. From 1928 the Sydney party headquarters counted among its duties systematic spying and informing on Chinese Australians who were critical of the nationalist government in China. The Sydney party headquarters was closely monitored by the nationalist government's consul-general in Sydney who held an *ex-officio* position on senior Australasian KMT committees. Chow believed that nationalist spies were tailing him in Sydney, on his travels north to Grafton and to his home town of Lismore, and that senior officers in the Sydney KMT headquarters – including business leader William Liu, editor of the KMT's *Chinese Times* Gee Ming Ket and W Gock Young, Chairman of the Society of Chinese Residents in Australia – were hounding him during his time in Sydney. The consul-general unsuccessfully petitioned the Commonwealth government to have Chow arrested and deported the moment he stepped ashore.

For Vivian Chow, the consul-general's failure to effect his expulsion tapped the deepest source of his pride in being born Australian. By right of birth he was entitled to the protection of the British tradition of rule of law. 'Even if I were a Communist practical and theoretical,' he reflected, 'the Commonwealth of Australia has no power to deport from the country a native born son.' The liberty that came with his Australian birthright made him proud to be Chinese and Australian. 'In that land of Anglo-Saxon liberty,' he wrote, 'I was brought up at once an Australian and a Chinese.'

A year later Chow left Sydney for Shanghai. When he returned home again in 1935 Chinese Consul-General KF Wang wrote to Prime Minister Lyons complaining that Chow 'is sheltering behind his Australian domicile in attacking my Government'. Chow's offence on this occasion was to publish an article in the Sydney *Sun* in December 1935 alleging that the Nanking government had condemned to death two Shanghai journalists for writing articles critical of the nationalist government's passive response to Japanese military aggression in north China. In light of the consul-general's failed attempt at deportation in 1932, the consul-general no longer petitioned for Chow's expulsion. Instead, he appealed to the Australian prime minister 'for his advice as to what redress I have against an offender who makes such false and damaging statements against the highest official of my Government — Marshall Chiang Kai Shek'. Whether Prime Minister Lyons chose to offer advice to Consul-general Wang is not recorded. Chow's Australian birthright once again preserved him from prosecution in Australia and possible execution in China if the consul-general had his way. Instead, Chow died of natural causes in Sydney, six years later, aged 35.[51]

Vivian Chow's reflections reveal a young man proud of his Chinese and Australian heritage and with an acute interest in what it meant to be counted Australian in the era of White Australia. Even though, for the most part, his Australian identity was a source of pride, still, he was painfully conscious of the limitations that White Australia placed upon his freedom of expression — not freedom of political expression in this case, but freedom to express his sense of pride in being an Australian of Chinese heritage. It was his only complaint. At one point he recalled that when he was a student at Lismore High School an Irish-Australian teacher took him aside and told him to stop harping on about his Chinese ancestry. 'Forget it, lad,' Chow records the teacher chiding him. 'Don't put on airs in being proud of your Chinese ancestry. There's nothing to boast about. What does China mean to you anyway?' Chow's reply deserves a hearing. 'I replied,' he wrote,

You were born in Australia, so was I. Your father came to this
country a pioneer, likewise my father. Your father was proud of his
country, likewise my father. May I give the retort courteous, sir, and
say to you: 'Why are you so proud of being Irish? Why is it that
you storm and agitate about Home Rule in Ireland, and what does
Ireland mean to you anyway?'[52]

Chow learnt from an early age that the homelands from which settlers set out to make a life for their families in Australia were not valued equally. Where transnational ties with the British Isles were tolerated and even encouraged he had a struggle on his hands to maintain his family's links with China.[53] Still, he insisted on discovering the grounds on which his Chinese heritage made him any less Australian than the son of an Irishman.

7
THE PACIFIC SHADOW
OF WHITE AUSTRALIA

*There is a school of thought, among ethnologists particularly, who
maintain that as the Pacific is to be the ocean of the future, so there is
now in embryo a new race who will one day inhabit the lands whose
shores are washed by its waters.*

SF Chow, 'The Chinese from Australia' (1933).[1]

In the 1920s a regulatory regime that had become familiar to Chinese
Australians since federation was extended to cover business and
movement in and out of the South Pacific Islands. Australian authorities
used their League of Nations mandate after the Great War to extend
the administrative reach of White Australia to Pacific communities that
had been relatively free from discriminatory constraints on movement,
property ownership and trade under German and British colonial
administrations. The Australasian KMT network then expanded
through the islands in the shadow of the Australian mandate, as a kind
of *doppelganger* of White Australia, helping Chinese residents to negotiate

the tangled web of regulations governing Chinese immigration and settlement in Australia's Pacific sphere of influence.

The KMT was particularly well suited to this role. White Australian regulation gave different Chinese-Australian business firms, labour organisers, Masonic lodges, church congregations and native-place associations good reason to pool their resources to secure freedom of movement for their members, family affines and business partners in and out of Australia. The KMT's uniquely privileged access to provincial governments in south China in the early republic, and to the nationalist government of China after 1928, lent that organisation a degree of authority that no other Chinese-Australian body could match. The KMT provided access to official Chinese and Australian government channels at the very moment White Australian regulations were beginning to limit Chinese freedom of trade and movement in the South Pacific.

As we have seen, Chinese Australians were exceptionally keen travellers, recording visits to and from Australia over the White Australia era well in excess of their aggregate number. Some were possibly travelling to China to live out their final years, as White Australian legend would have it, but many were simply commuting through Sydney en route to a variety of destinations in China, Hong Kong, Southeast Asia and the islands of the South Pacific on business and family matters. They were compelled to move around more than other Australians by a suite of federal and state legislation intended to limit their liberties by restricting access for Chinese residents to Australian citizenship, preventing wives and children joining their husbands and fathers permanently in Australia and, in some states, restricting their ownership of property and investment and their involvement in particular industries.[2] Due to these restrictions, travel became essential to Chinese Australians trying to run businesses and raise families.

The entrepreneurs of larger enterprises extended their business operations to colonial sites abroad where a familiar style of rule of law prevailed without the burden of discriminatory restraints on investment, trade and movement. Less prosperous shop assistants, market gardeners and labourers followed them along the same maritime routes leading to the Pacific Islands, Hong Kong, Canton and Shanghai, transnational manoeuvres facilitated by the Australasian KMT. It was a party of adventurous merchants and free labourers who were determined to travel, work, trade, invest and raise their families, despite the limits that confronted them. This chapter explores the links tying the Australasian KMT to Chinese business interests in Sydney, and to broader Pacific Island investment and trading networks, to show how its expansion mirrored that of White Australia.

Maritime networks and Pacific Islands trade

Historically speaking, Sydney's claim to regional leadership of the Australasian KMT was fairly slim. The city was selected in the 1920s as the preferred site for the party's Oceania regional headquarters in recognition of its current maritime links with Asia and the Pacific Islands, including its relations with the merchant marine and its links with island settlements in the South Pacific. Canton assigned the Australasian branch network responsibility for establishing branches on merchant vessels servicing ports in south-east Asia where KMT activity was outlawed. Within a few years of its creation the Sydney headquarters had recruited almost 1000 labourers through 15 sub-branches on merchant vessels sailing between Australia and ports in east and southeast Asia.[3] Sydney's maritime links also extended to island settlements serviced by traders based in Sydney. In the case of the Pacific Islands, the sea routes that linked KMT branches were the same channels through which Chinese-Pacific Island trading and migration networks were routed through Sydney.

Banana-trading companies, led by Heungshan merchants with links to the Pacific Islands, lay behind several of the great Chinese-Australian firms that dominated general retail trade in Shanghai in the Chinese republic. They were instrumental as well in the foundation and growth of the Australasian KMT. Sydney merchants imported bananas and tropical fruit from the Pacific Islands in return for trans-shipping processed foods and manufactured products, largely sourced from Hong Kong, to the islands. Green bananas were imported from Queensland and Fiji for ripening in Chinese-Australian company storehouses in Sydney before being distributed statewide and interstate through local company networks. It has been estimated that Chinese-Australian producers and importers with ties to Fiji handled between a half and three-quarters of all bananas ripened and traded in Australia over the first quarter of the twentieth century. The same Heungshan merchants were among the most significant of all foreign investors in Shanghai; it was they who built the second-largest KMT party organisation outside of China after French Annam. Their business and political activities were inseparable.[4]

One of these banana firms, Sang On Tiy, was founded in 1902 as a partnership among the three Sydney fruit merchandising firms of Wing *Sang*, Wing *On* and Wing *Tiy*. Wing Sang (*Yongsheng*) and Wing On (*Yongan*) were the respective parent companies of the Sincere, Wing On and, indirectly, Sun Sun department store chains later established in Hong Kong and China. Founded in 1890 by Heungshan natives in Sydney, Wing Sang was the largest trader of Queensland bananas in southern Australian ports over its early years. In time the firm expanded into owning and managing fruit plantations abroad, chiefly in Fiji, and diversified locally into general importing and exporting. Partners in the firm included Ma Ying-piu, founder of the Sincere Department Store chain, and George Kwok Bew (*Guo Biao*), a maternal cousin of the Kwok brothers (who founded the Wing On firm in Sydney and China) and a partner with Ma Ying-piu in Sincere. One of the Kwok brothers, James Gocklock, was an employee of Wing Sang before he ventured out on his own in 1897 to establish the Wing On Fruit Store in Sydney. Within two years James was joined in the venture by four of his brothers who together built up the substantial Wing On commercial empire in Sydney, Hong Kong and China. One of the brothers, Philip Gockchin, spent three years in Suva managing the Sang On Tiy banana combine before joining his brother in Hong Kong and later founding Wing On's flagship Shanghai store. The banana trade was the cornerstone of Chinese-Australian venture capital in the White Australia era.[5]

Chinese Australians and the Great War

White Australia introduced politics into the banana trade in the aftermath of the Great War. Up to this time Chinese-Australian involvement in local banana production and trading was generally uncontroversial and so it might have remained but for the race chauvinism generated by the Great War. At the Paris peace conference Prime Minister William Morris Hughes took credit for ensuring that no 'racial equality' clause was inserted into the charter of the League of Nations. On his return to Australia, Hughes likened his achievement at the Paris negotiations to that of the Anzacs who had preceded him to Europe. 'White Australia is yours,' he announced to the Australian federal parliament. '[Our] soldiers have achieved the victory, and my colleagues and I have brought that great principle [of White Australia] back to you from the conference, as safe as it was on the day when it was first adopted.' The Great War vindicated the champions of White Australia who were determined to ensure, in the prime minister's words, 'that none should enter in, except such as they chose'. Whatever the initial reasons for going to war, the allied victory in Europe was widely celebrated in Australia as a victory in the struggle to keep Australia white.[6]

Chinese Australians served in Australian forces in Gallipoli, France and Belgium, some with considerable distinction. William Sing of the Fifth Light Horse was famous for his marksmanship, on one occasion winning a duelling contest with an enemy sniper known as Abdul the Turk. William and George Loolong were both wounded in France and decorated for their gallantry. Albert Chan enlisted in August 1914 and ended the war with the Distinguished Conduct Medal (DCM) for conspicuous gallantry. Caleb Shang of the 47th Battalion of the AIF returned to Brisbane as one of the most decorated Anzacs of the war, earning a DCM for conspicuous gallantry at Messines Ridge in Belgium and a Military Medal and Bar to his DCM for covering his company's withdrawal on the Somme.[7] Alongside these Chinese Australians several hundred thousand labourers from China excavated and constructed the trenches in which Australian and allied infantry hunkered down on the Western front.[8]

Their contributions were little acknowledged and seldom appreciated in Australia. After the war, in response to agitation from returned service associations, Chinese Australians were chased off their leases in northern Australia to make way for returning white servicemen, and in some places banned from selected industries. Land tenanted by

Chinese on the Atherton tableland in northern Queensland was resumed by the Commonwealth for distribution to white servicemen returning from the war. Local chapters of the Australian Returned Services League (RSL) in Papua and New Guinea pressured the Australian government to prohibit Chinese residents from taking out licences as ships' captains and to prevent Chinese long-settled in the area from owning land in Australia's mandated territories. As one Chinese community member in New Guinea later recalled, 'The RSL members ... hated us Chinese most and oppressed us most'.[9]

After the Great War an alliance of local returned soldiers' associations and chambers of commerce launched a public campaign protesting the expansion of Chinese-Australian involvement in the banana industry in northern New South Wales. In 1916 the Tim Young Fruit Company had begun buying freehold land on the NSW north coast. Within three years the larger Sydney merchandising firms of Wing Sang, Wing On and Tiy Sang followed Tim Young in purchasing substantial banana plantations in the region. By war's end around 14 per cent of plantations in northeastern New South Wales, measured by area under cultivation, were in Chinese-Australian hands. Despite protests from white planters the NSW state government declined to take action against Chinese-Australian firms. When agitation spilt over the border into Queensland, however, that state government introduced in 1921 a mandatory dictation test to limit Chinese-Australian entrants into the Queensland banana industry.[10]

White growers in Queensland also agitated for a national ban on the importation of bananas from Fiji, which were chiefly cultivated on Chinese-Australian plantations in the islands. The embargo followed a bout of banana blight that all but bankrupted the Fijian plantations in 1919. Chinese plantations in Australia fared little better. By the 1930s, writes author Eric Rolls, 'fruit fly, bunchy top, cyclones and the White Australia policy had destroyed Chinese banana growing'.[11] Chinese-Australian banana traders survived by consolidating their investments offshore. As well as the department stores they set up, they also expanded their business into commercial and life insurance, banking, and textile manufacturing on a large scale. This is the subject of the following chapter.[12] Here we might note that the families who dominated the banana industry and, in time, the great diversified firms based in Hong Kong and Shanghai, were at the same time closely linked to the leading echelons of the Australasian network of the KMT.

Business and the KMT

Families and firms enjoyed close relations with every level of the KMT party organisation, ranging from small cells in the party's Pacific Islands network to its central headquarters in Shanghai. Sun Yatsen held a personal portfolio of Wing On shares purchased by his wife in 1916. The Wing On Company in turn made substantial loans and donations to Sun Yatsen's central headquarters in Shanghai.[13] Family and business ties linking the Sydney firms to local party branches in the Pacific Islands were more intensive still. George Bew was part owner of Wing Sang and Co. and at the same time a partner in the Sang On Tiy banana importing firm, a founding shareholder in Sincere, a cousin of the Kwok brothers who owned the Wing On firm and, from 1916 to 1920, state director of the NSW branch of the KMT. A founding partner of the rival Tiy Sang firm of Fijian banana growers, Peter Yee Wing, was elected party treasurer during George Bew's term as director and succeeded him in that office. George Bew and Peter Yee Wing between them were responsible for much of Fiji's annual banana production and held the reins of the NSW and Australasian KMT headquarters over its first 15 years of operation.

Yee Wing succeeded George Bew as head of the NSW branch from 1920 to 1925 when he was selected to head the reorganised Australasian party headquarters for three successive terms, beginning with the KMT's first regional party congress in 1925 and ending with the fourth congress, also held in Sydney, in December 1931. His withdrawal from positions of leadership in the Sydney headquarters can be attributed to his absence over much of his third term in China, where he supervised the purchase of land to build the Australasian party clubhouse in Canton, noted in the preceding chapter. Yee Wing surrendered control of the Sydney headquarters to take up a position as deputy supervisor of the Australasian KMT clubhouse building committee in Canton, to which he was elected by delegates to the fifth Australasian congress meeting in 1933.[14]

As we have seen, the Australasian KMT office in Canton was one of the most important initiatives undertaken by the Australasian KMT to meet the needs of Chinese-Australian travellers. The club functioned on the model of native-place *huiguan* set up by Cantonese émigrés abroad, although in this case it was set up in Canton by émigrés who thought of themselves as Australians or New Zealanders. The club performed many roles but its chief purpose was to provide a place for members to meet and do business, to help them in their dealings with customs authorities in China and to provide legal and administrative security for Australian, New Zealand and Pacific Island visitors who were unfamiliar with life in the Chinese republic. In Sydney, the Australasian KMT headquarters provided a range of services for party members commuting from the Pacific Islands comparable to those of the Australasian office in Canton. It served as a first point of contact for strangers, a place to eat and sleep in the party dormitory on the fourth floor of the new KMT building and as a reliable source of advice on immigration and business affairs.

Although dominated by a small coterie of leading merchant families, the Australasian KMT headquarters welcomed merchants of modest means who engaged in legitimate fields of trade within its jurisdiction. None responded more warmly than the owners of small and medium businesses in Fiji and New Guinea, who sought to extend their home-town connections and kinship ties through institutional networks operating around the Sydney KMT headquarters. One prominent retired member of the KMT in Sydney has recalled visiting the Australasian party headquarters shortly after alighting from a steamer from Fiji as a young man after the war in the Pacific. 'In Fiji I joined the KMT to extend my social networks,' he told a gathering of KMT historians in October 2005. 'We all did. We joined the KMT to make connections in a city where we arrived as strangers.'[15]

KMT Pacific Island branches

Sydney's place in maritime routes linking the Pacific Islands to Australia and China was instrumental in the founding of the Fiji and New Guinea party networks. According to official party records, the founder and early leader of the KMT in Fiji was Lew Ching (*Liu Qing*), a merchant from Suva who joined the party on a routine visit to Sydney in 1916 and returned to the islands with a charter to form a sub-branch in Fiji. In the case of New Guinea, legend has it that the first party branch was founded by a group of 19 members of the Seeto family who joined the KMT in Sydney while en route from New Guinea to their home county of Hoiping and were invited to establish a branch in Rabaul on their return to New Guinea.[16] KMT leaders in Sydney welcomed and encouraged these approaches. They were active Pacific Island traders themselves.

In time, party members based in ports along Pacific Island trading routes were able to draw on an extensive KMT maritime network to expand the range of their business connections in the Pacific Islands and approach government authorities to remove obstacles to investment, trade and movement in the region. In the late 1920s they were assisted by the Chinese consulate in Sydney, which enjoyed *ex officio* membership on the Australasian KMT executive committee after the consulate came under KMT nationalist government control in 1928.

FIJI

Fiji had few Chinese community organisations of note when the first KMT sub-branch was established in Suva in May 1917. Within a decade of the branch's founding Suva party members had built a substantial community hall – the only Chinese community building on the islands – and were operating a school, a theatre company, a netball club and a small Chinese library. In 1930 they launched a fortnightly newspaper, the *Chinese National News (Guomin banyuekan)*, which continued publishing into the 1970s. By 1929 four sub-branches had opened on the Fiji islands in Suva, Lavuka, Lautoka and Ba. In 1931 these four were placed under a consolidated Fiji islands branch in Suva that reported directly to the Sydney general headquarters. The extent and influence of the KMT network was evident to authorities in the islands. The governor of Fiji reported to London that the majority of Chinese residents of Fiji were sympathetic to the KMT and the Chinese nationalist government in China.[17]

The party's success in Fiji was, in a sense, premised on its occasional failure to act as an inclusive public association. Despite its reputation as a national political party, open to all Chinese residents, the Sydney headquarters retained strong nativist links with Heungshan County that were reflected in the party's operations in Fiji, a shortcoming in the eyes of its critics. Vivian Chow, himself of Doong Goong parentage, complained in 1933 that 'the Sydney Kuo Min Tang is dominated by the Heungshan natives or descendents of men from there' to the exclusion of people from other counties.[18] To many Chinese residents of Fiji, however, the KMT's Heungshan parochialism was a blessing.

The Chinese community of Fiji was dominated by Heungshan natives. According to KMT party sources, 45 per cent of Chinese residents in Fiji came from Heungshan, another 42 per cent hailed from the four See Yap counties combined, 10 per cent from Doong Goong, and the remaining 3 per cent from the Sam Yap counties neighbouring Canton. Ties of kinship were no less important than county connections in linking the Fiji community to the Sydney KMT network. The three Heungshan families that dominated fruit businesses and party affairs in Sydney were also prominent in Fijian party and business affairs. In 1931, for example, the Fiji party branch donated the considerable sum of £1500 to the anti-Japanese war effort in China. Responsibility for raising the donation was assigned to three leading Fiji branch party committee members – Guo Qinghe of the Kwok family, Ma Quanliang of the Ma family and Yu Jinrong of the Yee family – each with family ties to the three leading Heungshan KMT families of George Kwok Bew, Ma Ying-piu and Peter Yee Wing in Sydney.[19]

According to Fiji historian Bessie Ng Kumlin Ali, the earliest Chinese traders in Fiji were natives of Toishan County who moved to Fiji from Melbourne in the mid-19th century. Moy Park Ling left Toishan for Victoria in 1856 before moving to New South Wales in the 1860s, and in 1872 to Fiji, where he opened for business under the name of Houng Lee. In Fiji he maintained close and constant links with his old See Yap district networks in Sydney, not all of them from his own county. He established close business ties with the Tiy Sang firm in Sydney, for example, despite that firm operating under the control of the Hoiping native (and later KMT leader) Peter Yee Wing. Moy's son George was subsequently employed by Yee Wing's Tiy Sang firm.[20]

The catalyst behind this successful cross-county business arrangement was the Sydney entrepreneur Quong Tart who introduced Peter Yee Wing and his Tiy Sang Company to Quong's Toishan business connections in Fiji in 1899. Yee Wing and Quong Tart sought Moy's help in negotiating with local Chinese firms and the colonial secretary of Fiji regarding the possible importation of Chinese contract labour to the islands. The labour negotiations came to nothing, but Quong Tart's connections nevertheless helped to forge abiding business links between the two companies. Quong Tart, representing Tiy Sang, was himself a Moy from Toishan, as was Moy Park Ling.[21]

With the expansion of the banana trade over the following decades, Heungshan natives entered Fiji in considerable numbers under the sponsorship of the Heungshan fruit merchandising firms based in Sydney. Chinese residents trebled in number from the turn of the century to 305 in the 1911 census (10 per cent of them women) and trebled again to 910 by 1921 (7 per cent women). With the closure of the Australian market in the early 1920s large-scale banana production collapsed and was replaced by copra trading. At this time the population grew steadily to 1751 by 1936 (16 per cent women) and to 2874 (27 per cent women) by the end of the Pacific war. At this time around half of Fiji's Chinese residents were natives of Heungshan. The Heungshanese were on the whole more mobile than other Chinese residents of Fiji. Although making up 45 per cent of residents Heungshan natives accounted for 60 per cent of applications for Return Permits submitted to Fiji authorities between 1930 and 1931 (as we shall see, Return Permits were introduced to allow departing Chinese residents to return to the islands while excluding new immigrants from China).[22]

Unskilled labourers from China were relatively few in Fiji. Small business dominated the life of the local Chinese community. When local Chinese firms turned from bananas to trading in copra, Chinese labourers became shopkeepers, operating numerous small universal-provider stores throughout the islands. The two developments were causally related. When Chinese shareholding firms entered the copra market in the 1920s and 1930s their involvement was largely confined to trading. They purchased most of their copra from an expanding network of Chinese general stores in the villages that flourished by purchasing small quantities of copra from native producers for resale to Chinese traders, who on-sold to white trading companies or sold directly abroad. By 1924 three local Chinese firms accounted for almost one-quarter of the Fiji copra trade: Jang Hing Loong handled 14 per cent, Kwong Sang 8 per cent and Kwong Tiy 2 per cent of the copra trade. The synergy that emerged between large copra traders and small village stores greatly expanded opportunities for Chinese labourers to become small traders on the islands.[23]

According to official KMT records, by the early 1930s some 1600 Fiji residents were operating 230 small businesses and eight large firms on the islands, or roughly one independent business for every six or seven Chinese residents on the islands. Most of the independent businesses were small trading stores but the eight large firms included the Sydney-based firms Sang On Tiy and Tiy Sang as well as local firms such as Jang Hing Loong, Kwong Tiy, Fong Sam, Kwong Sam and Zoing Chong. Some of these firms were quite substantial, managing local factories and mills in addition to importing and exporting sea cucumber, copra, pearl, timber, rice, fruit and spices. A significant proportion of businessmen were KMT party members, including a majority of the highly-mobile Heungshan native traders. By 1930 almost one in three Chinese residents of Fiji was a party member.[24]

Mobility and party membership went together. White authorities in Australia and New Zealand effectively controlled Chinese access to the islands, initially, through poll taxes imposed on Chinese passengers en route to the islands, and later through the influence they could bring to bear on authorities in London and in Suva, the site of colonial authority over British territories in the southwest Pacific. One older party member in Fiji recalls that KMT branches were founded on the islands chiefly to assist Chinese residents in negotiating the increasingly complex immigration procedures imposed on short-term departures and re-entries from Fiji in the White Australia period.[25]

Over the period in question, commercial vessels travelling to and from Hong Kong or Singapore disembarked island passengers in Sydney for transfer to island steamers. Before federation, Chinese heading to and from the islands were obliged to pay NSW poll taxes. When Houng Lee prepared to take his wife and family to China in 1899 he faced a combined bill for non-refundable poll taxes to various Australian authorities of £600 simply for passing through their territorial jurisdictions. He appealed to the British prime minister to persuade the Australians to waive the tax for eminent people such as himself; he won

a reprieve for his family if not for others. On another occasion, at Quong
Tart's request, the governor of Fiji wrote to the governors of Queensland
and New South Wales seeking exemption from their respective poll
taxes for Chinese labourers transiting through Brisbane and Sydney to
the Pacific Islands. The colonial governors agreed to waive poll taxes in
return for a guarantee of £100 per head and, in the case of New South
Wales, on condition that just one Chinese could be carried per 100 tons
of cargo.[26] These concessions did little to lift actual constraints on direct
migration from China and or to ease the difficulties facing Chinese on
the islands who wished to commute or return to China.

Poll taxes and person:tonnage ratios were eliminated at federation
and replaced by direct legislation and administrative discretion as the
preferred instruments for limiting Chinese access to Australia's Pacific
territories and sphere of influence. Governors of Fiji were attentive
to white Australian sensitivities in weighing up competing requests
from local white planters to admit Chinese contract workers into Fiji
in defiance of Australian restrictions. White colonists were, on the
whole, sympathetic to the racist assumptions of Australian public policy
even while they questioned its application to Fiji. As early as 1879,
the *Fiji Times* echoed Sydney and Californian journalists of the day in
declaring that 'all men are born free and equal, except the Indians and
Chinamen'. As there were only 30 Chinese men and woman in Fiji at
the time of publication, apocryphal comments of this kind were uttered
more in sympathy with the trans-Pacific racism of the day than out of
immediate concern bearing on Fiji.[27] That said, white planters were no
less hostile towards unrestricted Chinese emigration to the islands than
the Australian labour movement in relation to Australia. Both sought to
limit Chinese entry to one or two categories of 'desirable' immigrants.
They parted company on the categories each considered desirable.

Fijian planters favoured granting admission to unskilled labourers to
work their plantations and frowned on the admission of merchants and
skilled artisans who could compete against them. Australian government
authorities, by contrast, were prepared to grant exceptions for certain
categories of skilled migrants and merchant traders but reluctant to make
exceptions for unskilled labourers. The matter was settled in favour of
the Australians. In 1913 the secretary of state in London instructed

the governor of Hong Kong that Chinese labour was no longer to be licensed for transit to any Pacific Islands under British jurisdiction.[28]

In the 1920s a series of ordinances followed that had the effect of severely limiting entry to new arrivals from China and requiring all those leaving Fiji to apply for permission to return before departing. New arrivals were limited by a requirement that they secure a visa for entry. Although consistent with Britain's treaty obligations with China this requirement facilitated 'discrete' discrimination whereby visa applications could be ignored or rejected by British missions in the Far East without explanation. Henceforth any Chinese departing with the intention of returning was required to apply for a Certificate of Identity and a Permit to Return prior to departure. Permits for re-entry were handled more generously than visas for new arrivals. In 1928 the KMT approached the Chinese consul-general in Melbourne seeking clarification of the impact of the new commuting regulations on Chinese departures and returns to Fiji. In his formal response, the governor of Fiji pointed out that no resident of repute had been denied re-entry after an absence of less than five years.[29]

For Chinese residents of Fiji the governor's message was reassuring on two counts. First, it indicated that they could come and go as they pleased so long as they complied with finger-printing and other intrusive requirements of the governor's ordinance bearing on Permits to Return. The governor's formal reply also showed that the KMT was capable of representing the interests of Chinese residents to government by virtue of its links with Australia, its status in dealing with the KMT Nationalist Government of China and its position as an institution representing the Chinese residents of Fiji. In the following year the Chinese nationalist government appointed a resident vice-consul to Fiji, the first of several KMT government representatives to serve on the islands before the Pacific war. The arrival of CL Cheng as resident vice-consul in 1930 further cemented the Sydney KMT's position in Fiji.[30]

NEW GUINEA

Another success story for the Sydney KMT headquarters was the network of five party branches sponsored in New Guinea in the early 1920s. Four of the branches were based in former German territories surrounding the Bismark Archipelago, stretching from Madang on the northern coast of the New Guinea mainland northward to the islands of New Britain and New Ireland and east towards the Solomon Islands. The KMT opened its first sub-branch in Rabaul, New Britain, on 20 September 1920; within three years the party opened a further three sub-branches in Kokopo (1920), Kavieng (also spelled Keawieng, 1921) and Madang (1923). A Solomon Islands branch opened in 1923. At the 1925 regional party congress in Sydney the Australasian headquarters elevated the Rabaul sub-branch to full branch status and placed the other four under its jurisdiction, an arrangement that persisted until 1931 when the Rabaul branch was renamed the New Guinea Branch and the Solomon Islands sub-branch reverted to Sydney's direct control. Throughout this period Rabaul remained the liveliest centre of Chinese community activity in New Guinea as well as the epicentre of the local KMT movement. By 1930 over 400 of the 1600 Chinese residents of the New Guinea islands were members of the KMT, the majority of them in Rabaul.[31]

The New Guinea KMT network was erected on different foundations from its Fiji counterpart. To begin with, the party was not the only Chinese community organisation of note in the territory. Seven or eight common-surname associations and district clubs preceded its establishment in Rabaul, most claiming memberships of no more than 10 to 20 men. New Guinea historian David Wu argues that the proliferation of so many small clubs in Rabaul and other settlements indicated a general lack of co-operation among Chinese residents in the islands, a division later reflected in the history of the KMT's New Guinea network. In this case the party was captured not by native-place networks, as in Fiji, but by a single clan association playing on subethnic tensions on the New Guinea islands, specifically, the Seeto family from Hoiping working with Hakka Chinese residents from Huiyang County against their See Yap rivals. Hoiping was itself a See Yap county.[32]

Further, the Methodist and Catholic churches each played a greater role in Chinese community life in New Guinea than in Fiji. The greatest single fracture dividing the multilingual Chinese community of New Guinea was the sectarian division separating Methodists from Catholics. The boundaries of this religious divide overlapped with clan and subethnic loyalties – the Hoiping Seetos were Methodists, along with most Hakka families, while other prominent See Yap families were generally baptised as Catholics – and in the case of the Methodists corresponded directly with KMT membership. Religion and politics served as convenient markers for subethnic and family divisions separating the Hoiping Seetos and Hakkas from other See Yap families. After founding their party branch in 1920, the Seeto clan entrenched the local KMT as a non-Catholic institutional network with the aim of wresting community leadership from the prominent Catholic families who had represented it to that time. These differences were further entrenched with the establishment of a KMT school in Rabaul in 1920, later absorbed into a Methodist Overseas Chinese School (*huaqiao xuexiao*) in 1922, and the foundation two years later of a rival Catholic school, St Theresa's Yang Ching school (*Yangzheng xuexiao*) in Rabaul. It was not until 1939 that the KMT played a part in bridging this religious and subethnic divide by calling successfully on 'patriotic' Chinese in New Guinea to support the anti-Japanese war effort in China.[33]

Where natives of Heungshan predominated in Fiji, Chinese residents of New Guinea were predominantly Hakka from Huiyang County northeast of Canton and natives of the four See Yap counties. David Wu's survey of Chinese-New Guinea residents in 1971 revealed 70 per cent See Yap heritage, 13 per cent Sam Yap and counties neighbouring Canton, and 12 per cent Hakka. The Heungshan natives who dominated party life in Fiji fell within the remaining 5 per cent of 'Others' in New Guinea. These figures probably reflect the population balance of the prewar period.

Hakka women were especially prominent in the party. One-third of all party recruits enlisted in Rabaul in 1947 and 1948 were Hakka women. Not surprisingly, the Mahs, Kwoks and other Heungshan families who dominated party affairs in Sydney and Fiji over the prewar period were not well represented on party committees in New Guinea, where KMT branch executives generally bore the names of prominent See Yap and Hakka families in the region, including Seeto, Chow, Tan and Chan.[34]

Institutionally speaking, the greatest difference distinguishing the New Guinea from the Fiji party network was its apparent lack of fit with the Australasian party headquarters. In Fiji, entrepreneurship and party membership were inseparable, as were ties linking Heungshan natives in Fiji with Heungshan business and family networks in Sydney. There were few Heungshan natives in Rabaul with ties to Sydney Heungshan KMT families. Many of New Guinea's wealthiest business families were Catholics who felt excluded from the 'Methodist' KMT.[35] The New Guinea KMT network ended up refracting existing community fractures along religious, ethnic and lineage lines. For all these differences, however, the New Guinea party offices maintained productive relations with the Sydney party headquarters. Maintenance of cordial relations between disparate family and native-place networks in the face of significant community fractures testifies to the flexibility of the Australasian KMT as an inclusive regional civic institution.

KMT achievements in New Guinea can be attributed to effective merchant leadership, the absence of contract labour on the islands and a common concern to find an authoritative voice to speak out against emerging threats from White Australia. Judging from the scale of voluntary financial contributions to the party the key factor appears to have been merchant involvement and leadership. Rabaul was a busy port with a substantial population of Chinese merchants operating in close contact with small traders. Party activities reflected the prosperity and generosity of the community. Not long after its founding in 1920, the Rabaul branch opened a school for the children of Chinese residents in the town, which consistently enrolled around 100 pupils. A second KMT school was established in Kavieng in 1924. Between 1920 and 1922, party members in Rabaul contributed £1000 towards erecting the most substantial building in Chinatown to serve as the party's branch office. When that building was destroyed in a devastating fire that laid to waste Rabaul's Chinatown in 1923, a further £800 was immediately raised to replace it. By 1930 each of the branches and sub-branches in Rabaul, Kokopo, Kavieng and Madang had purchased or constructed a dedicated party building, including a splendid party headquarters, costing £1800, in Kavieng that was opened in 1930.

Buildings and schools aside, the branch's most memorable achievement was its donation of £900 towards the KMT aircraft fund set up by local KMT luminary Seeto Kwan to purchase aircraft for Sun Yatsen's Canton administration in 1924. This was followed by a number of investments and contributions ranging from £800 to £1000 in support of patriotic causes in China raised between 1920 and 1932. In all, between 1920 and 1932, the 400 or so members of the New Guinea branch raised over £10 000 for building works, charitable activities on the island and various patriotic causes in China, representing an average donation of £25 from each local member over the period.[36]

The second condition for the KMT's success in New Guinea, the absence of contract labour, can be traced to the period of German occupation. Chinese traders had already settled in the New Guinea islands when Germany proclaimed the colonial territory of New Guinea (1884–1914). In the 1880s, the German-based Neuguinea Kompagnie contracted 1700 coolie labourers from Singapore to work in and around Madang, on the New Guinea mainland, which initially served as the administrative centre for the German territories. Chinese and German sources suggest that half of the workers died of exhaustion and disease within two years of their arrival. Chinese sources also point to rumours that workers who survived the disease were buried alive by their German overseers to prevent further spread of infection. This sobering experience put an end to the contracting of Chinese indentured labour in the 1890s and to the encouragement of free Chinese immigration from 1898 once the German colonial administration resumed control from the Neuguinea Kompagnie.[37]

When the Germans moved their administrative centre from the New Guinea mainland to Simpson's Harbour (later renamed Rabaul) in 1910, Chinese merchants were already well established in the area. Lee Tam Tuck (*Li Tande*), a Hakka from Huiyang County in Guangdong, came to the islands around the same time as the earliest German traders, the Hernsheim brothers, in the 1870s. Lee established himself as a shipbuilder and trader on the island of Matupit in New Britain, where he provided recruitment services for German traders wishing to recruit free skilled labour from China. Rather than repeat their failed experiment with indentured labour, German officials drew on the regional and lineage networks of men such as Lee Tam Tuck to recruit skilled labour for their new settlement. They encouraged free Chinese immigration. Many of the carpenters, tailors, cooks and servants who were recruited from China through these merchant networks stayed on in New Britain to become traders themselves and to act as trading agents for German and British firms in New Britain. By 1900 the number of Chinese agents in European employment was reported to have exceeded the number of Europeans.[38]

The German authorities recognised Lee's claim to property in Rabaul in return for his acknowledgment that it was held on lease from the German Crown. Lee was granted a 30-year lease over 17 acres, which developed in time into a classic Chinatown settlement and the main commercial centre of Rabaul. Given his role as chief labour recruiter and dominant landlord in the area, Lee was commonly referred to in Chinese not as a landlord but as the 'Lord of the Land'. A classic headman in the old triad mould, Lee was, in all likelihood, an elder brother of the Yee Hing secret society network. The Hakka association he founded was called the Chung Yi Wo (*Zhongyihe*) Club, or Hall of Loyalty Righteousness and Harmony, a name customarily reserved for Yee Hing lodges.[39]

The dynamics of the Chinese settlement changed when Australian forces seized Germany's New Guinea possessions during the Great War. White Australian administrators wasted no time imposing discriminatory restrictions on Chinese traders and limiting their freedom of movement. In 1917 they issued a Control of Chinese Trade Order that effectively banned Chinese wholesale trade in New Guinea. The order was rescinded following vociferous complaints from traders in Sydney who serviced the Chinese stores. Australian authorities then substituted a regulation prohibiting Chinese general stores from operating within two miles of copra plantations, placing them beyond the range of daily retail business and out of reach of native copra producers who were left with little choice but to sell their copra to British and Australian traders. When the League of Nations mandate came into effect in 1921 the Australians began transporting White Australian immigration restrictions to New Guinea as well, beginning with residency restrictions on Chinese wives accompanying their husbands to New Guinea, extending to prohibitions on new arrivals and involving certification of Chinese residents wishing to leave and return on family and business matters. No new immigrants from China could enter New Guinea other than in exceptional circumstances and with the express approval of the Australian government. There was no need to legislate these restrictions specifically for New Guinea as they were gazetted under Australian law, which applied locally from 1921 under the mandate.[40]

White Australian law impacted heavily on the resident Chinese community. As one Catholic community leader pointed out in a petition of 1924, Chinese men could no longer hold title to land, they could not bring their wives to join them (wives of 10 years standing were limited to an initial visit of three years and to second and further visits after further gaps of seven years between), they could not invite qualified teachers to educate their children, they could not request substitutes to replace them in business during their absence abroad, they could not leave with an expectation of returning without first obtaining a Permit to Return and they could not secure the necessary permit without undergoing humiliating procedures, including submission of a full hand-print.[41] In Papua, Australian authorities proceeded to implement a policy of racial segregation, separating 'Asiatics' from whites and natives in residential quarters, schools, parks, playgrounds, hospitals, libraries, baths, clubs and theatres, on an apartheid model not officially sanctioned within Australia itself. Given these restrictions on their customary rights to trade, invest, travel, mingle and raise their families, Chinese merchants from Rabaul to Madang were compelled to draw on their own social and business networks, particularly religious and political networks with links to Australia, to survive the transition to White Australia.

A special cause for concern was Lee Tam Tuck's 30-year lease over the Chinese settlement of Rabaul inherited from German times, which returned to haunt the Chinese community after Germany's New Guinea territories came under Australian control. Australian authorities initially agreed to recognise existing leasehold claims to the Chinese settlement of Rabaul, which by this time had grown into a substantial commercial precinct. According to Chinese sources, in 1925 the Australian authorities reversed their decision and compelled Chinese leaseholders in Rabaul to sign a 10-year agreement that would surrender their claims over their properties when the lease lapsed in 1934, five years short of the original German lease. From 1934 Rabaul's Chinatown was to revert to the use and discretion of the Australian government acting under its League of Nations mandate. The terms of the lease agreement were a constant source of irritation and consternation for the local Chinese business community over the decade to 1934.[42]

The establishment of KMT branches in the former German territories coincided with the Australian occupation of German territories in New Guinea, and the party's expansion was enhanced by its role in formal dealings with Australian government authorities over immigration and mobility. The KMT was called upon to represent the entire community in negotiating with Crown authorities over travel, property and family reunion regulations that hit residents hard following Australia's military occupation of German territories in 1914 and the formal transfer of sovereignty from Germany to Australia after the war. When long-term Chinese residents of New Guinea were finally eligible for Australian citizenship some decades later, the habit of calling upon the local KMT branch to represent them before the Australian government died hard. 'We as commoners are not in the position to fight the [Australian government]', one of David Wu's interviewees explained. 'It is the Kuo Min Tang's job to do something for us.'[43] This attitude can be traced to the role played by the KMT following the transfer of colonial authority over New Guinea from Germany to Australia at the outbreak of the Great War.

The Australasian KMT office in Sydney relished the opportunity to expand its operations into Australia's mandated territories. When things began to go awry in relations with Australian authorities in New Guinea, the Sydney KMT organisation was in a position to act on behalf on Chinese communities in New Guinea in their dealings with Australian and British authorities. In relation to the recovery clause in the 10-year lease of 1925, for example, KMT officers in Rabaul appealed to Australian government and Chinese consular officials to intervene on their behalf. Local KMT members came up with a further £700 for the construction of a KMT government vice-consulate in Rabaul should the Chinese and Australian governments agree to its establishment. When, in 1934, postwar authorities introduced legislation limiting copra production to growers it chose to license the KMT's Rabaul office made further approaches to the consul-general in Australia to prevent discrimination of the kind that had disadvantaged Chinese fruit-growers in Australia under the White Australia Policy. The KMT party network was one of the few institutions to which Chinese residents of New Guinea could turn to present their grievances to the Australian government.[44]

NAURU

By the 1930s Sydney KMT headquarters had extended its branch network to cover a number of islands with substantial Chinese resident populations within Australia's Pacific sphere of influence. One exception was Nauru. The absence of a significant KMT party network on the island of Nauru can be attributed to an exceptional feature of Chinese residents on the island: unlike Chinese residents of Fiji and New Guinea, they were overwhelmingly made up of indentured labourers, supplemented by service staff and interpreters

In other respects Nauru shared a great deal in common with German and Australian New Guinea. Like New Guinea, Nauru was under German jurisdiction when it was occupied by an Australian expeditionary force in 1914 and it came under a League of Nations mandate after the Great War, although in this case under the joint administration of Australia, Britain and New Zealand. There was a considerable Chinese presence on Nauru at the time the mandate came into effect, as there was in New Guinea, and the treatment of Chinese workers on Nauru offered little improvement on the treatment meted out to workers and traders in the New Guinea islands under the Australian mandate. Yet even in the mid 1920s, during its period of radical labour activism, the KMT did little or nothing on behalf of Nauru's Chinese workforce. The KMT seems to have had little interest in dealing with problems affecting indentured labour.

In this regard it differed significantly from the old imperial state. In 1908, the Qing government outlawed labour emigration to German settlements on the island as a mark of protest against German mistreatment of workers there. A party of indentured labourers contracted to work on Nauru had gone on strike the previous year claiming that they had been deceived over wages and conditions. The contracting company attempted to starve them into submission in a series of actions that resulted in the deaths of 250 workers from dysentery and beri beri. A similar outcome in New Guinea led to the replacement of indentured labour with free labour, recruited with the aid of local Chinese merchant Lee Tam Tuck. On Nauru, however, the contracting of indentured labour resumed in 1912 when the newly-installed republican government of China lifted the late imperial ban on Chinese emigration to the island. Indentured labour contracts were maintained with British and Australian support under the League of Nations mandate when the British Phosphate Commission assumed control of German mines on Nauru after the Great War.[45]

Conditions for Chinese miners barely improved under Australian and British control. In 1924, 900 indentured Chinese miners on Nauru went on strike and were locked in. Ahead of the Japanese landing on Nauru in 1942, 580 of the indentured miners were evacuated to central Australia and sent to work in wolfram (tungsten) mines before being placed under the military jurisdiction of General Douglas Macarthur's command headquarters in Queensland. After the war Chinese labourers were again contracted to work the phosphate mines of Nauru. When 1400 went on strike in 1948, British and Australian authorities arrested their leaders, surrounded their settlement and bludgeoned or overpowered contract workers who tried to break out of the blockade. Four Chinese were killed and 35 seriously wounded.[46]

The Australasian KMT rarely responded to systematic institutional abuse of indentured Chinese labourers in the Pacific. To be sure, the practice of contracting indentured labour for Nauru's phosphate mines long predated the implementation of Australia's League of Nations mandate and the creation of the Australasian KMT network. At that time Chinese imperial authorities were willing and able to intervene on the workers' behalf in the period of German colonial control.[47] In the mid-1920s, when the KMT was highly sympathetic to organised labour and was expanding rapidly throughout the British colonies and Australian mandated territories of the South Pacific, the Sydney office failed to extend its patronage to Nauru, despite levels of abuse endured by indentured labourers far in excess of that endured by free labourers and merchants in other ports. Indentured labourers appear to have fallen outside the self-appointed mandate of the Australasian KMT.

The party's neglect of Chinese labourers in Nauru does not seem to have resulted from a bourgeois orientation on the part of the Sydney KMT leadership. Rather, the Nauru case reveals ignorance and indifference on the part of the Sydney-based KMT network towards old-style indentured labour. This is not surprising. Indentured Chinese labour was largely unknown along Australia's Pacific coast over the second half of the 19th century. There were no indentured labourers in New Guinea from the late 19th century, and few if any among the Chinese residents of Fiji at the time party branches were founded on the islands (in contrast to 60 000 indentured labourers recruited from India between 1879 and the Great War and 300 from Japan in 1894).[48]

Contract workers had no place among the Australian KMT's merchant or labour constituencies. The Australasian KMT was a party of free merchants and free labour – a party of workers and traders who valued their freedom to move in and out of Australia, Asia and the Pacific Islands in the shadow of a White Australian regime that was determined to monitor and control their mobility. The Australasian KMT was a party of, by and for, mobile people.

8

ENTREPRENEURS, CLUBS AND CHRISTIAN VALUES

We are told that the people of Asia are good enough to enter the pearly gates, good enough to enjoy eternal life with Christ and with all just men, but not good enough to live a short life on the Australian continent with Messrs Chifley, Menzies, Calwell, Fadden and their followers.

Samuel Wong, 1950.[1]

Federation Australia nourished a particular breed of entrepreneurs whose impact on the commercial development of 20th century China was out of all proportion to their number. The success of these entrepreneurs is well known among international business historians and quite legendary in China.[2] This group of Chinese Australians made up the largest identifiable group of international Chinese investors in Shanghai before the communists came to power in 1949 – by one account contributing one-third of total Overseas Chinese investment – in addition to making substantial investments in Hong Kong, Singapore, Canton and Tianjin.[3]

Today the grand buildings they erected along Shanghai's Nanking Road compete for world-heritage listing alongside the Taj Mahal and the Sydney Opera House. In Australia, however, these entrepreneurs are all but unknown outside the family circles of their Chinese-Australian descendents.

The more prominent of these Chinese-Australian businessmen shared a number of characteristics. One was a distinctive investment strategy that involved raising capital from widely-dispersed networks of shareholders in Australia and elsewhere and investing shareholder capital in large-scale enterprises under the control of family-managed firms. A second feature was their capacity for social networking through inclusive civic associations in addition to their family and home-county networks. All came from Heungshan County in Guangdong but the majority were active in one or another local chamber of commerce, Masonic lodge, philanthropic society, political party or Christian church in Sydney and had links throughout the region. Through these civic associations they extended their social and business networks beyond the range of their immediate families and home-town friends. Third, all were Christians, and most commenced their business careers in Sydney. This chapter explores the reasons underlying the success in Hong Kong and China of this small group of Chinese Christian entrepreneurs from Sydney by tracing their roots to the religious, social and business environment of turn-of-the-century Sydney and by following these roots to their intertwining networks abroad.

This chapter is not, strictly speaking, a study in business history. It focuses on the routes and strategies through which Cantonese immigrants to Australia created business, political and religious networks linking far-flung rural and urban communities in Australia to one another and to similar networks in Hong Kong and south China. A number of questions that business historians raise in the course of their work are worth noting all the same because they set the scene for the arguments that follow. One bears on the development of business firms in isolation, so to speak, and probes the historical transition from social networks to modern corporate firms. Another set of questions has to do with the institutional settings in which business firms operate, including the rule of law (especially contract and company law) and the development of capitalist instruments such as money, formal contracts, deeds, and the like. This second set of questions points to a separate historical process of development leading from business transactions governed by rituals and networks to transactions governed by contract under law. Rule of law, contracts, networks and business firms converged in Chinese-Australian history in a distinctive fashion that accounts for the remarkable success of networked family firms in developing into large-scale transnational enterprises.[4] Put simply, Australian-Chinese entrepreneurs elected to do business through family firms working in association with modern civic institutions that expanded their business networks.

White Australia provides the background to this story. For all its discrimination and restrictions Australia offered a stable legal foundation for business development and provided a style of civic life conducive to free and open association. Chinese Australians appreciated the values that underlay this system no less than other Australians and they fought to participate in Australian public life as full and equal citizens. In the face of discriminatory legislation, we have noted, they opted to extend their business operations to other British colonial sites in the Pacific, and East and Southeast Asia where a familiar British style of rule of law prevailed without the added burden of discriminatory restraints on property ownership, trade and movement. With one or two exceptions they expanded their business networks along pathways mapped out within the colonial borders of British rule of law in East Asia and the Pacific Islands.

Chinese-Australian entrepreneurs were, on the whole, conservative risk-takers. When it came to risking capital they favoured Hong Kong as their point of entry into the China market. In the Crown colony they could start up their business ventures under British legal jurisdiction and make useful connections through Cantonese-speaking civic associations not unlike those they had set up for themselves in Australia. Hong Kong's success as a regional hub for business and industry was arguably founded on the local Chinese community's capacity for self-government (in dispute resolution, policing, health care, social welfare and making representations to government) no less than upon the *laissez-faire* policies and rule of law of the British colonial administration.[5] Across Hong Kong, an extensive institutional apparatus of Chinese hospitals, philanthropic associations, clubs and churches developed alongside the colonial administration to provide social and business services to Chinese residents of the city. This development was matched on a modest scale in Australia by an institutional arrangement of churches, clubs and societies that were set up to manage local community affairs and mount claims through the press and to the government for equality of treatment in Australia. Although smaller in scale, the complex of civic institutions that developed in Sydney was commensurable with the complex that developed independently in Hong Kong.

Chinese-Australian entrepreneurs were conservative in another sense as well, preferring to expand their business operations by developing extensive networks of trust among fellow countrymen rather than by evolving into formal corporate hierarchies.[6] They innovated in relatively conservative fashion, expanding traditional networks based on kinship and native place to embrace membership of inclusive civic associations that reached well beyond kinship and place. The NSW Chinese Chamber of Commerce, the Sydney Presbyterian Chinese Mission, the Chinese Masonic Society and the Australasian Kuo Min Tang were each inclusive bodies that reached beyond the limited family networks on which the entrepreneurs founded their business ventures. Through participation in churches and societies, the Sydney entrepreneurs extended their connections beyond Australia to embrace counterpart bodies in Hong Kong and southern China as well as umbrella organisations, such as the Tung Wah community hospital in Hong Kong, which provided social services for Chinese Australians moving to Hong Kong or transiting through the colony on occasional visits to their family villages.[7] Their involvement with inclusive civic associations enhanced their credibility, extended their networks of trust and expanded their options for raising capital and doing business. Their engagement with inclusive associations substantially expanded the range of social networks available to Australian entrepreneurs in Australia, Hong Kong and China without risking the quasi-familial relationships of trust on which their firms were ultimately based.

Finally, their involvement with churches and societies allowed Australian entrepreneurs to move effortlessly in elite circles extending from their home communities in Heungshan and Sydney to new sites in Hong Kong and Shanghai where they arrived as strangers but rapidly established themselves as community leaders through their civic connections. Their elite status in turn enabled them to raise capital for investment from large and small investors in and beyond Australia, to press for freedom of trade and movement in and out of Australia, China and the Pacific Islands, to offer opportunities to other network members to travel, live and work in Hong Kong, Shanghai and Oceania and to support their families and communities in Sydney and their home counties while extending their business ventures abroad. In the founding and development of Chinese-Australian civic clubs from the 1890s to the 1930s we find formally constituted community-wide institutions transcending familial and regional boundaries and working closely with networked firms to their mutual advantage. Their experience with churches and societies in Australia was an important factor enabling Chinese-Australian entrepreneurs to scale up their operations to levels that exceeded all but a few comparable firms in Hong Kong and China.

Clubs and businesses

Chinese-Australian merchants were among the earliest in the diaspora to recognise the value of inclusive clubs and societies for community management and business networking. The NSW Chinese Chamber of Commerce (1903) was founded some years after the Hong Kong Chamber (1896) but ahead of comparable chambers in Singapore and the Straits settlements, the Dutch East Indies, North America and even in China itself.[8] The underground Yee Hing network of New South Wales was transformed around the same time from a loose rural affiliation of secret-society lodges into a tightly focused urban institution with a prominent public profile. As we have seen, when it went public in 1911 as the Chinese Masonic Association of New South Wales, the Yee Hing network was led by the wealthy wool broker and investor, James Chuey. Similarly, the Oceania regional branch of the KMT opened in Sydney in 1921 under the direction of some of the wealthiest and most able Chinese business leaders of the time. And some of the earliest and most inclusive organisations of the day were Chinese-Christian church congregations, including the Presbyterian congregation under the pastoral care of the Reverend John Young Wai, whose parishioners included members of the Masonic Society, the KMT, the Chamber of Commerce and many of the Chinese-Christian leaders who went on to establish businesses in Hong Kong and China.

Networks of trust based on lineage and native-place ties were supplemented in Sydney by broader civic networks from the late 19th century. The Lin Yik Tong (*Lianyitang*) was founded in 1892 as a joint initiative involving the Gibbs Bright shipping agency and eight Sydney Chinese firms under the direction of WRG Lee (*Li Yihui*) and his firm On Yik Lee (*Anyili*). Membership of the merchant Tong was confined to a small fraction of Chinese firms operating in Sydney at the time. Nevertheless, the founders of the Lin Yik Tong moulded the organisation into a relatively representative body by enrolling corporate members from firms linked to each of the eight major émigré counties represented in the city (Heungshan, Doong Goong, Changsheng, Goyou and the four See Yap counties) and by rotating the management of the organisation among board representatives from each of the eight firms involved. The operation of the Lin Yik Tong, as CF Yong first pointed out, was both inclusive and democratic.[9]

With fees and commissions raised through its shipping arrangements with the Gibbs Bright shipping agency, the Lin Yik Tong profited its member firms and generated a comfortable surplus for charitable works in the community at large. Within a decade of its founding, however, the Tong entered into a series of bitter legal disputes with the leaders of the new Empire Reform Association, Thomas Yee Hing and Ping Nam. These disputes were widely rumoured to have lain behind the savage knife attack on Quong Tart who was a champion of the Lin Yik Tong. Quong Tart never fully recovered from the attack and died in July 1903. The reformers launched a new and even more inclusive chamber of commerce in the same month. The Tong dissolved three months later.[10] Given its restricted membership and its overt hostility to the reform party's agenda, the Lin Yik Tong cannot be considered a linear antecedent to the more inclusive and reform-minded NSW Chinese Chamber of Commerce (*Huashang huishe*), but it does offer the earliest instance of a corporate structure among Chinese-Australian civic associations.

Chambers of commerce

The first Chinese-Australian chamber of commerce was set up in Sydney following the visit to Australia of the Chinese reformer Liang Qichao, traced in an earlier chapter, over the summer of 1900 and 1901 at the invitation of the Society to Protect the Emperor. Before coming to Australia Liang was associated with the earliest attempt to establish chambers of commerce in China. Along with his mentor Kang Youwei and a party of like-minded reformers, Liang helped to launch the ill-fated One Hundred Days Reforms at the imperial court in 1898. One focus of their reforms was greater government involvement in commercial and industrial development; another was the co-ordination and consolidation of local business enterprises through a national network of chambers of commerce. Although the reformers enjoyed the support of Emperor Guangxu, their reform agenda was cast aside in a conservative coup encouraged by Empress Dowager Ci Xi. Some of the reformers were executed; others, including Kang and Liang, fled abroad, and the emperor himself was placed under house arrest within the palace complex in Peking. But for his enforced exile, Liang Qichao is unlikely to have visited Australia from October 1900 to May 1901 to garner international support for the exiled reform party's return to China. Were it not for his visit to Sydney members of his reform party may not have acted quite so early to found the NSW Chinese Chamber of Commerce in 1903, the second of its kind among Chinese communities in the world.[11]

A year after Liang Qichao departed Sydney for Yokohama, the group of Sydney businessmen who initially invited him to Australia convened a series of meetings to plan a non-partisan commercial chamber in Sydney. Some years earlier two of these men, Thomas Yee Hing and Ping Nam, called on 50 leading business figures to form a local arm of the exiles' reform organisation, the Society to Protect the Emperor, in order to cement their links with the reform party in Yokohama and Vancouver. Thomas Yee Hing promoted this early venture through his newspaper the *Tung Wah Times*. After the Empire Reform Association was launched in January 1900 the *Tung Wah Times* (later renamed the *Tung Wah News*) was converted into an official organ of the reform party. It was supported by the NSW Chinese Chamber of Commerce, indicating the linear relationship between the society, the chamber, and the leading Chinese-Australian business newspaper of its day.[12]

There were a number of local incentives for founding a chamber at this particular time, including mounting concern within the merchant elite over signs of resurgent anti-Chinese sentiment in New South Wales and discriminatory legislation coming before the new Commonwealth parliament. From the turn of the century white storekeepers in rural New South Wales pressed for a boycott of Chinese stores in country towns. Around the same time, Sydney businesses launched a campaign alleging a Chinese monopoly in the fruit and vegetable markets.[13] At the federal level, the Commonwealth parliament passed the Immigration Restriction Act in 1901, all but ending legal Chinese emigration to Australia, and in 1903 legislated to deny all but a small number of the 30 000 Chinese residents the same rights of naturalisation and citizenship available to white immigrants. These legislative initiatives carried serious implications for Chinese residents seeking to recruit employees, start up businesses, expand their business investments, or raise their families in Australia.[14]

Circumstances leading to federation also played a part in the formation of the chamber. In preparation for federation the editors of the *Tung Wah News* called for greater co-operation among parochial Chinese networks to meet the challenges of a federated Australia. The paper urged its readers to overcome their familial and native-place differences though inclusive civic organisations that could focus the energy, ideas, wealth and enthusiasm of Chinese residents from all counties and provinces in China to benefit themselves and the new Australian Commonwealth.[15] Both motives – a concern to combat racism and a determination to unite the fractious Chinese-Australian community – were echoed in deliberations leading to the foundation of the chamber itself. Chinese merchants, the chamber pointed out, had 'come to feel scattered and isolated after several decades residing in many different parts of Australia, and were occasionally subject to the ridicule of others'. Their business motives were equally strong. The reform party launched the Chinese Chamber of Commerce with the aim of consolidating the Chinese community of New South Wales and 'protecting and invigorating the spirit of commerce'.[16]

The chamber welcomed representatives of Chinese firms based in New South Wales drawn from every region in China. The single condition of entry was that they should adhere to the aims of the organisation. Around 60 firms joined the chamber over its first year of operation. In 1913 its name was revised to the New South Wales Chinese General Chamber of Commerce of Sydney Australia (*Aozhou niuxiuwei xueli zhonghua zongshanghui*) to comply with regulations issued in Peking for the governance of overseas chambers of commerce. In 1915 the title was amended again in compliance with the Chamber of Commerce Law of the Republic of China. These amendments entitled the chamber to send a representative to the first republican national convention in Peking. Membership of the chamber grew to over 200 firms in 1914 and to more than 400 firms and individuals by 1921.[17]

Little Bourke Street merchants founded a chamber of commerce in Melbourne in 1913, a decade after the Sydney chamber. Over its early years the Melbourne chamber more than matched its Sydney counterpart, attracting 400 members by 1914 and growing to almost 1000 members by the close of the decade. This was consistent with the history of Chinese firms in Victoria. In 1865 the business names of 146 firms were carved onto a stone tablet erected to mark the renovation of the See Yap temple in South Melbourne. Long as this was, the list was not comprehensive even for Victoria insofar as it excluded firms associated with natives of other counties and districts. The colony hosted an impressive Chinese business community from its earliest days.

Chinese businessmen in Melbourne were also precociously modern in their outlook and orientation. The See Yap temple was renovated in the early 1860s in the very latest style. The merchants remodelled the exterior of the building to resemble a modish Victorian mansion – two storeys in height, flat-fronted and surrounded by a colonnaded verandah – and for the interior decorations they fused traditional religious iconography with self-representations of the globe-trotting businessman. Above the figure of the god Kwan Ti (*Guandi*) in the main hall, the society erected a large bas relief of two Chinese gentlemen dressed in top hats and tails with their arms outstretched encompassing a circle, in a profound sense a symbol of eternity but in a more profane sense the compass of their imagined trading world in the 1860s.[18]

In later years Melbourne failed to keep pace with the growth and endeavour of the Sydney commercial chamber. The Chinese population of the city declined relative to Sydney and, according to CF Yong, by the 1920s Melbourne merchants were a less cohesive group than their counterparts in Sydney. The Melbourne Chamber of Commerce nevertheless played a similar role to the Sydney chamber in petitioning Australian authorities to ease discriminatory immigration restrictions, in making representations to the Chinese government on patriotic issues and in donating to worthy causes in China, including a subscription of £2000 to drought relief in north China in 1920. It also encouraged investments in Chinese-Australian business ventures. At the urging of the local chamber, Melbourne merchants bought £5600 worth of shares in the China–Australia Mail Steamship Line in 1921.[19]

China–Australia Mail Steamship Line

The establishment of the China–Australia Mail Steamship Line is a remarkable chapter in the story of Chinese Australia. Its collapse is no less noteworthy. As a tale of corporate failure, the history of the China–Australia Mail Steamship Line offers a dramatic illustration of the risks attendant on particularistic clubs working together to establish a hierarchical corporate firm. The company was launched in 1917 on the assumption that the level of co-operation shown among civic associations such as the NSW Chinese Chamber of Commerce, the Australasian KMT and the Chinese Masonic Society could be replicated in a large-scale business venture. The motives of the partners were fairly straightforward: massive increases in the costs of maritime trade between China and Australia during the Great War, largely conducted on Japanese-registered vessels, were costing businesses dearly. By attributing blame for the increased cost of doing business in wartime to Japanese profiteering, Chinese-Australian business leaders conjured a patriotic motive sufficiently powerful to bring their disparate organisations together. Even so, the formal corporate structure of the new firm failed to harness the particularistic groups that comprised it. CF Yong's narrative account of the history of the China–Australia Mail Steamship Line can usefully be supplemented by approaching the history of the firm as a case study of particularistic social networks experimenting with substantial investments in a hierarchical firm, and of the fallout of corporate failure for relations among the same networks.[20]

The Great War delivered a virtual monopoly over Australia–China freight to Japanese shipping lines when German vessels were withdrawn from the area and British ships were requisitioned for war service. As the war dragged on, Japanese lines increased freight charges out of Sydney bound for China tenfold from £1.10.0 to £11.10 per ton. Japan was regarded as a common enemy of China and Chinese communities abroad after the Sino–Japanese war of 1894–95. Evidence of Japanese ship owners apparently profiteering at their expense incited conservative firms associated with the NSW Chamber of Commerce to set aside their differences with progressive businessmen in the KMT and move towards a common resolution, founding a shipping line of their own. The founders saw prospects for substantial profits on the Sydney–Hong Kong run comparable to those they imagined Japanese shipping firms were registering in Tokyo. If they could not reduce shipping rates they would at least profit from wartime conditions. Over the Australian summer of 1917–18 the partners raised £108 000 from shareholders in Sydney, Melbourne, Hong Kong, New Zealand and Fiji, and purchased two ships, the *SS Gabo* and the *SS Victoria*.[21]

The ships were registered in the name of William Liu, a 24-year-old Chinese Australian of mixed parentage, for fear that under Australia's capricious immigration and property laws the company's ownership of the vessels would not be recognised if the registering party was anything but a native-born Australian. Liu was also general manager of the line. Not long after they were registered as Australian vessels, however, the two ships were requisitioned for war service at an estimated loss to the company of £20 000 in addition to revenues foregone. By the time the ships were returned to service in late 1919 and early 1920, the line faced intense competition from British vessels re-entering the route. The line was caught in a prolonged and costly price war and, despite further capital injections from shareholders, collapsed in 1924.

The company's financial problems precipitated a bitter management dispute among shareholding partners. The underlying problem was arguably one of business planning rather than of business management. Failure to anticipate requisition, in particular, doomed the project from the start. But the problem played out as a dispute over control of the board between rival factions in Sydney commercial circles. Conservative businessmen associated with the NSW Chinese Chamber of Commerce held a majority on the board over its early years, a time when they generally enjoyed the support of other board members associated with the KMT and Chinese Masonic Society. After the company announced a loss of over £60000 in 1921, William Liu was replaced by KMT leader Peter Yee Wing. The conservatives never forgave Yee Wing or the KMT for their part in the company brawl. They withheld further financial support for the line.[22]

The familial, regional and factional differences exposed by this corporate collapse were laid bare in February 1922 in a sustained attack on William Liu's management of the line penned by Percy Lee (*Li Xiangbo*) in the republican newspaper *Chinese Republic News*.[23] Lee attributed the collapse not to the firm's poor business fundamentals but to management problems arising from the family relations linking William Liu and his father-in-law Gilbert Yip Ting Quoy, and compounded by careless supervision on the part of the board. The highly partisan tone of the article reflected one facet of a many-sided dispute. Still, Percy Lee's claims are instructive in revealing the underlying tensions dividing the social networks that came together to form the line.

According to Lee, at the meeting of the board that initially nominated William Liu as sole owner of the company's vessels, Gilbert Quoy announced that he had received formal notification that ownership and registration of vessels in Australia was limited to native-born Australians. In fact, Percy Lee pointed out, naturalised Australians were no less entitled than native-born subjects to own and register sea-going vessels based in Australian ports. Three seasoned businessmen with seats on the board were naturalised Australian subjects: James Chuey, Peter Yee Wing and Phillip Lee Chun (*Li Chun*). By virtue of their long experience in business these men were better equipped to own and manage the company's assets than the young William Liu. Gilbert Quoy deceived the board, the article concluded, to the advantage of his personal and family connections and to the detriment of the company.

Gilbert Quoy also took advantage of his relations with William Liu, by this account, to profit his family and ruin the line. Percy Lee alleged several abuses of privilege by Quoy, including several free first-class trips with eight or nine members of his family to China. Quoy was also reported to have been personally responsible for the most costly business decision taken by the company, the charter of a Chinese government vessel in Hong Kong, the *SS Hwah Ping*, on a lease costing almost £60 000 per annum. In the face of stiff competition the chartered vessel cost the line £36 000 over its first year in operation.[24] As the scale of the loss threatened to wipe out most of the company's paid-up capital within a few years, the board decided to terminate the lease at the end of the first year. According to Percy Lee, on notifying the relevant shipping agents in Hong Kong, members of the board discovered that the charter had been renewed by Quoy on the authority of William Liu.

Similar charges were levelled against Liu himself, including claims that he signed several costly contracts with uncompetitive suppliers, that he hired and fired staff without regard to their performance, that he exceeded his expense allowance and that he failed to recognise or to act upon problems as they arose. Lee also claimed that Liu deliberately misled Adelaide shareholders into parting with £5000 for a parcel of his own shares at an inflated price, and pocketed the difference. In fact one Adelaide shareholder took Liu to court in Sydney around this time alleging that he had misled prospective shareholders at a meeting in Adelaide where he promoted the company with extravagant claims of future returns at a time when he should have known that the company was trading near to insolvency.[25]

The claims levelled against Gilbert Quoy and William Liu are unverifiable and largely scandalous. Nevertheless, they highlight critical lines of fracture on the board at a crucial moment in the company's history. One fracture cut along lines separating rival institutional networks. Gilbert Quoy was one of several representatives of the mainstream conservative faction of the NSW Chinese Chamber of Commerce seated on the board. Of the three naturalised subjects allegedly misled by the claim that they could not themselves register shipping in Australia, James Chuey was head of the Chinese Masonic Society, Peter Yee Wing was Australasian director of the KMT and Phillip Lee Chun was a rare KMT sympathiser on the otherwise anti-KMT chamber of commerce. The article implied that Gilbert Quoy effectively disempowered the KMT and Masonic networks on the board when he deceived the board to secure the appointment of William Liu as inaugural managing director.

The parties also fractured along native-place lines.[26] James Chuey and Peter Yee Wing came from two of the four See Yap counties. KMT sympathiser Phillip Lee Chun hailed from Heungshan county whose natives, whatever their political inclinations, had a soft spot for the KMT (the party's founder Sun Yatsen was a Heungshan native). Gilbert Quoy was a leader of the Doong Goong community in Sydney. His son-in-law William Liu came from a See Yap family but his divided loyalties compounded Percy Lee's charge of nepotism. Liu was open to the charge that he subordinated his native-place allegiances to family ties when he married into Quoy's Doong Goong family.

In light of the opinionated tone of this newspaper account we need to place its author among these overlapping and conflicting networks. Percy Lee was a sturdy champion of the sole pro-labour KMT radical on the board, Samuel Wong, whom he maintained had consistently drawn the attention of the board to problems in William Liu's management style and to his unhealthy relations with Gilbert Quoy. Lee presented Sam Wong's case against the three major institutional networks on the board – the chamber of commerce, the Masonic Society, and the business leadership of the KMT – in sympathy with small shareholders and in support of Sam Wong's perennial defence of the working man. These differences subsequently played out in bitter disputes within the KMT and in relations among the KMT, the Masonic society, the chamber of commerce, and the different native-place networks based in Sydney.[27]

Networked firms

An alternative, particularistic model of Chinese-Australian business development was elaborated with greater success by Heungshan County merchants in Sydney operating networked family firms. The long arm of the British empire beckoned enterprising Chinese-Australian businesses to spread their investment along a chain of British ports stretching from Sydney to Shanghai, with the result that well-connected émigrés from Heungshan county drew on their local networks to develop substantial enterprises in East Asia and the Pacific Islands. Less well-connected labourers and tradesmen who did not enjoy ready access to these networks took up shareholding partnerships with friends or firms that did. The results were spectacular: Chinese-Australian businesses flourished in the domestic fruit and vegetable trades in eastern Australia at the time of federation and their owners went on to build some of the largest commercial conglomerates in Hong Kong, Canton and Shanghai before the outbreak of the Pacific war. As noted, entrepreneurs from the Sydney fruit and vegetable markets were the most significant of all international Chinese investors in Shanghai before the communists took the city in 1949.[28] Firms with roots in Australia came to own and manage some of the most prominent commercial, industrial and financial enterprises in China, including one of its two largest textile enterprises, several hotels, banks and insurance companies, and the country's most prestigious department stores.

Department stores for Chinese customers were partly an innovation of the Australian retail pioneers who founded the Sincere (*Xianshi*) and Wing On (*Yongan*) department store chains in Hong Kong, Canton and Shanghai. Ma Ying-piu and his partners opened their first Sincere Department Store in Hong Kong in 1900, the first in Canton in 1912 and their grandest store of all in Shanghai in 1917. The Gock brothers' Wing On Company opened for business in Hong Kong in 1907 before setting up a flagship store in Shanghai in 1918. In time these department store chains were joined by two other Chinese-Australian retail firms along Nanking Road, the Lee and Liu families' Sun Sun Department Store (*Xinxin*) in 1926 and The Sun Company Store (*Daxin*) opened by the Choy family in 1931. Other Australian stores opened in south China, including the Chan family's Chung Wah Store in Hong Kong and the Wong brothers' two stores in Canton, the Jan Gwong (*Zhenguang*) and the Gwong Seung (*Guangshang*) stores. To Shanghai residents the four Chinese-Australian stores came to be known as the Four Great Companies. All of their founders hailed from Heungshan County, adjacent to the home counties of the Cantonese operators of Western Goods Stores that had long dominated Shanghai's retail trade before the arrival of the Australians. With their business roots in Sydney they retained extensive personal and business connections with Australia, raising much of their capital from investors in the country and offering opportunities to fellow Heungshan natives (and fellow Australians) to experience life and work in Shanghai.[29]

The shareraising strategies of the Four Great Companies followed the well-worn path of smaller Chinese-Australian business ventures that set a local precedent for shareholding partnerships in successful business ventures within Australia. W Warley and Co., for example, opened in 1903 in Glen Innes with 19 registered partners of whom just five were local residents. Twelve Warley shareholders were based in Sydney, one in Canton and one in Hong Kong. In a study of Chinese stores in rural New South Wales, historian Janis Wilton has noted that this distinctive pattern of networked shareholder partnerships was shaped in part by current styles of business networking in China and partly by the particular conditions applying to Chinese business investors in White Australia. Beginning in 1901, restrictive immigration practices limited the pool of family members who could reside in Australia but offered possible exemptions to Chinese who could demonstrate business investments in the country. The limited pool of family members compelled entrepreneurs to seek capital outside their immediate family circles, and the prospect of exemption from the Immigration Restriction Act encouraged working men and women to take up shares in local business ventures.[30] By the time the Four Great Companies were canvassing shareholding investments around Australia, the practice of making low-risk investments in profitable commercial ventures through extended networks of trust was well established among Chinese Australians.

The successful expansion and extension of Chinese-Australian general stores in New South Wales was as remarkable in its own way as the growth of the Four Great Companies in Hong Kong, Canton and Shanghai. As Wilton has shown, Chinese general stores throughout the state adapted to local conditions by servicing white-Australian consumers with well-stocked stores, based in small to medium settlements and operating commercial delivery services marketing goods to remote areas. Kwong Sing and Co. of Glenn Innes was established in 1886 by a businessman known locally as Wong Chee. Wong later transferred management of the store to a Heungshan native of Shekki district, Percy Young (Kwan Hong Kee), who, with the aid of nephews sponsored to Australia, expanded the shop into a department store. By the 1940s each of the departments of the Glen Innes store was managed by a different member of the Young (Kwan) family. By mid century the Young family owned and operated a dozen stores in ten regional centres in New South Wales.[31]

Kwong Sing's founder, Wong Chee, helped to launch another retail store chain in northern New South Wales when he introduced Sydney-born Harry Fay (Louie Mew Fay; *Lei Miaohui*) to the owner of the Hong Yuen general store in Inverell. By 1916 Fay had become a managing partner of Hong Yuen. Over the following two decades he sponsored family members to work in the Inverell store and encouraged them to take up shares in the business. By the early 1930s he was employing 60 permanent staff and claimed an annual turnover of £100 000. By the 1940s, Hong Yuen shareholders – without exception members of Harry Fay's immediate family – had expanded their operations to other regional towns in New South Wales, including Moree, Texas and Warialda.

The expansion of the Kwong Sing and Hong Yeun family networks in rural New South Wales paralleled the expansion of the Four Great Companies on a scale commensurate with the demography of the rural New South Wales and the relatively limited financial and human resources of the families that controlled them. Wider partnerships were required to operate successfully on an international scale. The founder of Kwong Sing and patron of Hong Yuen, Wong Chee, sold up his shares to join forces with a wider network of Heungshan natives to launch more substantial international ventures.

Wong Chee is better known in Chinese business history as Wong Poon Narm (*Huang Bingnan*), one of the five original partners who founded the Sincere Department Store in Hong Kong in 1900, the Canton store in 1912 and the Shanghai store in 1917. Early in the 1920s he famously parted company with Sincere to join Liu Xiji and Charles Lee in forming the Sun Sun Company, which opened its first department store in Shanghai in 1926.[32] By this time Wong was operating well beyond his immediate family circle. Along with the Mas, Kwoks, Lees, Choys, Lius and other prominent Heungshan merchant families in Sydney, he expanded his available pool of potential investors to communities in Australia and abroad who were willing to risk their savings in larger international business ventures. Chinese Australians contributed the majority of investment capital raised by the four great Australian companies operating in China. The Sydney entrepreneurs also drew on partners and investors in Hawai'i, California, Hong Kong and New Zealand.[33]

The four great stores of Shanghai

Their experience in Australia exposed Ma Ying-piu and the Gock brothers to a style of retail marketing not currently available in Hong Kong or Canton. According to Sincere Company sources, during his time in Australia Ma Ying-piu was 'greatly impressed by the Western methods of business, more especially as applied to the large department stores which are such features in the various state capitals of the Commonwealth'.[34] Customers entering Anthony Hordens in downtown Sydney were treated to a range of fixed-price goods displayed in glass cases ranged over several floors and presented in a common corporate style. They were offered courteous service by trained staff wearing standardised uniforms and they enjoyed convenient access to tea rooms and bathrooms. Sincere founder Ma Ying-piu and Wing On founder James Gocklock (*Guo Le*) both 'credited Sydney's flagship store, Anthony Hordens & Son, as the model for their own creations'.[35] Wing On drew directly from the Anthony Hordens corporate ethic to craft its own service ethic of 'quality, reasonable price, satisfaction and courtesy'.[36]

The physical appearance of Sydney's retail stores was no less striking. New-style department stores were reshaping the visual field of modern commercial cities all over the world, advertising their products and services through their massive presence on the street and their neon lights on the skyline. The Australian department stores did the same for Shanghai. Charles Lee, son of the Sun Sun founder and manager of the Shanghai store in his turn, recalls his youthful impressions of the stores:

> *Whenever a train reached the outer suburbs of Shanghai, or a boat turned into the Huangpu River, away in the distance all of the passengers could see the tall spires and gleaming lights of the Four Great Companies ... Their eye-catching company insignia shone like stars on the horizon, shedding their beams in every direction, so that every woman and child in Shanghai knew their names. [The*

> *buildings] were the most successful advertising tool adopted by the*
> *Four Great Companies.*[37]

Anthony Hordern, the story went, started out as a pedlar and ended up a retail magnate in Sydney.[38] Ma Ying-piu and the Gock brothers hoped to do something similar. Around this time, however, white storekeepers in New South Wales were agitating for a boycott of Chinese shops and white businesses in Sydney were mounting a public campaign, alleging that Chinese residents held a monopoly over the city's fruit and vegetable markets.[39] The Commonwealth was legislating to restrict Chinese immigration and to deny Chinese residents access to naturalisation and citizenship. White Australian publicity campaigns and legislative initiatives had implications for Chinese residents seeking to recruit employees, start up businesses or expand their business investments in Australia. As historian Wellington Chan has observed, Ma and Gock readily appreciated that any attempt to expand their business investment in Australia 'had no chance of being accepted by the majority of white Australians'.[40] They invited their fellow kinsmen and townsmen in the Australian community to become partners in their family companies with a view to expanding their Sydney retail businesses to Hong Kong and China.

SINCERE

Like Anthony Hordern, Ma Ying-piu worked as a labourer before he found employment as a store clerk and launched out on a business career of his own. Born in 1864, Ma was a second-generation Australian sojourner with a network of relatives and fellow villagers from Shechung (*Shachong*) village in Heungshan County on hand to greet him when he arrived in Sydney as a young man in 1883. His father had been a gold miner in the 1850s. In 1890 Ma founded the Wing Sang (*Yongsheng*) Company, an import–export firm based in Sydney's Haymarket, with a number of business partners from his home district, including Choy Hing (*Cai Xing*) and George Kwok Biew. After a decade or so in Australia he made the first of several journeys to Hong Kong, where he eventually decided to settle and set up his new business.

A devout Christian, Ma sold his shares in the Sydney Wing Sang store to raise funds to spread the Gospel in Hong Kong with his wife,

Huo Qingtang, the daughter of a Christian minister. Their illuminated lantern-slides and piano in tow, the couple toured village markets in Hong Kong and neighbouring Guangdong province singing praises to the Lord and illustrating his good works. Their first business venture in Hong Kong was a Christian credit union, launched with start-up capital of Y20 000 raised from Christian business partners in parcels of Y5 shares. He next opened an émigré store and banking service, the Wingchongti (*Yongchangtai*) Gold Mountain Store, which dealt in imports, exports and remittances to and from Australia and elsewhere. Finally, in 1900, Ma called on his long-standing links with business partners in Sydney (including Choy Hing and George Biew) and more recent links in Hong Kong and the United States to raise Y25 000 to fund the development of the Sincere Department Store in Hong Kong.[41]

The first Sincere fixed-price department store opened on Queen's Road in Hong Kong in January 1900. It introduced elaborate window displays on the Anthony Horderns model and cultivated professional courtesy among service staff as part of its modern corporate style. Some years later the partners opened a larger store on Des Voeux Road and in 1909 incorporated Sincere as a limited liability company under British law. By 1916 the company boasted paid-up capital of HK$2 million raised from 'Chinese who had resided at one point or another in Australia and North America'. This was the largest public subscription of capital to that time for a single commercial project anywhere in China or Hong Kong. Before the decade was out the company had opened branches in Canton (1912), Singapore (1917) and, its grandest store of all, on Nanking Road (1917). Over time the Canton store and production facilities became a drain on the company as local warlords and successive Kuo Min Tang administrations imposed excessive charges and penalties on investments in that city. The Shanghai store was a commercial success from its day of opening when 10 000 customers passed through its doors.[42] The Sincere Department Store was the first of the four Chinese-Australian stores that turned Nanking Road into the most prestigious retail strip of its day in China.

WING ON

The second to open was the Gock brothers' Wing On Department Store, which flattered Sincere by imitation. Like Ma Ying-piu, James Gocklock and Philip Gockchin started out in business in Sydney, managing the successful Wing On Fruit Wholesalers in the Haymarket. From 1902 they worked with Ma's Sydney partners in establishing the Sang On Ti banana combine in Fiji, over which Philip Gockchin presided for three years in Suva as company manager. The brothers drew on their Wing On business in Sydney for start-up capital, which they complemented with investments from a small group of relatives and friends in Australia and the United States. Moving abroad they followed Ma's example more closely still, opening their first store in Queen's Road in 1907 before moving to Des Voeux Road. They incorporated under Hong Kong law and, like Ma, managed to accumulate paid-up capital of HK$2 million by 1916. In 1918 they opened a store in Shanghai that stood one storey higher than Sincere Department Store on the opposite corner of Nanking Road. Like Sincere, Wing On was an immediate success. On any trading day the store is said to have recorded sales equivalent to the annual receipts of all general stores operating in Shanghai before the opening of the new Australian department stores on Nanking Road.[43]

The Gock brothers also learnt from Ma Ying-piu's mistakes, making a number of decisions that insulated their firm from sovereign and business risks more successfully than did Sincere. They largely confined their commercial operations to colonial territories in China where British rule of law prevailed, chiefly Hong Kong and the International Settlement in Shanghai. They declined to follow Sincere's heavy investments in Canton, where Wing On made relatively few investments.[44]

Diversification beyond the company's core retail business was a second distinctive feature of the Wing On strategy; Yen Ching-hwang has calculated that revenues from real estate investments accounted for one-quarter of the firm's income in 1934. The Gock brothers also expanded into commercial and life insurance and opened a highly successful bank in Hong Kong in 1931. Their largest non-core investments were in textile manufacturing. Beginning on a modest scale with the purchase of the Weixin underwear factory in Hong Kong in 1919, the Gock brothers expanded their textile investments to $12 million by the early 1930s. They built three large textile mills in Shanghai and surrounding districts over the decade. With 14 000 employees, 240 000 spindles and 2000 weaving machines, the Wing On textile group was the second largest Chinese textile manufacturer on the Chinese mainland before the communists came to power.[45] Their products serviced the Wing On department store network.

SUN SUN

The Sun Sun Company store, the third Australian department store to open in Shanghai, emerged from an acrimonious rupture within the Sincere group of companies. Founder Ma Ying-piu fell out with his assistant manager Liu Xiji over the level of returns to the highly profitable Shanghai branch store from consolidated accounts shared with the less profitable head office store in Hong Kong. The two stores operated as a single firm, with profits from Shanghai making up for trading deficits in the Hong Kong store from year to year. As senior manager of the Shanghai operation, Liu Xiji was dissatisfied with this arrangement. He joined forces with another partner in the Sincere group, Wong Poon Narm, the original founder of the Kwong Sing store in Glen Innes, and a third partner who had recently departed Townsville, Charles Lee, to form the Sun Sun Company. The partners succeeded in raising between $1 and $2 million in China through commercial sources. In 1923 their Queensland recruit, Charles Lee, returned to Australia where he raised a comparable sum from small investors across the country marketed at $10 per share.

Construction of Sun Sun's Shanghai building got under way in July 1922 and was completed within three years. After being fitted out, the store opened for business in November 1926. Two years later Charles Lee was appointed general manager. During his eight years in this position the company followed the Wing On pattern of diversification, branching out to invest in hotels, theatres and – a Sun Sun innovation – radio broadcasting. At the outbreak of war with Japan in 1937 the company was valued at $40 million. At seven storeys high, the Sun Sun building stood one storey higher than Wing On and two higher than Sincere on an adjacent block on Nanking Road.[46]

THE SUN COMPANY

In 1936 Choy Chong and Choy Hing opened The Sun Company, the fourth Australian department store on Shanghai's Nanking Road.

Choy Chong established a footing for the firm in Hong Kong before expanding his business to Canton in the 1910s. He constructed a magnificent head office for the firm on the Canton waterfront which dominates the Pearl River Bund to this day. Choy Hing was a friend of Ma Ying-piu from their Sydney days and served for a time as chair of the board of directors of Ma's Sincere Company. The two Choys teamed up in the 1930s to build the grandest department store of all on Nanking Road, a ten-storey edifice boasting a number of innovations, including central heating and elevators connecting three floors of the shopping area. William Liu, employed as the firm's English secretary, oversaw the installation of the elevators. To this time Liu had been shunned by Ma Ying-piu and the directors of the other companies for his alleged role in the failure of the China–Australia Mail Steamship Line, but with the support of the Choys, Liu contributed significantly to the growth and success of The Sun Company.[47]

Networks and opportunities

The Australian department stores on Nanking Road offered opportunities for villagers from their founders' home counties in Guangdong to find work, acquire an education and participate in the life of big-city Shanghai. At any one time the Wing On store in Shanghai employed hundreds of staff from the Gock brothers' ancestral hamlet of Chuk Sau Yuen (*Zhuxiuyuan*) and neighbouring hamlets in Shekki district in Guangdong. The Sincere firm did the same for the Ma family hamlet of Heungmoi (*Hengmei*) a few miles southwest of Chuk Sau Yuen in neighbouring Liangdu district. The Sun Sun department store employed no less than 500 natives of Heungshan County over the life of the business and, according to one historian, never dismissed an employee drawn from the owners' home county. When the communists seized the store's records in 1949 they found over 200 natives of Shekki district in Heungshan County on the Sun Sun payroll.[48]

The four big companies also provided opportunities for young Chinese Australians to acquire business skills and work experience in Hong Kong and Shanghai that helped to launch them on their careers in Australia. The Sincere Department Store sponsored Australian-born

Joe Mah to travel to Shanghai, Janis Wilton records, to acquire skills he would later put to good use in his uncle's store in northern New South Wales. Wong Chee's successor at Kwong Sing and Co., Percy Young, served for a time as manager of Sincere's Tianjin store.[49] The stores also served as patrons for Australian employees seeking official certification from Australian authorities to return to Australia after spending time in China or seeking to extend their approved periods of absence. Poon Gooey entered Victoria at the age of 18 in 1894 where he lived for long periods in Horsham and Geelong before moving to Sydney. From Sydney he made four trips to China between 1918 and 1924, each time securing a Certificate of Exemption from the Dictation Test (CEDT) before departure. When he sought extensions of the time limits that applied to his CEDTs he wrote on Wing On Company paper. His requests were successful.[50]

Another stream of activities linking family stores in Australia and the Big Four in China was capital investment. Representatives of the Four Great Companies visited Australia from time to time to capture commercial investments and small savings for expansion of their businesses in China and retained close connections with these Australian investors over time. They also founded small-town banks in their native district of Shekki to handle financial transactions between China and Australia, and drew upon their banking networks in Australia and China to finance their major investments.[51]

Marriage and children further reinforced the firms' intercontinental connections. Historian Shirley Fitzgerald has published snippets of private correspondence exchanged between William Liu's wife Mabel in Shanghai and her cousin Henry Yet in Sydney at a time when The Sun Company building was under construction. In her letters home Mabel complains of the high prices and inclement weather in Shanghai and writes of her yearning to be back for Christmas. Mabel returned to Sydney with her children on the next available boat. The letter is a rare published sample of the extensive private correspondence through which families divided between China and Australia maintained personal contacts over the late 19th and early 20th centuries. Network ties were maintained occasionally through capital raisings, partly through shared employment and, above all, through everyday contacts centring on the stuff of family life.[52]

Firms and Christian networks

The business ethics of the Four Great Companies were cultivated in a small Sydney Christian congregation under the charismatic leadership of a young man from Canton, the Reverend John Young Wai (*Zhou Rongwei*). Kuo Mei-fen has traced some of the family, business and political networks linking Chinese community leaders in Sydney and China to John Young Wai's Sydney Presbyterian Mission in the 1890s and early 1900s.[53] A number of the Australian retail pioneers were associated with Young Wai's church and school in the Haymarket and with his wider Protestant connections in Hong Kong and south China. The Gock brothers, Ma Ying-piu, Ou Bin and Choy Hing, were all members of this extended circle. The major exception was Charles Lee.

Charles Lee lived and worked well outside the range of John Young Wai's Presbyterian circle. Born in Heungshan in 1881, he set sail for Melbourne at the age of 17 in the company of an old friend of the family, Leong Kunhe (*Liang Kunhe*), and followed Leong overland to Ayr, in Queensland, where he took up work as a labourer on Leong's sugar-cane plantation. Not long after arriving, Lee was befriended by the local Church of England pastor, Allen Miller, who informally adopted him into his family and taught him to speak, read and write in English. Charles Lee was baptised under the Anglican rite in 1904. In the following year he married Evens Leong, Leong's Australian-born daughter. We touched on their wedding in an earlier chapter.

Evens was, by all accounts, a bright and independently-minded young woman who exercised considerable influence over her husband's business affairs. At her prompting, the couple sold off the Ayr properties they inherited on her father's death in 1908 and invested the capital in an import–export business and retail store in the regional city of Townsville. This decision shaped their short life together. Charles and Evens made a number of profitable property investments in Townsville in partnership with a local lawyer named Edward Mepharson, but the bureaucratic annoyance surrounding these investments discouraged them from investing further in Australia. Charles could not purchase property in his own name in Queensland because property ownership was confined to Australian subjects and naturalisation was not open to him under 1903 Commonwealth government legislation denying resident Chinese rights of naturalisation. The couple went in search of investment opportunities abroad. Evens encouraged Charles to take her with him when he next visited his native village in Guangdong. She fell ill on the visit, her first outside Australia, and died; she was 33. Charles Lee married again and stayed on in China where he invested the family's savings in a new venture, the Sun Sun Department Store in Shanghai.

Charles Lee carried his Christian convictions with him. Before leaving Ayr, he was recruited as a lay preacher for the local parish of the Church of England, and was reputedly the first Chinese Australian to minister for the Anglican church in Queensland. On founding the Sun Sun store in Shanghai he revived his pastoral mission by establishing a Cantonese-speaking Anglican church in the city to complement the private chapels set up within the walls of the Wing On and Sincere stores. He also funded the training of ministers for the church. Charles Lee died in 1936 at the age of 55, a prominent member of the Chinese Christian community of Shanghai.[54]

The Sydney Christians adopted a different course of action, converting staff of their department stores, insurance companies and industrial enterprises into Christian congregations. After leaving Sydney, as we have seen, Ma Ying-piu spent some time as a Christian missionary in Hong Kong and south China, and he established a firm in Hong Kong to promote Christian businesses in the colony. His missionary zeal did not abate when he moved into department store retailing. In 1907 Ma set up a Moral Education Department (*deyubu*) for employees of his Sincere store in Hong Kong to promote ethical behaviour among his employees and to win converts to Christ. Along with the firm Sincere's Moral Education Department expanded from Hong Kong to Canton, Shanghai and Tianjin, winning converts along the way. According to the official company historian the firm's Christian-instruction units 'were set up in succession in every branch of the department store and every factory with the result that the number of converts among our employees grew daily'. The Moral Education Department conducted weekly religious services in Sincere's assembly halls, attracting several hundred worshippers to each service. Ma Ying-piu conducted these services himself in the early years; as the business expanded he employed ordained Christian ministers to carry on the work. Business and conversions flourished, the company report concludes, 'with the Grace of God'.[55]

Wing On adopted similar practices. The company's service motto of 'Quality, reasonable price, satisfaction and courtesy' was elaborated as a comprehensive ethical philosophy in company publications and widely promoted through a company-sponsored Christian Union in every store and on every worksite. Wing On's Christian Union made much of the happy convergence between the company's egalitarian service philosophy and the Paulian axiom that all people are one in Christ. The first tenet guiding the stores' business philosophy was recognition of the equality of all who entered the doors of the emporium: 'Whoever the customers happen to be they should all receive equal treatment. There is to be no slighting of one customer and privileging of another'. Inclusive commercial egalitarianism was an extension of Christian ethics.[56]

Wing On's Christian Union drew upon the precedent set by Sincere to the extent of borrowing Sincere's Chinese title for its Moral Education Department for the Chinese title of Wing On's Christian Union (*deyubu*). Like Ma Ying-piu, Philip Gockchin and James Gocklock were prime movers behind the foundation of the Christian Union, participating in its activities and appearing in company photographs promoting the work of the Union. The Christian Union also operated as an ethical service-training unit within the Wing On stores. Like its counterpart at Sincere it convened weekly Christian services for store personnel.

Wing On and Sincere carried their Christian philosophy beyond the walls of their stores and factories through their church and philanthropic activities. Philip Gockchin was Treasurer of the Building Fund of the Hong Kong Chinese United Church and his brother James Gocklock contributed to Christian and non-Christian charities in south China throughout his life. The firm contributed directly to Christian charities in China, including the Young Men's Christian Association (YMCA), and assisted with the renovation of the Tung Wah Hospital in Hong Kong, being largely responsible for construction of a new eastern wing for the hospital in the 1930s. Wing On also donated generously to emergency relief funds following periodic floods and famines in China.[57]

The Sincere Company ran an equally extensive philanthropic program, supporting schools and hospitals in Heungshan County, supporting college and university education in Canton and providing substantial emergency relief for floods and famines in north and south China. As early as 1909 Ma Ying-piu funded the construction of an infirmary and a hostel at Lingnan Christian College in Canton, the finest college in south China at the time and a forerunner of the renowned Sun Yatsen University that now occupies the Lingnan site. The two buildings were named in his honour: the Ma Ying-piu Infirmary and the Ma Ying-piu Guesthouse.[58]

In their community services the two firms sometimes worked together. Ma Ying-piu was appointed to the board of Lingnan Christian College in 1918 and some years later was joined on the board by a son of Philip Gockchin, also a Lingnan benefactor. Sincere also supported branches of the YMCA in its stores and factories. Ma's wife Huo Qingtang founded the Hong Kong branch of the Young Women's Christian Association (YWCA) in 1918, and two years later was elected founding director of the umbrella women's Christian organisation in the colony, the Hong Kong Chinese Christian Women's Association. Ma and the Gock brothers each founded branches of another Christian group, the Chinese Christian Association, in their home district of Shekki, which they continued to support over the years through regular levies on the profits of different arms of the Sincere and Wing On enterprises. Senior managers of both firms held positions on the boards of peak civic associations, major hospitals, and schools and universities, from Hong Kong to Canton, Shanghai and Tianjin.[59]

The Christian ethics that drove their community activities served the entrepreneurs well. The church and community initiatives undertaken by the owners and managers of the Chinese-Australian department stores, as Lai Chi-kong has pointed out, assisted in promoting a commercial service ethic among staff of the firms, in facilitating co-operation between management and staff within the firms and, on occasion, in stimulating co-operation among the firms in, for example, their joint management of the Nanking Road Chamber of Commerce, the common positions they adopted on controversial matters of state in the Chinese republic and the investments they made in one another's commercial ventures.[60] To these we might add the advantages conferred by membership of church organisations that ultimately transcended family and native-place ties. From their early days in Sydney to their halcyon days in Hong Kong and Shanghai, the Christian entrepreneurs maintained extensive links through their churches to networks of people to whom they might otherwise have not have enjoyed access. Their experiences in Sydney equipped them to move easily into Chinese elite circles in Hong Kong and to work confidently with colonial authorities as the need arose.

Despite the material and commercial benefits their beliefs conferred, the profession of Christian faith by the Sydney entrepreneurs cannot be reduced to instrumental profit-seeking. The Mas, the Gocks, the Lees and the Lius, were, as historian Denise Austin has shown in an extensive study of Chinese-Australian Christian entrepreneurs, true believers,[61] their Christian faith and business ethics shaped by their association with the Presbyterian church of the Reverend John Young Wai in Sydney.

Reverend John Young Wai and his descendants

John Young Wai was born on 7 October 1849 and came to the Victorian goldfields as a young man of 18. His family belonged to the Hakka community of Changsheng County and, according to family lore, was active in the Taiping Rebellion of the mid-19th century. Young Wai's personal family history in Australia is better documented than is his early life in China. According to church records he was baptised on the goldfields and studied for the ministry in Melbourne. On graduation he served in a number of rural parishes before taking up a position at Beechworth in northeastern Victoria. In 1882 he transferred to Sydney where he built his first church in Foster Street, Haymarket, in 1893 and was ordained a full minister in the same year. His time in Sydney coincided with the early business ventures of Ma Ying-piu, Choy Hing, George Bew and the Gock brothers.

On a visit to Hong Kong in 1887 Young Wai met and married Sarah Ti See Man, a young graduate from the German Christian mission school in the colony. Like himself, Sarah was a Hakka. On the couple's return to Sydney, Sarah Young Wai supported the mission through her work with Chinese women and with the white-Australian wives of market gardeners and stallholders in the fruit and vegetable markets.

Historian Kuo Mei-fen reports that Sarah met women immigrants on their arrival in Sydney and offered them advice on health, housing and managing family finances. If they needed medical attention she supplied introductions to local hospitals and offered to care for their families.[62]

John Young Wai's first services were conducted on the premises of a store owned by another Changsheng native who traded under the name of Goon Ping & Co. Early in the 1890s the Reverend Young Wai opened a church and night school to preach the gospel and offer English lessons to all who wanted to learn. Despite its Changsheng native-county connections the school attracted Heungshan workers and retailers from the Haymarket and Paddy's Markets. The Gock brothers were among Young Wai's earliest converts and students. In his 1949 memoir, James Gocklock credited John Young Wai's preaching for his own conversion and for that of his Heungshan colleagues in the Wing On Company. Reflecting on his experiences at the night school, Gocklock recalled that he had been initiated into the English language on arriving in Australia with a durable lesson handed down from generation to generation of Chinese vegetable hawkers: go door to door calling out to housewives 'Mrs – Cabbage?' He mastered formal English at Young Wai's Presbyterian night school without ever managing, he later ruminated, to shake off his vegetable hawker's accent.[63]

The church struggled in its early years. The Foster Street church and school were demolished within a decade of opening when Sydney City Council reclaimed the surrounding area for slum clearance. Drawing on proceeds from the compulsory resumption of the Foster Street property, Young Wai built a small church in Campbell Street, where the building stands to this day, and transferred his night school to the new site. The Reverend Robert Jackson, moderator of the NSW General Assembly, formally opened the Campbell Street church in December 1910 in the company of five leading elders of the provincial church. Reverend John Young Wai delivered his sermon to the congregation in Chinese.[64]

Philip Gockchin and Ma Ying-piu were not on hand to celebrate the opening of the Campbell Street church as they had left Sydney for Hong Kong while the old church was still in use. On their return visits to Sydney, John Young Wai approached his communicants to draw on their personal and company funds to extend the work of the Sydney mission to Hong Kong and to their home districts in Heungshan

County. Ma Ying-piu built a sister church in Hong Kong and drew on company dividends to support an affiliated church in Shekki district in Heungshan.

Ma's colleague at Sincere, Ou Bin, was a catechist at the Campbell Street church, as was Choy Hing, founder of the Da Sun Department Store in Shanghai. Choy Hing contributed the bulk of funds for building Reverend Young Wai's first church in Foster Street.[65] Each of the business families maintained close relations with Young Wai's family over the years. When Philip Gockchin's wife died unexpectedly, leaving behind a 14-month-old son, Sarah Young Wai offered to care for the child until Philip was in a position to care for the boy himself. 'I could never forget the charity and good will of Mrs Young Wai,' Philip recalled 50 years later. As the Wing On corporation expanded over these 50 years, Gockchin repaid her charity indirectly through a lifetime of philanthropic activities in Sydney, Hong Kong, Heungshan and Shanghai. Reverend John Young Wai died in 1923, survived by his wife Sarah and six children.

Young Wai's personal and family links with republican political networks were as extensive as his connections with business. After the 1911 republican revolution he served as English secretary for the Sydney republican organisation and in 1914 persuaded the grand master of the Chinese Masonic Society and local republican sympathisers to co-operate in establishing *Republican News*, the pre-eminent Australian republican newspaper of the period. His daughter Carrie married Yu Junxian, a leading figure in the KMT's powerful Organisation Department in China. The couple married in her father's Campbell Street church.[66]

Yu Junxian went on to become a figure of great eminence in the nationalist government of China. He was born in 1902 in Pingyuan County in Guangdong, one of two boys and five girls in the family of a local school principal, a graduate of Chaojia Teacher's College in Canton, who founded the first modern-style school in his home county. As a child, Yu Junxian attended his father's school but left on his father's death to support his mother and siblings. After he resumed his education he was rewarded with a place at Sun Yatsen University in Canton. On graduating in 1926 he allied himself with the right-wing KMT faction led by Chen Guofu, which launched the anti-communist

Party Purification Movement over the following year. Towards the end of 1927 Yu Junxian was assigned to KMT party work in Java where he oversaw the creation of the KMT general headquarters for the Dutch East Indies and served briefly as director of its propaganda department. In 1928, at the instigation of the Japanese consul, he was imprisoned for eight months by Dutch authorities for advocating an anti-Japanese boycott in protest against Japanese military interventions in China. Expelled from the Indies in 1929 he returned to China to take up a position in the KMT Organisation Department.

It was in this capacity that Yu Junxian toured Australia, New Zealand and the Pacific Islands in 1931. His bride Carrie accompanied him back to China where Yu was appointed special envoy to the Canton City Party Standing Committee in 1936 and to the Guangdong Provincial Party Standing Committee in the following year. When war with Japan broke out he smuggled his wife and children through Hong Kong back to Sydney, Carrie leading the way and her two young children close behind, concealed in wicker panniers on the back of a donkey. Yu Junxian declined to follow his family to Sydney and instead followed Chiang Kai-shek to Taiwan, where in 1973 he was elected president of the Investigation Yuan, one of the five most senior positions on the national cabinet. On meeting up again with his Australian son in Taipei, after a lapse of 35 years, there was little the ageing minister in Chiang Kai-shek's cabinet did not know about the young man's extraordinary career in Australia. The nationalist consulate in Sydney had filed regular reports on the family to party headquarters in Nanking and Taipei.[67]

Reverend John Young Wai left a remarkable legacy of family engagement with Australian public life extending to the present day. His six children – Joshua, Rachel, Samuel, Kezia, Carrie and Alfred – continued to lead classes in Chinese and English in the small school attached to the Presbyterian mission for much of their lives. One of his two grandchildren who were smuggled out of China in a wicker basket in 1937 was John Yu, son of Carrie Young Wai and Nationalist Minister Yu Junxian. Safely home in Australia, John grew up in the home of his grandfather and went on to study medicine at the University of Sydney where he specialised in paediatrics. As chief executive of the Royal Alexandria Hospital for Children, Dr Yu pioneered new methods in paediatric care that propelled the Sydney hospital to the forefront of international hospital care for children in the 1970s. On his retirement Dr Yu went on to serve in an honorary capacity as chancellor of the University of New South Wales (to 2005), chair of the Australia-China Council of the Department of Foreign Affairs and Trade (to 2006) and deputy chair of the Board of the NSW Art Gallery. Dr Yu was also appointed inaugural chair of the Commission for Children and Young People in New South Wales. In 1996, Prime Minister John Howard bestowed upon him the award of Australian of the Year.

9

BEING AUSTRALIAN

[Leaders of] Australia will look back with regret and shame ...
superior to the desire of snatching a fleeting popularity at the expense
of a few strangers.

Reverend Cheok Hong Cheong (1888).[1]

The Gock family lived out the Second World War in Japanese-occupied territories in China and Hong Kong. When the war was over Philip Gockchin reaffirmed his control over the Wing On businesses in Hong Kong but bade farewell to the company's assets in China – appropriated by the communists – and paid his first visit to Australia after many years away. The country he found on his return in 1951 was clearly prospering but the Chinese community seemed, to his eyes, to have dwindled to insignificance. At a time of considerable growth in Australia the resident Chinese population had fallen to around 10 000 souls, a mere fraction, Gockchin reflected, of the 50 000 who could have been found clearing the land, working in mines, building railroads or growing and marketing fruit and vegetables across Australia at the close of the goldrush era.

Their numbers had declined not of their own design but in consequence of the White Australia Policy.[2]

Gockchin derived little consolation from observing that the fate of the Chinese in Australia reflected the situation facing Overseas Chinese (*huaqiao*) everywhere in the world at that time. He observed that

> The Overseas Chinese hired themselves out as labourers, opened up wastelands with their sweat and blood, and built the foundations for future prosperity. In the end, however, it is others who profited from their efforts.[3]

He might as well have been speaking of China, where the people's government had seized the fruits of his family's labour and investment over the preceding 50 years.

What especially concerned him in Australia was the startling contrast between the growth and prosperity of one group of Australians and the absolute decline of another. People of Chinese descent were left with little choice but to leave Australia as he had done, he concluded, if their families were to prosper. Rather than urge his children and grandchildren to settle in Australia, Philip Gockchin advised them to study in the United States, which had begun to open its doors to Chinese immigrants immediately after the Pacific war. Few of the Gock family settled back in Australia.

Gockchin's account of Chinese hard work, thrift and industry, profiting others more than themselves, bears little likeness to White Australian stories of Chinese sojourners tearing riches from the earth and squandering them on opium or smuggling them back to China. Still, his account confirms the general impression that no more than a few Chinese stragglers were left behind in the postwar era to live out their lives without hope or prospects in White Australia. The English-language archive of Chinese Australia amounts to little more than a record of absence and exclusion: indexes to petitions seeking redress for unequal treatment, filing boxes of old departure records, thumbprints and photographs pasted onto immigration files and black-and-white images of sunburnt market gardeners, pinned up in local museums over captions identifying 'the last known Chinaman in the district'. Chinese-language sources are rarely consulted. In consequence, although the

Chinese chapter in the history of Australia is recounted with a variety of inflections, it invariably ends as the story of a vanishing people.

The response of White Australia to the apparent disappearance of the men from China, even when notably triumphant, was often tinged with nostalgia. At the time Gockchin visited Sydney, whites had already taken to collecting discarded opium tins, dirt-encrusted medicine bottles and shards of broken pottery from hundreds of sites of Chinese settlement across the continent, in some cases razing the site with a back hoe once the exotic artefacts had been extracted to ensure its erasure. Today these artefacts adorn mantelpieces and glass cabinets across the country. Some of the finer pieces are preserved in local museums to demonstrate this or that district's historical or cultural links with China. As a rule they commemorate not the Chinese heritage of Australia, but White Australia's exotic links with a remote civilisation in China. The names of the men who bought, sold and used these artefacts while breathing the sweet, chill air of the typical Australian morn – as Vivian Chow once put it – are generally omitted from public displays.[4]

At times White Australian nostalgia turned bizarre. In the late 1930s a party of Freemasons gathered in Melbourne to redress what they saw as the lamentable decline of Chinese traditions throughout the world. By this time the local heritage of fraternal connections linking Anglo-Celtic Freemasonry to the Chinese Yee Hing was largely forgotten. The men who gathered in Melbourne were keen, in the absence of men from China, to preserve Chinese traditions in Australia and under the false impression that the quasi-Masonic lodges of the Yee Hing network were on the verge of extinction.

At the initiative of Clive Loch Hughes-Hallett, an Englishman resident in Melbourne, a white Australian version of the Triad Society was founded 'as it might have been centuries ago' to keep Chinese traditions alive on Australian soil. As Hughes-Hallett later recalled:

> So in 1937 a lodge was constituted, carefully following the native traditions of the society. There were Five Founders corresponding to the Five Monks, each styled Provincial Grand Master, one for each continent, again according to the tradition. A sixth Founder was admitted, who was to stand aside and apart in the mysterious role of Wan Yun Long, the Commander-in-Chief, to co-ordinate the work of the other Founders and to warrant new lodges.

With his fellow founders, Hughes-Hallett undertook a systematic investigation of the 'history, teachings and rituals of the Chinese Triad Society' by consulting sinological experts on the ceremonial procedures of the Hung League, including Gustave Schlegel's *The Hung League* (Batavia 1866), and *The Hung Society* (London 1925), authored by JSM Ward and WG Stirling. These definitive works, as noted in an earlier chapter, were widely believed to provide a reputable scholarly foundation for the claim that the Hung League was a Chinese equivalent of European Freemasonry.

Members of the Melbourne-based triad lodge undertook their responsibilities with missionary zeal in the belief that Australian Freemasons bore a special burden of responsibility to preserve authentic Chinese heritage by virtue of their close proximity to Asia. 'Even under the best conditions,' their leaders conceded, 'their work may not bear fruit for 50 years.' Still,

> it is both significant and fitting that the initiative in setting up such
> a research organisation should have been undertaken by Australian
> rather than by the United Kingdom or American freemasons.

At their formal meetings the white triads dressed up in elaborate Chinese robes and practised the rites set out in the colonial canon on Chinese ritual practice. Initiates were dressed in straw sandals and invited to pass through the Red Flower Pavilion – represented as a model set upon on an altar in the City of Willows – before arriving at the Hung Gate where they swore blood oaths of fealty and gained admission to the Hung League. In time these initiation ceremonies were held for 21 initiates in Melbourne, 22 in Sydney and one based in Brisbane. Registered members received a standard certificate written in Chinese and English, headed by the triangular symbol of the Hung League, signalling the lodge's association with the Chinese triads.

The founders' investigation of Chinese ritual practices picked up apace with the recruitment of a certain Captain Albert Francis Warrington, who claimed to be a retired sea skipper, and who was inducted into a Chinese lodge of the Hung League while stationed in Burma. Warrington certified that the ceremonies adopted by the Victorian lodge were 'alike in many points' to those practised in the triad lodges he had known in

Southeast Asia (Chinese triad leaders in Melbourne, Sydney and Cairns were not consulted). The Chinese history that Captain Warrington affirmed was duly appropriated for Australian history, or at least for the history of the Freemason's Triad Lodge of Melbourne:

> *The opening words of our Traditional History place the foundation of the Triad Society in the reign of the Emperor Khang Hsi. It is with the object of trying to discover the basis on which the modern ritual rests, that the original study group was formed in Melbourne in the 1930s. But to return to the facts of history.*

The lodge was dissolved within two decades of its founding, in December 1957.[5]

What were the facts of history? Warrington's warrants notwithstanding, the assumptions underlying this episode in the history of antipodean sinology were wide of the mark. There was little evidence to suggest that Chinese secret societies were in decline or that their traditional rituals were at risk of disappearing, whether in Southeast Asia, China or, indeed, in Hong Kong, to the consternation of the colonial constabulary. The notion that they were disappearing from Australia was equally misleading. Although greatly reduced in size, Chinese-Australian fraternities remained conscious of their heritage and their members were not of a mind to abandon the rituals and traditions they had invented for themselves in Australia to cement their identities as Australians of Chinese descent.

Nor were Chinese Australians on the point of disappearing. Most Chinese Australians of the White Australia era lived out their lives in the comfort and security of privacy, as did most other Australians. Some of their descendents, however, are very well known. The television chef and author Kylie Kwong is one of 800 Australian descendents of a prominent businessman in Darwin and northern Queensland, Kwong Sue-Duk. Jeff Fatt, who plays the sleepy character in a purple pullover on the ABC children's television program, *The Wiggles*, is a grandson of the brother of Percy Young, Kwan Hong Fatt, who operated a branch of the Hong Yuen general stores in New England. Helene Chung-Martin, a child of the Chung family who ran the KMT branch network in Tasmania before the war, was a well-known ABC journalist before her retirement, serving as the national broadcaster's correspondent in Peking in the 1980s. She has written two books on her time in China and is currently working on a history of the Chung family in Tasmania. The world-renowned guitarist John Williams is a grandchild of the Melbourne QC William Ah Ket, who fought gallantly against discriminatory immigration restrictions in Victoria at the time of the federation. As we have seen, Olympic gold-medallist Cathy Freeman acknowledged hers when celebrating the award of the 2008 Olympics to Beijing.[6]

Other families of the White Australia era made substantial contributions to public life in Australia. After Charles Lee, founder of the Sun Sun Company, died in China in 1936 his son Charles Cheng-Che Lee succeeded him as director of the company before retiring to Australia and recording the history of Chinese-Australian business enterprise. Cheng-Che Lee has published many books and articles on the subject. Writing in Sydney in the 1990s he reflected that 100 descendants of Charles and Evens Leong were living and working in Australia at the time he put pen to paper. William Liu, manager of the merchant steamship line, is well remembered by his descendents in New South Wales, some of whom married into Harry Fay's family and worked with the Hong Yuen chain of general stores in rural New South Wales. Quong Tart has a distinguished list of descendants who continue to cherish the memory of his family and business life. And as we have seen, Reverend John Young Wai left an extraordinary legacy of family engagement with Australian public life from the 19th to the 21st centuries. Today, 500 000 Australians of Chinese ancestry can claim a living heritage that no museum can possibly capture.

Being Australian

We could end the story here by mounting additional evidence of Chinese community engagement with White Australia and enumerating the contributions that Chinese Australians have made to their communities and to the country since the earliest years of colonial settlement.[7] But the point at issue is not how much a particular individual or family contributed to Australia or whether one community contributed more than another. Rather, the challenge is to establish how different communities came together to constitute Australia as a nation at federation and how their transnational social, cultural and economic connections succeeding in linking Australia to the world over the century that followed. Immigrant communities as a rule transcend the boundaries of their host nations in ways that connect them to wider global networks and make modern immigrant trading nations such as Australia possible.[8]

There has always been room in Australia's national story for the transnational networks maintained by British and Irish communities, from the earliest claims made for the 'crimson threads' binding Australia to empire, to postwar studies of Irish-Australian engagement with home rule in Ireland, to more recent studies of long-standing community ties maintained by British Australians with their home counties.[9] Similar networks were maintained by Chinese communities linking Australia to the Pacific Islands, California, the Straits settlements and southern China through family ties, business networks and community organisations. The meaning of their history is not to be gauged by their contributions alone but by the ways in which they helped to constitute Australia as a national community and as a national hub of transnational communities whose members called Australia home. The big question, then, is not who did this or that for Australia but how it was that different communities came together to *be* Australian, and how their coming together is acknowledged and commemorated to this day.

Historian John Hirst has canvassed the sentimental motives for Australian federation in his centenary history *The Sentimental Nation*. 'In looking for the motives of Australian federation, historians usually are far too instrumental in their thinking,' he remarks in the opening chapter. 'It was *the making of the nation*, apart from anything it might do, that was sacred.'[10] The idea that they participated at the making of the nation appealed to communities scattered across the continent who momentarily shelved their differences and came together around a common conviction that they shared not just one economy, or even one continent, but also One Destiny.[11] Federation was seen by the white community as a good in itself.[12] So it was seen by Chinese Australians. Australia's Chinese communities participated in nation-making at federation through their own public debates, philanthropy and pageantry. They wanted to be and to be seen as Australians.

As a sentimental system, nationalism is grounded in the politics of recognition, that is, in struggles for recognition of common equality among citizens, among peoples and among states. In Australia's case the claim for recognition at federation entailed not merely recognition of Australia as an autonomous state but also a struggle for status equality among the communities that made up the nation. The sentiments that inspired nation-making at federation were those of a national people seeking to cast off the prejudices and inequalities of their old countries to embrace fairness, equality and natural justice. Chinese communities shared these sentiments to the point of suggesting that they should be extended beyond the limits of White Australia. They shared a vision of universal progress that linked individuals, families and nations to the global community of the 'family of man', as Alfred Deakin characterised Australian aspirations at the moment of federation.[13] Why, they asked, did white Australians assume that the modern principles of liberty, equality and fraternity made sense only to white egalitarians?

Their place in Australia was more readily acknowledged under British colonial rule than in White Australia after federation. In colonial Victoria, Chinese played prominent roles in local community pageants, parading their dancing lions and dragons before trails of Scottish pipers, benevolent society matrons and district fire brigades in annual fairs and festivals. As historian Amanda Rasmussen has shown, the Chinese community of Bendigo negotiated its relations with the white community of the gold-mining district through annual participation in the town's grand Easter Parade. The Bendigo festivities were supplemented around the colony by Chinese communities in Beechworth, Ballarat, St Arnaud and Maldon, who linked their celebrations of traditional festivals with local carnivals and charity fairs. Kuo Mei-fen has drawn attention to a similar phenomenon in Sydney where Chinese residents took part in Queen Victoria's jubilee celebrations in 1897. The public acclaim they received confirmed for Chinese community leaders that being Chinese did not disqualify them from being part of the larger Australian pageant. Historian Kevin Wong Hoy has observed that Chinese feasts and festivals were widely appreciated in north Queensland in the late 19th century, as they were in Adelaide, according to fellow historian Patricia Monaghan-Jamieson. And in Melbourne, city authorities invited Chinese community organisations to participate in the grandest parade of them all to celebrate Australian federation in the new federal capital. In January 1901, 200000 Melbourne residents lined the streets to applaud the lions, dragons and Chinese celebrants of federation as they wound their way through the centre of town. Public celebrations of this kind were not about *doing* something but about *being* something – in some cases being a rural community, in others a metropolitan community and, in the case of federation, about being a united and sovereign nation. Chinese Australians participated in public pageants at every level in the lead-up to federation.[14]

In the federation era, the wider values of empire were domesticated as national values once a new tier of government was set up at the Commonwealth level to patrol the territorial and cultural boundaries of the new Australian nation. This process was no more uniquely Australian than the values that inspired it. National–state boundaries were hardening around the world in the concluding phase of the Atlantic century, a phase roughly corresponding to the federation period in Australia. Sixty million Europeans crossed the Atlantic to the Americas over the century preceding the Great War. Over the long 19th century international flows of people, capital and merchandise were as great and as rapid as anything in our own time. Cross-border capital flows and population movements were even higher than today, relative to population and national product, and transport and transaction costs fell further and faster than anything comparable in our own time. In the United States the ratio of foreign debt to GDP exceeded the levels that pushed Brazil and other Latin American states to the brink in the debt crisis of the 1980s. This intense Atlantic phase in the development of the global economy cooled off from around the turn of the century with the introduction of passports and immigration controls and the imposition of national trade barriers.[15] The ideal of the isolated national state capable of exercising absolute control over its economic, demographic and cultural boundaries was largely a product of this phase of state closure around the turn of the 20th century.

Australian federation was shaped by its times. The paramount concern among all parties at the time of federation was the defence of Australia's continental boundaries.[16] Fissures emerged in debates leading up to federation over disputes between free traders and protectionists and, to a lesser degree, between champions of greater or lesser immigration restrictions. In both cases disagreement turned on the hardening or softening of state boundaries. A key issue in the trade debate was whether differential tariffs and trade barriers between the colonies would be removed at federation and, if so, whether they would be replaced by harder or softer boundaries at the unified national level. Basically, the question was whether the federated Commonwealth should exercise its newly-won sovereignty to tighten the movement of merchandise at its borders. The debate over Asian immigration turned on the same question. Should the new state look upon its territorial border as an enclosing fence, regulating the entry of certain categories of people, or as an open gate welcoming people in?[17]

Across the Pacific the answers to these questions came down hardest on the issue of immigration. Australia, New Zealand, Canada and the Unites States all introduced national immigration regimes to limit the entry of immigrants from China. Washington excluded Chinese because they were Chinese. Canada and New Zealand imposed discriminatory head taxes that effectively limited entry to those who could afford to pay. Australia imposed a dictation test to assess, symbolically as it were, the familiarity of Chinese migrants with national culture and values. This was a ruse to police the entry of 'coloured' peoples and political undesirables. But the Commonwealth came to believe its own propaganda claims, to the effect that certain kinds of people had to be kept out of the country not because of who they were but because they failed to understand and appreciate Australian values. The Commonwealth government developed an immense administrative apparatus that institutionalised the values of White Australia as the corporate ethic of the Australian national state.

Voice and values

There is no point pretending that White Australia was other than it was, a place extremely hostile to non-white Australians. Nevertheless, there is something to be said for retracing the history of Chinese Australians around iconic Australian values to show how narrowly these have been construed over time as, basically, Anglo-Saxon values. Here we have been tracing historical voices along two different tracks – one echoing comments by white Australians on the place of Chinese in Australian history, the other tracing what Chinese Australians have said and done themselves about their place in Australia over the first half of the 20th century. The two tracks rarely meet. Chinese Australians have rarely been invited to participate in Australian conversations on national values.

In White-Australian publications of the late 19th and early 20th centuries, Chinese residents were pictured as depraved, self-interested, menial, unhealthy and generally despicable characters who had no place alongside free white settlers under the Australian sun.[18] Few of these claims are taken seriously today. Still, a more refined version of this crude characterisation continues to hold sway. This is the culturalist argument that Australia was host to a clash of civilisations between slavish, dependent and hierarchically minded exiles from an unchanging Chinese empire on the one side, and individualistic, egalitarian and patriotic white settlers fresh from battle with the tyrannies of Old Europe on the other. The culturalist argument purports to explain popular racism. In fact it elevates popular racism to a matter of high principle, converting an elementary clash of material cultures into a clash of civilizations and values. The history of Australia has been greatly impoverished by the old White-Australian presumption that universal values are the particular preserve of whites.

This exalted form of anti-Chinese sentiment coexisted in White Australia alongside popular racism. It may even have been more pervasive than popular racism. Evidence uncovered by archaeologist Barry Macgowan indicates that Chinese diggers lived, shopped and caroused in closer proximity to Europeans on the goldfields than the historical record of anti-Chinese agitators has led us to believe.[19] Historical anecdotes support the archaeological evidence. Joe Byrne, partner of the famous outlaw Ned Kelly, is said to have spoken Cantonese after picking up the language as a boy while playing in the Chinese camp on his parents' farm at the Woolshed Diggings near Beechworth. His nickname was Ah Joe.[20] There are plenty of stories of friendship and co-operation between European and Chinese Australians in country towns and in the inner-city suburbs of Melbourne and Sydney.[21] But white Australians who shopped and joked on weekdays with Ah Lum the greengrocer could work up a sweat talking about the Chinese menace to Australia on a Sunday afternoon at the Domain or at the Yarra Bank. The lived experience of local communities at the level of town and neighbourhood was translated into the higher language of Australian values through an educated sinological discourse on the faults of the Chinese character. Translated into the language of Australian values, Ah Lum the local greengrocer became Ah Lum the Chinaman.

This elevated style of anti-Chinese sentiment operated above the everyday concerns of towns and neighbourhoods at a level where public figures contemplated higher questions of nationality and values. In the imagined community of the colony and the Commonwealth, the great men of politics raised daily concerns into national anxieties by invoking the national interest and Australian values.[22] This was especially true around the time of federation. Federation, author Donald Horne has argued, took place 'without proper rhetorical warning'. The White Australia Policy gave it retrospective meaning:

> *When the newly elected MPs met in Melbourne in their borrowed houses they had to act like statesmen, who had some important occasion for their coming together. They needed a great self-defining debate: that ritual debate happened to be on immigration policy.*[23]

At the level of nation building, the clash of cultures thesis went on to play an important role in defining Australian values and sanctioning the White Australia Policy.

This role has yet to be exhausted. In *The White Australia Policy*, Keith Windschuttle argues that an underlying clash of cultures between Chinese and white Australians supplied a primary motive and sufficient cause for Chinese exclusion from Australia for the better part of a century from the 1880s to the 1960s.[24] Chinese were excluded not because they were Chinese, the argument runs, but because they did not share the Australian national imaginary. They had to be excluded in order to preserve a fragile public commitment to fair play, mateship and egalitarianism. Insofar as Australian national values have been defined, challenged and upheld through public debate, many historians of White Australia, including Windschuttle, have helped to certify their lineage as white. The lineage of national values can thus be traced through successive attempts to exclude people of Asian background from the Australian continent.

For evidence of the insuperable cultural divide separating Chinese Australians from the white majority, some historians point to an apparent indifference on the part of Chinese immigrants to the religious, educational and cultural life of their communities. Chinese immigrants to Australia, as one historian has put it, 'had no interest in matters pertaining to the education of children, and little in the affairs of the Christian churches. This social isolation was one of the reasons for the resentment that some people felt toward them ...'[25] Even sympathetic observers who condemned anti-Chinese rioting at Lambing Flat in 1861 felt obliged to conclude that 'Europeans and Orientals would never be able to exist harmoniously on the goldfields because of the gulf between their respective ideas and habits'.[26] This value gap is presented as a reasonable and adequate explanation for Chinese exclusion from White Australia. Popular resentment over Chinese values, the story goes, bred anti-Chinese sentiment, which fed into legislative processes to keep Chinese out of White Australia in the federation era.

In fact the legislative restrictions imposed on Chinese immigrants after federation bore little relation to the claims of cultural incompatibility mounted on the goldfields of Ballarat or Lambing Flat. There were certainly grounds for misunderstanding. Chinese workers fraternised on a scale and in a style unfamiliar to white miners. It was not their lack of aptitude for working co-operatively that distinguished them but rather the scale of co-operation that gave white diggers cause for alarm. Much of the surviving archaeological evidence indicating large-scale co-operative work on the pre-industrial goldfields, including dam building, water sluicing, the layering of earth for gardens and the like, can be traced to Chinese engineering work laid down 150 years ago. The historical record again supports the archaeological evidence. 'On the whole,' historian Charles Price concluded from extensive research into the working practices of Chinese miners, 'their mining was co-operative on a larger scale than European mining.'[27] A capacity for hard work and hardy co-operation characterised the fraternities of working men who came to Australia from China. They arrived in parties of fraternal brotherhoods that were egalitarian, democratic and in many cases anti-monarchical in character.

By any measure Chinese immigrants were as fraternal as Scottish Freemasons and no less egalitarian than Irish Hibernians. Their evident difference from Scots and Irish should not be allowed to obscure their similarities. Yet even assuming that these similarities were little understood at the time, goldfields Australia was not White Australia. By federation the country had moved on to the point where their similarities were more obvious and substantial. Twenty-eight per cent of Chinese respondents to the 1901 census described themselves as Christians.[28] The commitment of Chinese Australians to 'the education of children' and to 'the affairs of the Christian churches' counted for little to the architects of White Australia at federation. Christian educators and businessmen of Chinese descent were subjected to the same restrictions as other Chinese Australians. They could not travel abroad without being photographed and fingerprinted, they could not invest in certain industries and territories in Australia, they were not eligible for citizenship and most men were separated from their wives and children, who remained in China.

Even today, historians of Australian federation make an exception for Chinese Australians in their understanding of sentimental nation making. National sentiment at federation is said to have embraced ideals of mateship and equality directed towards the unification of the continent and overcoming the petty prejudices carried over from the class society of Britain. Chinese participation, on the other hand, is thought to have rested on the rational calculation of particularistic interests rather than the values and sentiments that drove white Australians. Historians Roslyn Russell and Philip Chubb highlight a paradox of 1901 when Chinese participated enthusiastically in the great parade that wended its way through Melbourne's streets at the opening of the first Commonwealth parliament, and the first Act of parliament that restricted further Chinese immigration. 'Did Melbourne's Chinese citizens really have anything to celebrate with the advent of the Commonwealth?' they ask.[29] The question is a reasonable one. It assumes that Chinese participation in public life rested on rational calculation of particular interests rather than on shared ideals or sentiments. It overlooks the prospect that Chinese Australians celebrated federation because they were sentimental dreamers too.

Chinese-Austalian aspirations

The dreams of Chinese Australians were not atavistic throwbacks to an idealised Chinese past. From their founding in the 1850s, Chinese clubs and societies in the Australian colonies were unabashedly modern and international in their style and orientation. In the 1850s, the See Yap Society began policing the dress and habits of its members to ensure that they conformed to the vestimentary standards of the modern British male.[30] Early in the 1860s this society also renovated its temple in Melbourne in the latest Victorian style and, as we have seen, framed its aspirations in a bas relief of two men in top hats and tails with their arms outstretched encompassing the world. By the 1880s the once-ubiquitous blue breeches and coveralls brought over from southern China were giving way among Chinese-Australian males to European coats and jackets. In the cities, the queues that Han Chinese men were obliged by their Manchu conquerors to wear were hidden beneath a fedora and, on special occasions, a top hat. By the turn of the 20th century the most conservative of Chinese-Australian organisations were urging their members to cut their queues. These cultural innovations were not simply instances of cross-cultural dressing or assimilation: Chinese in Australia wanted to be modern and cosmopolitan and they imagined that there were few better ways of being modern and cosmopolitan than being an Australian subject of the British empire.[31]

In keeping with these aspirations, Chinese-Australian merchants were among the earliest anywhere to recognise the value of modern civic institutions in strategic business planning. Their success can be attributed to a characteristically Australian capacity for extending the reach of traditional networks of trust through engagement with modern civic institutions, including chambers of commerce, political parties and Christian churches. Chinese-Australian businessmen turned in the first instance to their families and fellow townsmen to build their networks. In time they extended these connections through church congregations, chambers of commerce (including one of the earliest Chinese chambers in the world), Kuo Min Tang party branches and Chinese Masonic lodges. Individual entrepreneurs and firms extended their social and business networks incrementally to the point where they accounted for a significant proportion of trade between Australia and the Pacific Islands and came to dominate modern retail trade in Hong Kong, Canton and Shanghai. Their grafting of modern commercial ethics onto existing social networks equipped them to recognise and to seize emerging business opportunities and to achieve unprecedented efficiencies of scale in wholesale and retail trading. The expansion of these traditional social networks through corporate civic institutions enabled them to raise significant capital for investment from large numbers of small shareholders while reducing the transaction costs of doing business in an unfamiliar environment.

Chinese-Australian networks had an ethical foundation. Australian entrepreneurs were renowned in Hong Kong and Shanghai not just for their business acumen but also for their Christianity, their egalitarian ideals and a recognisable spirit of co-operation that sharpened their competitive edge abroad. They favoured the principle of equality under the law rather than grace-and-favour politics, generally preferring to set up their businesses under the legal jurisdiction of British colonial administrations in East and Southeast Asia. They practised a modern commercial service ethic directed towards meeting the needs of their customers. By encouraging the use of phrases such as 'Welcome', 'Please' and 'Thank you' among their employees, they popularised a new civic code of politeness through their department stores in Hong Kong and China. They also co-operated with one another in penetrating new markets. To Chinese observers these everyday indicators of equality, fraternity and Christian politeness made up a distinctive set of Chinese-Australian claims on the egalitarian ethic of modernity.

Neither the NSW Chamber of Commerce nor the NSW Masonic Association could compare with the Australasian branch of the KMT as an instrument for extending business connections beyond Australia and for representing merchant interests to government. The KMT eclipsed the Chinese Masonic Society in Australia after federation, when an expanding web of federal regulation governing migration and mobility brought business, labour and Chinese patriots together around the Australasian KMT headquarters in Sydney. The expanding arc of Australian regulation in the Pacific encouraged business firms, labour organisers, community organisations and political parties to pool their contacts and expertise to secure greater freedom of movement for people, cargo and investments to and from Australia, Asia and the Pacific Islands.

The Kuo Min Tang took up the challenge. The growth of the KMT in the 1920s closely shadowed the consolidation and expansion of White Australia on the Australian continent and its effective extension into the South Pacific. In facilitating mobility and business the KMT drew on its privileged access to office holders in China and their representatives in Australia, China and the Pacific Islands.

Compared with the individuals, firms, clans and native-county networks that drew on its services, the KMT was a relatively open organisation. Senior positions in the party leadership were captured by particularistic family interests and native-county networks from one site to another – by Heungshan natives in Sydney and Fiji, by the Seeto family and Hakka communities in New Guinea – but the party was not limited to serving any one of these particularistic networks at the expense of another. Senior leadership positions in Sydney were shared among owners and managers of rival firms, and KMT services in dealing with customs officials and government officers were available to all members. The Australasian KMT clubhouse in Canton welcomed visitors from all states and territories, and its officers were prepared to defend a See Yap native from the depredations of 'local bullies and evil gentry' as readily as a Heungshan native. Similarly, the Sydney KMT offices and dormitory provided services to members drawn from different clans, ethnic groups and regions scattered among the Pacific Islands. As an inclusive institution the party was open to social networks seeking to extend their reach beyond their particular families, native places or sites of residence in the South Pacific. It proved sufficiently large and flexible to accommodate all particularistic networks.

Despite their modern aspirations, universal values, business success and engagement with civic communities, Chinese Australians could not escape being characterised as servile, hierarchical and self-interested aliens in White Australia. The attribution of slavery to Chinese society and culture by 19th century ethnographers and 20th century historians is related to the language in which political conflict was expressed over the period; it owes little to close observation of China or of Chinese working practices. Their style of work gave rise to a widespread allegation that Chinese diggers toiled night and day like teams of slaves or convict gangs under the whip hands of their headmen. In fact, Chinese labourers worked as members of voluntary associations operating as fraternal networks that valued equality, fraternity and fairness as keenly as did other Australian workers. They referred to one another as 'brother'. Far from being strangers to the delights of honest toil, the attractions of individual freedom, the appeal of the egalitarian ethic or the bonds of mateship, Chinese diggers were as fraternal, egalitarian and independent as their counterparts in the white labour movement. What distinguished them was a distinctive material culture associated with their colour that placed them outside the pale of Australian values.

Chinese Australians argued against their exclusion on the very grounds that were deployed against them, that is, by reference to fair play, egalitarianism and fraternal association. The ethical language in which they argued for their rights was partly derived from a moral 'little tradition' preserved in the fraternal associations that organised their immigration and settlement, partly acquired in Australia through contact with the everyday street language of mateship and fair play, and elaborated through observation of the institutional operation of the British empire, including its ethic of the rule of law.

White Australia and Red China

At few points in their lives were Chinese immigrants invited to comment on their so-called servility or to speak out on what they thought of the values of fairness, equality and mateship. Historian Charles Price has argued that if Chinese-Australians had protested their exclusion more forcefully their interventions may have made a difference.[32] In fact, when Chinese community leaders did mount reasonable claims in their own defence, their voices fell on deaf ears. Indifference to Chinese-Australian voices was a condition for their exclusion from the jurisdiction of Australian values. The silence that enveloped them in Australia bred defensiveness, resentment and, in the case of Philip Gockchin, a spirit of resignation and retreat. In a significant number of cases it encouraged Chinese Australians to look to China for some kind of symbolic redress in the belief that white Australians treated them with derision because China was so weak that they could treat the country and its people with contempt. The spread of Chinese nationalism among the diasporic community owed a great deal to Australian, North American and European racism.

This is an important point. The brutal regime of Mao Zedong is offered by Keith Windschuttle as unassailable proof of a primordial Chinese cultural predisposition for subservience and slavery.[33] To the contrary: Mao Zedong was a Leninist of a very modern streak, who rose to power on the back of a nationalist movement to recover China's unity and dignity as an equal and autonomous state. Arguing by analogy, the modern nationalist struggle for recognition that yielded White Australia produced Mao Zedong in China.[34] In fact, the association between White Australia and Mao Zedong is not merely analogous: there are a number of direct connections, some of them trivial, some profound.

At the trivial level we can consult Dr Li Zhisui's scandalous memoir, *The Private Life of Chairman Mao* (1994). Dr Li was Mao Zedong's private physician and his memoir is generally read and remembered for divulging scandalous court secrets about the founder of the People's Republic. Coincidentally, it reveals the private thoughts of an educated Chinese doctor who happened to be living and working in Australia in January 1949 when news came through that the People's Liberation Army had occupied Peking. Dr Li was making 'good money' in Sydney, he recalled, 'but I could never become a citizen. My pride and self-respect cried out against this racist policy.'[35] He found a cure for his depression in Peking where he returned in time to take part in the triumphal founding ceremony of the People's Republic at Tiananmen on 1 October 1949, and accepted an invitation to serve on Mao Zedong's personal medical staff. After his experience in Sydney he felt proud, like many other people of Chinese descent living under racist regimes abroad, that China had 'stood up'. It was some time before he recognised Mao for the monster that he was.

Australian historian Sean Brawley has pointed to a more profound connection linking the White Australian vision of Prime Minister William Morris Hughes to the genesis of Maoist-style nationalism in China. The Australian prime minister was a wily politician, fluent in the local dialect of Australian nationalism and possessed a special gift for reading the mood of the electorate and finding words and images to turn fleeting popular sentiment to political advantage. He presented himself as an honest, sincere and practical man of action, whose duty it was to advance the Australian national interest. The national interest meant keeping Australia white.[36]

Prime Minister Hughes had little time for high-sounding principles or for dreamers, and little patience for the principle of racial equality promoted by idealist US President Woodrow Wilson at the Paris Peace Conference. He set out deliberately to undermine international efforts to uphold racial equality as a universal principle in order to preserve a foundational premise of Australian sovereignty – the right to defer to race in order to determine who could come into the country. To concede the principle of racial equality was to concede that the Commonwealth government could not exercise racial discrimination in determining who could and could not enter Australia. Racial equality was a utopian ideal and the terms of the peace agreement, Hughes declared, 'must deal with the world and human nature as they are, and not as they would have them be'.[37] For the Australian prime minister, racial equality was idealist bunk.

In the spring of 1919 the Japanese delegation put forward a proposal to insert a racial equality clause into the preamble of the Covenant to the League of Nations.[38] President Wilson was sympathetic, Lloyd George prevaricated, but the Australian prime minister was forthright in his opposition. Any statement asserting the principle of the equality of races would have placed in jeopardy the vision of White Australia for which Australia's young men were said to have fought and died on the battlefields of Europe. The Japanese delegation reported to the Japanese foreign ministry that 'The fate of our proposal lies in the hands of one man, the Australian Prime Minister'.[39] In the end the Australian delegation garnered sufficient support at the conference to reduce the vote in favour of inserting a racial equality clause into the preamble to a simple majority. That was enough to scuttle it.

The defeat of the racial equality clause was a triumphal demonstration of Australian national sovereignty in the White Australia era. For Japan it was a humiliation. Major EL Piesse, Australia's director of military intelligence, noted at the time that Hughes' attitude caused grave offence in Japan and that memories of this humiliation could have long-term consequences for Australia. Hughes, wrote Piesse,

> *has chosen to emphasise the national distinctions between the Japanese and ourselves in a way that could not fail to be offensive to a high spirited people ... their effect in Japan has been most serious.*[40]

It has certainly had a long-term effect on Australia's reputation in Japan. William Morris Hughes is all but forgotten in Australia but in Japan his exploits in Paris continue to be retold, again and again, in popular and textbook histories of Japanese nationalism and Australian racism. The Little Digger, as Hughes was known, is considered the quintessential Australian – rude, ignorant of world affairs, narrow-minded and deaf to the demands of international good citizenship.[41]

The ramifications in China were equally grave. The American delegation came up with a face-saving gesture to compensate the Japanese delegation for Hughes' defeat of the racial equality clause. According to Brawley, the Americans made a secret concession to the Japanese delegation in the closing days of the convention – to concede Japan's request to take control of German possessions in China. By trading Chinese territory for the principle of racial equality, Brawley writes, 'Wilson had to give Japan "what they should not have" because he could not give them what they *should* have' [author's emphasis], an international commitment to the principle of the equality of races.[42] When Wilson could not deliver on racial equality he promised to deliver part of China to Japan instead.

For China's domestic politics this secret agreement was one of the most far-reaching decisions ever taken in an international forum. Now it was the turn of the Chinese people to feel humiliated. China's delegation in Paris, representing the new republican government, protested, to no avail. China's nascent liberal parliamentary movement could not compete with Leninist parties in the wake of the fateful decision sealed at Versailles. Billy Hughes' pragmatic interest in scuttling the racial equality clause at the Paris Conference led to the downfall of the Chinese liberal republic and its replacement by a Leninist party state.

On hearing the news from Paris, students took to the streets of Peking in May 1919 to launch a movement that is still remembered in Chinese communist historiography as the founding moment of the communist revolution – the May Fourth Movement. While protesting the surrender of Chinese territories to Japan, students brandished signs calling for the removal of the democratic government of China and an end to all foreign imperialism. Leading public figures in Shanghai, Canton and Peking emerged to denounce the republican government for failing to defend the country's national sovereignty. Russian agents and representatives of the Communist International moved in among students, teachers, workers and political reformers, setting up networks of radical cells that would introduce a new and more powerful form of government to rid China of Japanese, British, US and other foreign imperialists forever. Within a few years, Sun Yatsen abandoned his commitment to liberal democracy, signed up with the Russians, reorganised his Chinese Nationalist Party into a Leninist party and set up a single-party state in Canton, a precursor to the communist party state. In 1921 the Comintern's small political cells converged to form the Chinese Communist Party. As a party of the working class the communist movement was of little consequence. Once it learnt to harness mass discontent over racism, foreign humiliation and colonial infringements on China's territory, the communist movement grew to become the most powerful political organisation in the country.

It would be drawing a long bow to attribute the birth of Red China to the words and actions of an Australian prime minister in Paris. Still, we can place White Australian intervention at the peace conference into a clear causal sequence stretching from Paris to Tokyo and across the Sea of Japan to Peking, even if these international outcomes were only partly of White Australia's making. Australia was just one of several sites of anti-Chinese racism on the Pacific Rim, but only the Australian government adopted a principled and patriotic position openly hostile to the ideal of racial equality. Publicly enunciated as White Australia, Australia's unique brand of patriotic racism was a source of constant humiliation to people in China and to people of Chinese descent in Southeast Asia, the Americas and in Australia itself. So it remains to this day. Humiliation is a powerful instrument of nationalist politics. Mao Zedong used it well to secure victory in 1949 and to win international acceptance among Chinese communities the world over for decades to come.

National values and racism

Australian values were not necessarily diminished by the Australian prime minister's artful defence of racism after the Great War any more than the Australian flag is diminished in the 21st century when it is draped over the shoulders of a White Australian bigot. Broadly speaking, the country's values and symbols are big enough for everyone. Mateship, equality and the fair go were sufficiently universal to appeal to Chinese Australians in the colonial and federation eras and they have proven sufficiently flexible to make provision for the abolition of race-based criteria for immigration in the post-Second World War era. Beginning in the 1960s, mateship, equality and the fair go were recast as the ethical foundations for a new ethic of social acceptance and cultural tolerance within an evolving multicultural Australia.[43] By the turn of the 21st century, Chinese Australians were serving in the same representative forums that had once legislated against them – as mayors of major capital cities, elected members of state legislatures and representatives and senators in the Australian federal parliament.

In light of these achievements it is timely to call into question crude assumptions about innate Chinese values that are no more tenable in the 21st century than they were 150 years ago. Back then, most of the claims mounted in defence of the proposition that there was a fundamental clash of cultures between Chinese and white Australians conflated self-evident differences in material culture (physical appearance, dress, customs, food, rituals and the like) with implied differences in ethics and values (servility, oriental despotism) while showing little regard for the causal nexus between material culture and ethical values.

What is this nexus and how does it work? Whatever the majority white community in Australia happened to make of the language, appearance or customs of the men from China who chose to settle among them, there was little that they would have seen in their language or behaviour that would have told them that Chinese were conditioned to slavery, venality, mendacity or dependence by a cultural preference for oriental despotism. This had to be learnt from experts with a smattering of knowledge about the 'real' and 'unchanging' China whose judgments overrode the claims of local Chinese Australians that they, like other Australians, were struggling in their own way to free themselves from the status hierarchies of their old society and be counted equal members of a new world in colonial and federation Australia. Australian racism had to take lessons from Anglophone ethnography of China – from the venerable tradition of expert writing about Chinese customs and values that situates China in a unique cultural space outside of history and beyond the pale of universal human values – before it could target the armoury of Australian values on 'the Chinese Question'.

Drawing on the traditions of Anglophone sinology, Keith Windschuttle and other historians before him, including Myra Willard and Charles Price, have consistently argued that ethnic discrimination of the kind practised in White Australia was not racist because it was based not on racial criteria, but on reasoned judgments about the principles and values that distinguish Chinese from others. Their judgments have been largely based on two prior assumptions, one about the incompatibility of Chinese and Australia values, the other about racism itself.

On the first point there is little historical foundation outside the flawed archive of sinological ethnography for Keith Windschuttle's claim that Australia hosted two incompatible immigrant cultures in the 19th century, one a British community 'freeing itself from the hereditary status and privilege of Old Europe', the other a Chinese community 'steeped in the servility of oriental despotism'.[44] As we have seen, the ethnography of White Australia is fundamentally flawed in picturing Chinese settlers as servile, hierarchical and averse to democracy. On the second point, Windschuttle's definition of racism is equally suspect. In this case nothing short of a principled commitment to racial supremacism grounded in biological determinism counts as racist. Even the most virulent forms of anti-Semitism associated with the fabrication and misuse of *The Protocols of the Elders of Zion* would not count as racist on this criterion, since *The Protocols* make no reference to biological determinism.[45]

In some countries discrimination of the kind practised in White Australia would be considered racist; the 'White' in White Australia suggests as much. It certainly seemed racist to Chinese Australians. At the end of the day, however, few Chinese Australians cared greatly whether the discrimination exercised in favour of whites and against people of colour was driven by racism, culturalism or ignorance: they were chiefly concerned to receive due recognition of their equal entitlements to reside, work, own property, do business, travel and enjoy the comforts of family life as residents of Australia and equal subjects of the Crown. Taking its cues from Chinese Australians, this study has focused on their struggle for equal recognition in each of these spheres, rather than on the racist character or intent of the White Australia Policy.

In concluding, however, the problem of racism cannot be ignored. Windschuttle does his readers a service by drawing attention to the long-standing reluctance of many people in Australia to concede that the 'White' in White Australia actually meant what it said – that Australia was a nation of and for whites. Simply eliding the word 'white' from White Australia has done little to redress long-standing problems of denial regarding the racial character of Australia's immigration and citizenship legislation in the White Australia era. In this sense Windschuttle inadvertently draws attention to the more daunting prospect that if the 'white' in White Australia is not racist then the 'Australia' possibly is. Take away the 'white' and Australia is still defined by a distinctive suite of national values that are regarded as the unique preserve of Australians rather than by a common set of universal human values.

In fact, there is little to distinguish Australian values from universal human ones apart from the idiomatic insistence that they are peculiarly Australian. *Liberté, egalité* and *fraternité* are translated into Australian dialect as freedom, egalitarianism and mateship. In the act of translation, the association of Australian values with a particular Anglo-Saxon heritage, rather than with the universal heritage of humankind, limits their application to people of Anglo-Saxon descent and to those instructed by Anglo-Saxons to appreciate that the values that made White Australia 'Australia' rather than merely 'white' are to be valued as uniquely Australian values.

This need not be so. The Australian historical record is sufficiently rich and varied to allow for the possibility that Australian values may be recast as universal human values without abandoning the Australian idiom that frames them. Much turns on how values are defined and on the terms invoked to describe them. When a prime minister defines Australian national values as 'respect for the rule of law, democracy and the institutions of state' it is difficult to imagine who could possibly be excluded apart from criminals, dictators and lunatics.[46] When national values are defined more finely to include respect for Anglo-Saxon traditions and local cultural icons, then the net is cast closer to the shores of White Australia. In April 2006, for example, Federal Parliamentary

Secretary for Immigration and Multicultural Affairs Andrew Robb suggested that intending citizens should be tested for their familiarity with Australian values and customs before they could be admitted as Australian citizens. He commended the Melbourne Cup as an event that aspiring citizens should be expected to know before they could qualify to call themselves Australian.[47]

If White-Australian experience is any guide, testing for knowledge of the Melbourne Cup is likely to tax the ingenuity of immigration officials. A frayed SP bookmaker's ledger held in the Launceston Museum, dating from the White Australia era, lists Melbourne Cup odds in Chinese figures alongside the names of punters in Chinese characters. At a time when Australian national values were being crafted as cultural antibodies to the alleged hierarchy, slavery and cruelty of John Chinaman, John was taking bets on the Cup. Had he known that betting on the Cup would improve his chances of inviting his wife and children to join him in Australia he might have kept a double ledger in English. But of course he was not to know. The genius of defining a nation by reference to a particular code of national values, rather than by universal human values, is that those who do the defining can amend the code at any time to appeal to popular prejudices about those whom they wish to exclude.

NOTES

PREFACE

1 Cf. Paul to the Galatians 3: 28 and the Remonstrance by Cheok Hong Cheong et al. protesting anti-Chinese sentiments of the 1888 Inter-Colonial Conference: 'We protest in the sight of Heaven that this is a crime, not as committed against us only, but against the great Creator of all "who made of one blood all nations of men"'; Cheong (1888); Welch (2003); see also chapter 8 below.

2 Stephenson (2005), p. 367; Ganter (2006).

3 *Australian Dictionary of Biography* Online Edition <http://www.adb.online.anu.edu.au/biogs/A140553b.htm>; The company's international ranking in noted on the LJ Hooker company website <http://www2.ljhooker.com.au/content/content_one.php?sect_id=24&cat_id=1>

4 Ganter (2006).

5 Among heritage activists Dr Henry Chan has done more than anyone to draw national attention to Australia's Chinese heritage. Among authors, Eric Rolls has done the same; see Rolls (1992), (1996).

6 When William died in 1904 his own father was entered on the death certificate as Hung-Hock Lew Shing (Lau Hung-Hock, or Liu Hongxue in Mandarin). The name 'Lew Shing' means 'surnamed Lew' (pronounced Lew, Liew, Lau or Liu, depending on local dialect).

7 Rolls (1996), pp.132–33.

8 Button (2006).

9 Patricia Foord tells and illustrates the Lew Shing family story on the Chinese Heritage website at <http://www.chaf.lib.latrobe.edu.au/lewshing.htm>.

1 BELONGING AND EXCLUSION

1 Mason (1924), p. 172.
2 Continuing interest is indicated in debate surrounding the publication of Windschuttle (2004) and Tavan (2005). The White Australia Policy was a policy framework endorsing discrimination in favour of whites through regulation of immigration and ad hoc legislation bearing on industry, commerce and citizenship, and covering all aspects of Indigenous affairs; see Markus (2001).
3 Gyory (1998); Pan (1999), pp. 261–73. The 1882 Act is available online at the US government archival website at <http://www.ourdocuments.gov>.
4 The Immigration Restriction Act of 1901 did not specify which groups were to be excluded. This was to be decided by administrative discretion and executed through assignment of a dictation test. The conditions governing Chinese naturalisation varied from colony to colony before federation. In 1903 the Australian federal government legislated to prohibit Chinese becoming Australian subjects of the Crown under the Commonwealth Nationality Act; see Choi (1975) and Markus (2001), p. 18.
5 Compare Pan (1999) and Markus (2004), pp. 51–58. Adam McKeown argues that statistical foundations for comparisons of in-migration among states such as Canada and Australia are skewed by categories of immigration, and argues for wider uses of statistics drawn from sites of emigration. McKeown (2004), pp. 155–189; see also Sinn (1995), pp. 11–34.
6 Chinese Canadians in British Columbia were disenfranchised in provincial and federal elections from 1875 to 1947. Pan (1999), pp. 234–47.
7 Willard (1923); Yarwood (1964), (1968); Palfreeman, (1967); Choi (1975); Viviani (1992); York (1995).
8 Price (1974); Markus (1979); Cronin (1982).
9 For the earliest national study, see Yong (1977); for the earliest regional social history see May (1984).
10 Cushman (1984), pp. 100–13.
11 Recent social histories include S Fitzgerald (1996); Wilton (1998), (2004); Ryan (1995); Chan, Curthoys and Chiang (2001); for connections linking immigrants' home counties and sites in Australia, see Williams (2001).
12 An exception is Curthoys (2001).
13 See, for exampe, Curthoys and Markus (1978). The exclusion of Chinese voices from Australian history is noted in Shen (2001).
14 Jones (2004), p. 219; on laws and statutes, see Jones (2001), pp. 215–21.
15 Price (1974), pp. 269–70. The first major study to abandon the clash of cultures thesis appeared five years after the publication of Price (1974); see Markus (1979).
16 Markus (2001), pp. 4–5; on culturalism as a new form of racism, see Barker (1981).
17 For a summary of these accounts, see Price (1974), pp. 104, 116–17.
18 Windschuttle (2004), pp. 174–81.
19 ibid. (2004), p. 178.
20 Rolls notes that Chinese employed by furniture manufacturers generally earned more than Europeans employed in the same industry, Rolls (1996), pp. 114–15.
21 Macintyre (1999), p. 103.
22 See Rowe (1989); Elvin (1974); Perdue (1987); Will (1990); J Fitzgerald (1996).

23   Schama (2005), pp. 19–25.
24   Charles Harpur (1845), cited in Alan Atkinson (1997), p. 194.
25   Berlin (1961), (1972).
26   The claim that an historical clash of cultures accounts for the White Australia Policy is indirectly challenged by the avowed white supremacist Andrew Fraser, a latter-day advocate of White Australia, who openly espouses the racist maxim that races are not equal; Fraser (2005).
27   See Price (1974); Markus (1979).
28   Selle (1948); Pearl (1967); Thompson and Macklin (2004).
29   Lo (1976–1978).
30   Tart (1911); Travers (1981); cf. Chinese-language biography of Arthur Lock-Chang by Huang (1999).
31   S Wang (2001), p. 197.
32   The registered population possibly disguised replacement immigration as Chinese returning to China were permitted to nominate substitutes. Markus (2004).
      The failure of US exclusion laws to achieve their stated purpose is explored in McKeown (2003).
33   Jones (2001), p. 217.
34   Jones (2005b), pp. 56–57.
35   Australian Bureau of Statistics (1925).
36   Jones (2005b), pp. 56–57.
37   On women and wives, see Sophie Couchman (2004b), Rule (2000), (2002), (2004); Bagnall (2004a), (2004b); Chou (1995).
38   Ah Ket (1999).
39   Thompson and Macklin (2004), p. 330.
40   Mo and Mo (1991).
41   Hwuy-Ung (1927).
42   Pelissier (1963), (1967).
43   Pelissier (1967), pp. 44–45.
44   ibid, p. 212.
45   Huck (1960).
46   Couchman (2004d); Hess (2004).
47   Goldsmith (1762).
48   Dickinson (1903).
49   Bryan (1906).
50   J Fitzgerald (1996), chapter 3.
51   Shen (1982).
52   Tim Flannery, for example, includes excerpts from the fabricated Hwuy Ung text in his book, *The Birth of Melbourne*, Flannery (2002). I wish to thank Sophie Couchman for drawing this to my attention.
53   Commission (1855), p. 14.
54   Lai (2004).
55   See chapter 2.

2 MATESHIP AND MODERNITY

1   Cited in JD Fitzgerald (1914), p. 2.
2   A full inventory of Australian values would probably include egalitarianism, mateship, fair play, rule of law (and disrespect for law), individualism, freedom,

common sense and pragmatism; see National Multicultural Advisory Council (1999), p. 101. These values are generally abbreviated to freedom, egalitarianism, mateship and fair play. Curiously, the value placed on leisure is rarely listed.

3 Price (1974), p. 106
4 Clark (2006), p. 111.
5 Secretary (1908), reprinted in Jones (2005a), p. 106; Bellamy (1888).
6 The US Chinese Exclusion Act of 1882 expressly forbad the entry of 'Chinese persons' without certification into the United States. The harshness of certification procedures gave the impression it was directed against Chinese as a race when it was designed to exclude Chinese labourers while making exceptions for merchant traders. A clause in the Act prohibiting courts in the United Sates from granting citizenship to Chinese of any description confirmed this impression. The Act was made permanent in 1902 and not repealed until the outbreak of the Pacific War; see US government archival website at <http://www.ourdocuments.gov>, 31 October 2006.
7 Couchman (2006), (2004d).
8 Lea-Scarlett (1974).
9 Couchman (2006).
10 Cited in Mark Williams (2005), p. 32
11 Molony (2000); Ward (1958).
12 Bean (1933); Ward (1958); Beaumont (1995).
13 On mateship, see Democrat Senator Aden Ridgeway (*7:30 Report*, 11 August 1999, ABC TV at <http://www.abc.net.au/7.30/stories/s43232.htm>), Labor MP Gareth Evans (speech to the House of Representatives, 24 March 1999, *Hansard*, pp. 3582–584) and historian Marilyn Lake (*Sydney Morning Herald*, 24 March 1999). On the tension between egalitarianism and excellence, see the Draft Preamble crafted by poet Les Murray: 'We value excellence as well as fairness', but the ideal of equal dignity should never be 'invoked against achievement' (Draft Preamble, 23 March 1999, Office of the Prime Minister of Australia John Howard, Preamble to the Constitution at <http://www.pm.gov.au>, 31 October 2006).
14 Brett (2005).
15 Taylor (2004a); Camilleri (1998).
16 Taylor (2004a).
17 —— (2004b).
18 Alan Atkinson (1997), p. 90.
19 ibid., p. 80.
20 C Harpur, 1845, cited in ibid., p. 194.
21 Markus (1979).
22 Macintyre (1999), p. 103.
23 Calhoun (1997), (1994), pp. 9–37, 304–36; Taylor (2004a).
24 Markus (1979); Price (1974).
25 See, for example, Price (1974), pp. 69, 105–06.
26 Liang (1903); cf. Sun Yatsen's brand of nationalism, J Fitzgerald (1996).
27 On European sources of these ideals see 'Introduction' in Taylor (1975) and Callinicos (2000).
28 Berlin (1961), (1972).
29 Sakai (2006).
30 J Fitzgerald (2006a), (2006c).

31   Price (1974); Markus (1979); Goodman (1994).
32   Markus (1979). References to race and bloodlines surfaced in public policy in the White Australia era: 'The extent to which Chinese blood has been mixed with the white race is shown by the figures for half-castes in the preceding tables.' Australian Bureau of Statistics (1925).
33   Markus (1979), pp. 236–41. On mooted links between race, servile labour and the emancipation narrative in the Americas, see Jung (2006).
34   Markus (1979), pp. 257–59; Macintyre (1999), p. 103. On exchanges between Australian and US prophets of racial doom and triumphalism, see Walker (1999) and Lake (2003).
35   Cited in Markus (1979), p. 40.
36   ibid., pp. 40–41. Chinese settlers in the US were emboldened by federal laws and treaties to challenge discriminatory legislation in the US federal courts in the late 19th century. Price (1974), p. 273; McClain (1994).
37   Markus (1979), pp. 35–43
38   Goodman (1994).
39   Willard (1923), pp. 20, 24–25.
40   Markus (1979), p. 28; Price (1974), pp. 68–69.
41   Willard (1923), pp. 29, 41–42.
42   Adam McKeown, personal communication, 3 July 2006.
43   Barker (1998), p. 13.
44   Bate (1978), p. 150.
45   *Fiji Times*, 9 August 1879, cited in Ng Kumlin Ali (2002), pp. 38–39.
46   McKeown (2001), chapter 2.
47   Markus (1979).
48   *Tung Wah Times (Donghua shibao)* 8 October 1898, 15 April 1899, 7 June 1899, 19 July 1899, 22 November 1899, 3 January 1900, 20 June 1900, 18 September 1901, 9 and 19 October 1901, 16 November 1901.
49   Price (1974), pp. 79, 100–01. Another observer noted that Chinese settlers in Sarawak had not initiated the violence. Morrell (1940), p. 260, cited in ibid., p. 101
50   Heidhues (2003), p. 32.
51   ibid., p. 31. Immigrants to Australia and California were sourced from southern Guangdong, while those who immigrated to west Kalimantan were largely Hakka people from northern Guangdong.
52   Cooke and Li (2004).
53   Trocki (2005), p. 149.
54   ibid., pp. 151–53.
55   ibid., pp. 163–64.
56   Hu-Dehart (2005). p. 173.
57   For indentured labour in New South Wales, see Darnell (2004); for Western Australia, see Anne Atkinson (1988).
58   Trocki (2005), pp. 159 ff.
59   This pattern continued into 20th century China; Faure (2006), p. 18.
60   Heidhues (2003), pp. 32, 54–55, 60.
61   ibid., pp. 85–97.
62   ibid., pp. 58–59, 62.
63   G Wang (1992a), (1996), (2000).
64   Wang (2000); Philip Kuhn, personal communication, 17 November 2006.

65 McKeown (2001), pp. 35–40, 43.

66 Richards (1992), pp. 64–104, citing King (1978).

67 Thus the 1892 *Australian National Dictionary*: 'All good Australians hope to go to England when they die'; see Inglis (1992), p. 107.

68 O'Farrell (2000), p. 56.

69 ibid., p. 65.

70 idem. This was despite rates of return immigration from North America to Ireland being among the lowest of European source regions, and rates of sustained female migration among the highest; McKeown 2004b.

71 Richards (1992), pp. 65–66.

72 ibid., pp. 68–75.

73 Cf. Wang's estimate that 'more than half' returned to China between 1852 and 1889. S. Wang (2001), p. 200.

74 Cronin (1982), pp. 124, 135.

75 The rate of return passage through Hong Kong was, on average, higher than the rate of departure from that port from 1861–1939. McKeown's tabulation of return passage to Hong Kong relative to departures for this period shows returning passengers exceeding departing passengers by 29 per cent in any five-year period. The rate of return through other ports (Xiamen, Shantou, Qiongzhou) was consistently lower than departures from those ports as returning passengers preferred to transit through Hong Kong; McKeown (2004a).

76 The definitive encyclopaedia of the Australian population estimates that 'more than 100 000' Chinese arrived in the 19th century; S Wang (2001), p. 197. Chen Zexian's detailed estimates of international labour migration from China to foreign destinations list 72 000 migrant labourers departing for Australia in the 19th century. Merchants and other categories of migrants were possibly excluded from this calculation; see Z Chen (1963) and S Wang (1978), pp. 313–14.

77 Huck (1968), p. 5.

78 Native-place associations (*tongxianghui or huiguan*) were established by people migrating within China or overseas to provide common sites of worship, enduring social networks and everyday assistance to members. Membership was based on a migrant's place of origin, hence the term.

79 On regional mobility, see May (1984), chapter 1; Trevarthen (2006). Stuart Macintyre notes that colonial Australians were generally mobile; Macintyre (1986), p. 22.

80 Tables 1.3 and 1.6, in Michael Williams (2001), pp. 63–64.

81 Jones (2001), p. 217.

82 May (1984), pp. 8–14. On the legislative restrictions affecting Chinese in Queensland, see ibid., chapter 2 and appendix N.

83 C Lee (2000), pp. 7–8.

84 Chapter 8 below.

85 C Lee (2000), pp. 10–15.

3 IMMIGRANT LABOUR AND GOLDFIELD FRATERNITIES

1 Cited in McLaren (1985), p. 14.

2 The Yee Hing Company (*Yixing gongsi*), also written Gee Hing or Ngee Hing, refers to a secret fraternal organisation that passed under different local titles including *Hongshuntang* (Hung Obedience Hall) in Sydney and Hung Men

(*Hongmen*). On 19th century rebellions see Meadows (1856); Spence (1996); Clark & Gregory (1982). On their 'revival' in the 20th century see Armentrout (1976).

3 Y Wu (1996), pp. 322–23. The name Wong Tock Gee (*Huang Dezhi*) is inscribed on a tablet commemorating donors to the See Yap Temple in South Melbourne in the 1860s. Sophie Couchman alerted me to mention of Tock Gee in the Alfred Grieg Papers of the Royal Historical Society of Victoria. Wu suggests Tock built the Chee Kong Tong (*Zhigongtang* or Chinese Masonic) Temple extant in Bendigo.

4 Yong (1977) pp. 157–8.

5 Sleeman (1933).

6 Yong (1977), p. 158.

7 Commission (1855); Cai (2004); Kok (2003), (2005), (1996–2005); Noonan (2006).

8 Chow (1933e).

9 ibid., p. 426.

10 Chow claimed General Ho Long 'was born in South Australia and had served in the Great War, having been present at the Gallipoli evacuation'. *Sydney Morning Herald*, 6 March 1935. The Chinese consul-general in Australia refuted the claim. Longfield Lloyd, Inspector Investigation Branch, to the Director, Commonwealth Investigation Branch, 7 March 1935, National Archives of Australia, Series C32091 Item CIB 676.

11 Chow (1933e). Wai Lee was a prominent businessman and Chinese Mason in South Australia; Kai Koon was naturalised in Grafton in 1858. Among wealthy merchants Chow lists Tam Chuen (*Huang Zhu*, see chapter 4) and Quong Tart.

12 McKeown estimates 7 million Chinese émigrés on the basis of published reports and Hong Kong exit figures; McKeown (2004a). Lynn Pan estimates 2 million over the second half of the 19th century; Pan (1999), pp. 60–63. Australian figures are derived from S Wang (2001), p. 197.

13 T Li (2006); Cooke and Li (2004).

14 S Wang (1978).

15 Markus (1998).

16 Kuo Mei-fen brought this novella to my attention. Richards (1992), p. 69. For California, see Campbell (1923), pp. 33–34; S Wang, (1978), p. 109. A contemporary estimate found that 'the great majority' travelled to California and Australia at the expense of relatives and friends already settled in those territories. S Wang, ibid., p. 114.

17 Cited in Huck (1968), pp. 3–4.

18 S Wang (1978), pp. 91, 113; Just (1859), cited in ibid., p. 114. *Report of the Select Committee* (1856–57).

19 Cited in Huck (1968), pp. 3–4.

20 S Wang (1978), pp. 109–11.

21 ibid., p. 117; on Lowe Kung Meng, see Dundas (1877).

22 S Fitzgerald (1996), pp. 54–60. Way Kee visited Launceston in 1882. Rolls (1992) pp. 226, 259.

23 —— (1996), pp. 54–60.

24 Similarly, the Nomchongs of Braidwood apparently derived their name from the family's Nomchong (*Nanchang*) firm; see also Houng Lee in Fiji, chapter 7. For Way Lee, see Petition (1891).

25 Price (1974), p. 59; Lea-Scarlett (1974).

26 Cited in S Wang (1978), pp. 99, 101–02. Colonial government reports in

Australia were occasionally less sanguine; idem.

27 For Long's Chinese characters, see Liu and Tian (1958), p. 131.

28 VY Chow (1933h), (1933g), (1933e).

29 On rascals and Chinese, see Bramble (2000), pp. 19–23.

30 *Sydney Morning Herald*, 7 August 1874.

31 JD Fitzgerald (1918), pp. 137–42. John D. Fitzgerald (1862–1922) grew up in Bathurst and worked for the *Sydney Evening News* before travelling to Britain and Europe in 1890–91 on behalf of the Trades and Labour Council. On returning to Sydney he was called to the Bar in 1900, edited the lay Catholic *Freeman's Journal* from 1899–1904 and served as a Sydney City Council alderman from 1900–04. In 1916 he was expelled from the Labor Party for supporting conscription. His publications include two novels, *The Ring Valley* (1922) and *Children of the Sunlight: Stories of Australian Circus Life* (1923), and three non-fiction books, *Greater Sydney and Greater Newcastle* (1906), *Studies in Australian Crime* (1924) and the first book on Australian Labor history, *The Rise of the Australian Labor Party* (1914).

32 Fitzgerald was born in 1862 and by 1886, Chow's implausible date for Loong's death, he was not a boy but a man of 26.

33 Fitzgerald (1918); Chow (1933e); *Daily Examiner*, 4 November 1932, cited in *United China* 1.11 (October 1933), p. 450.

34 NSW Registry of Births Deaths and Marriages, Deaths Index 3805/1874.

35 Loong Hung Pung's father and Vivian Chow may have borne the same surname Chow (*Zhou*). Informant Sam Yung may also have been related to the Chow, family which was registered in Australia under the name of Yung.

36 See chapter 4.

37 On Yee Hing symbols and animalia in Australia, see Kok (1996–2005).

38 Chow (1933f); Sleeman, (1933), pp. 138–40; Schiffrin (1970).

39 —— (1933f) p. 440; Chow Toong Yung was known variously in English as Frederick Foon Yung (Birth Certificate for daughter Isadore, NSW Registry of Births, Deaths and Marriages, Births, Reg. No. 23406/1904), Frederick T. Yung (Birth Certificate for daughter Lavinia, NSW Registry of Births, Deaths and Marriages, Births, Reg. No. 13138/1898), Toon Yung (Birth Certificate for son Luther, NSW Registry of Births, Deaths and Marriages, Births, Reg. No. 4354/1895) and in Mandarin as *Zhou Tongyang*; Liu and Tian (1958), p. 131. Chow wrote that his father hailed 'from the same village near Canton' as GT Quoy (Yip Ting Quoy or *Ye Tonggui*). The Yip family came from Chin Mei (*Cunmou*) village in Doong Goong. Compare Chow (1933f), p. 439 and S Fitzgerald (1996), p. 170; see also the *Daily Examiner*, Grafton, 2 November 1932, reprinted in *United China*, vol. 1, no. 11, p. 449; NSW Registry of Births, Deaths and Marriages, Reg. No. 3090/1894; NSW Registry of Births, Deaths and Marriages, Marriages, Reg. No. 2982/1877; NSW Registry of Births, Deaths and Marriages, Deaths, Reg. No. 8201/1943; Liu and Tian (1958), p. 1.

40 *Daily Examiner*, Grafton, 4 November 1932, reprinted in *United China* 1.11 (October 1933), p. 451; Chow (1933e). On his certificate of naturalisation, Kai Koon stated that he had arrived in New South Wales in 1851 and that he was 36 years of age at the time of his naturalisation. Phillip Bramble gave me a copy of Kai Koon's Certificate of Naturalisation dated 16 November 1857.

41 *Richmond River Free Press*, 22 September 1922, Yung (n.d.).

42 In 1932 Luther married Alice Ying-ding, a Ningbo native educated in Shanghai. They had two daughters, Jessie and Margaret. Under the Japanese occupation

Luther was detained as a British national and spent the war in detention. Alice and the girls remained free as Chinese nationals. Luther resumed work at the end of the war but his family returned to Sydney to escape the communists. Jessie and Margaret were attending the University of Sydney when Luther returned in 1954. He was active in the Australia–China Friendship Society; Yung (n.d.); Chow (1933f), p. 436; *Daily Examiner*, Grafton, 2 November 1932, reprinted in *United China* 1.11 (October 1933), p. 449. Vivian wrote in English under the names of Vivian Chow, VY Chow and Vivian Yung, and in Chinese as *Zhou Chenggui*.

43   Wasserstein (1998), p. 178.

44   ibid., pp. 179–80.

45   *United China* appeared monthly from December 1931 to May 1933, when it lapsed for five months. On resuming publication it appeared quarterly from October 1933. The masthead carries the Chinese title *Tuanjie zazhi*; *United China*, vol. 1, no. 2 (January 1932).

46   Chow (1933c).

47   ibid. (1933e).

4 REVOLUTION, RESPECTABILITY AND CHINESE MASONRY

1   Cited in Chow (1933f), p. 443.

2   Royal Commission (1891–92); S Fitzgerald (1996), pp. 70–74; Yong (1977), p. 15. In Queensland the Cairns lodge of the Yee Hing became a 'respectable' public organisation in 1911 and the Atherton lodge built a new public headquarters in the same year; May (1984), pp. 66–68.

3   McCalman (1985), p. 22.

4   Grand Master of the Chinese Masonic Lodge (1933). The title '19½', chosen out of respect for Loong Hung Pung, relates to the numerical hierarchies of Yee Hing leadership in which grand masters of provincial lodges were ranked 21. By implication, succeeding leaders declined to rank themselves at or above 20 out of respect for Loong; see Booth (1999), p. 220.

5   Chow (1933h), p. 427.

6   Sun (1943).

7   Chow (1933b); Chow (1933f), p. 436.

8   James See notes that he had three sisters and two younger brothers. Four are recorded in the Births registry of the NSW Registry of Births Deaths and Marriages under the surname See or Ah See:

    1438/1870 Sydney   See, Ah Father Ah, Mother Sam

    1366/1872 Sydney   See, Tan Hi Father Ah See, Mother Sam Que

    12109/1876 Grafton   Ah See, Thomas Father Ah See, Mother Sam

    13251/1878 Grafton   Ah See, Samuel Father Ah, Mother Sam.

The first listed was also known as Sarah; the second was Tse Tsan Tai himself, also known as James Ah See; the third was known in Chinese as Tse Tsi-shau (*Xie Zixiu*). Tse (1924), pp. 6, 7, 24; Chow (1933b); Chow (1933f), p. 444.

9   Chow (1933f), pp. 443, 450; Chow (1933d); Tse (1924).

10   —— (1933b); Tse (1924), p. 7.

11   —— (1933g), p. 462. An 1891 photograph features James See and Yeung Ku-wan seated in the middle of ten young men; Chow (1933e), p. 425.

12   Tse (1924), pp. 19–20; Noonan (2006).

13   Tse (1924), pp. 16, 18.

14 *United China* 1.10 (May 1933), p. 402. Jocelyn Chey alerted me to the connection between Shanghai Man Ning and Hong Kong Mannings.

15 Buck (1937).

16 *Bendigo Advertiser*, 17 April, 10 August 1896.

17 *Aozhou zhigong zongtang yibai wushinian jinian tekan* (2004), p. 1.

18 The official history of the Sydney lodge supports Yong's leadership sequence but not his dates. It reads John Moy Sing (1854–98), James Chuey (1898–1930), Yu Bin (1930–57), Guo Zilin (1957–60), Lau Ting (1960–93), Stephen Huang (1993–). *Aozhou zhigong zongtang yibai wushinian jinian tekan* (2004) pp. 26–27; *Hongshantang* referred to the Guangdong Lodge of the Hung League as distinct from the Fujian *Qingliangtang* (Green Lotus Hall) Lodge and other provincial lodges; see Lim (1999). The term *Hongshantang* appeared in newspaper publicity in the 1910s; see *Minguo bao* (Chinese Republic News), 12 November 1916. The term *Zhigongtang* (Zhigong Lodge) derives from the four-character epithet *zhi li wei gong* ('exert strength for public benefit') and means 'Exerting Public Benefit Lodge'. The term initially referred to a particular lodge in Victoria (Canada) and San Francisco but was extended to embrace the North American network after that lodge came to exercise loose hegemony over others in North America. By the early 20th century this hegemony extended to Australasia. Armentrout Ma (1990), pp. 24–22; Yong (1977), p. 160.

19 Yong (1977), pp. 161–62; Trocki (1993), pp. 89–119.

20 Chapter 3 above; see also J Fitzgerald (2005).

21 Armentrout Ma (1990), pp. 28–29. In British Columbia the earliest recorded Chee Kong Tong lodge was founded in Barkerville in 1862, and in other goldfield settlements in 1876 and 1882. Lyman et al. (1964), p. 531. Rural sites in New South Wales for which we have evidence of lodges include Bathurst (site of the Loong Hung Pung legend), Albury and Tingha; Wilton (2004).

22 Schlegel (1973) p. ix; Ward and Stirling (1925), vol. 1, p. i.

23 Yong indicates networking among Chinese Masons and Freemasons without providing details; Yong (1977), p. 160.

24 At the time Quong Tart joined the lodge it was registered as number 1552 under the English Constitution. After the consolidation of 1888 it became Lodge 42 under the Australian Constitution; Cumming (1995), p. 6.

25 The first recorded Freemason of Chinese descent was Teh Boen Keh, initiated in Surabaya (Java) in 1857, the second, Tsung Lai Shun, initiated into the Hampden lodge in Massachusetts in 1873; Cumming (1995). For the funeral cortege, see *Guangyi huabao (Chinese Australian Herald)*, 8 August 1903. Wai Lee was admitted to the United Tradesman's Lodge No. 4 in Adelaide, Sun Johnson entered Lodge Southern Cross no. 91 on 14 August 1892 and William Lee joined a Freemason's lodge in 1903. I wish to thank Patricia Jamieson, Kevin Wong-Hoy and Kuo Mei-fen for assistance on these points; cf. Yong (1977), p. 160.

26 Petition (1891).

27 *Jubilee History of Lodge Wentworth 1881–1931* (n.d.), p. 29. This source neglects to explain the withdrawal; see *The First 90 Years of Lodge Wentworth* (n.d.).

28 The grand master who presided over his initiation was Mr G Gabriel; Nickless (1961).

29 *Guangyi huaboa*, 13 January 1896; *Tung Wah Times* 31 July 1901.

30 Fitzgerald (1918). The Chinese Masonic network was an exception to the rule of particularistic ties; Armentrout Ma (1990) and Y Chen (2000).

31   Adam McKeown drew my attention to the phrase *zhonghuaguo* in documents
produced in Peru some years earlier noted in H Chen (1980), vol. 1, part 3,
p. 965. Delegates of the Qing state recognised the term *zhonghua* (without *guo*)
for Chinese community organisations in San Francisco; Armentrout Ma (1990),
p. 72. The Bendigo banner reads *Zhonghuaguo* (Chinese state, or China). The
naming of China remains a matter of curiosity. In an earlier study I quoted Liang
Qichao from 1900 as saying that the word '"China" (*zhongguo*)... is what people
of others races call us. It is not a name people of this country have selected for
ourselves'. Qu Weiguo pointed out to me that in abbreviating Liang's statement
I misrepresented it. In the section elided from my text, Liang was referring not
to the term *zhongguo* but to other terms used by foreigners, such as 'China'. My
point still holds. Liang was arguing that his country had never been named by
the Chinese. In the same paragraph Liang wrote: 'Hundreds of millions of people
have maintained this country in the world for several thousand years and yet to
this day they have not got a name for their country.' See J Fitzgerald (1996),
p. 117; Liang (1960), p. 15; and private communication from Professor Qu
Weiguo of Fudan University, July 2006.
32   Vivian (1985), vol. 1, plates 5, 24.
33   Chow (1933h), p. 430.

5 CHINESE AUSTRALIA AT FEDERATION

1   Liang (1928a).
2   Chang (1987), pp. 29–30, 46–48.
3   Reynolds (1993); Karl and Zarrow (2002).
4   *Sydney Morning Herald*, 29 May 1880, reprinted in Yarwood (1968), p. 90.
5   *Qingyibao* (1900).
6   L Chen (1999), p. 155. Sun Yatsen's book collection in the Shanghai French
Concession included Wise (1913) and Morrison (1895).
7   Quartly (1999), pp. 221 ff.
8   See *Tung Wah News*, 2 January, 24 May, 7 and 24 June, 1 July, 5, 23 and 26 August,
20 and 23 September and 22 November 1899.
9   ——, 20 September 1899.
10   ——, 3 May 1899 and 6 September 1899.
11   ——, 5, 9, 12 and 16 January 1901.
12   The following extracts are drawn from Zhongguo liguo (1912).
13   Vattel (1883), Preliminaries, clause 18; see also J Fitzgerald (2006c).
14   Cf. Hobsbawm (1985) and J Fitzgerald (1986); on nationalism and status
inequality, see Calhoun (1997).
15   Hevia (1995).
16   J Fitzgerald (2004a).
17   Dikotter (1992).
18   Cannadine (2002).
19   Crossley (1999), p. 343.
20   Lowe et al. (1879), p. 28.
21   The editorial on the commissioners' visit began by citing Marquis Tseng's article;
Argus, 30 May 1887.
22   Tseng (1887); it first appeared in *Asiatic Quarterly Review* in January 1887 and was
republished in *London and China News* before appearing in *Chinese Recorder* in April;

see also Hummel (1943), pp. 746–47; *New York Times*, 18 February 1887.

23 Marquis Tseng was 'so well known' in England that his father, China's leading statesman Tseng Kuo-fan (*Zeng Guofan*), was identified as the 'father of the Marquis Tseng'; Weale (1905), p. 64.

24 Chinese Imperial Commissioners (1887).

25 To the Honourable (1888).

26 The report of the commissioners was taken seriously in Peking. When the Australian colonies united to erect a continental barrier to the entry of Chinese in the late 1880s the Qing court approached the British government to intervene. Liu Ruifen, Qing minister in London, lodged a protest based on the report of Chinese commissioners about conditions affecting Chinese in Australia; Andrews (1985), pp. 24 ff.

27 Gyory (1998), pp. 212–16.

28 Tongwen (1889).

29 Report to Zongli Yamen (1889).

30 Correspondence (1889).

31 Lowe et al. (1879), pp. 9, 20, 23.

32 Letter to *Sydney Morning Herald* (5 May 1888), cited in Russell and Chubb (1998), p. 95; emphasis added.

33 *Sydney Morning Herald*, 29 May 1880, cited in Yarwood (1968), p. 90.

34 Gongfa xuehui xu (n.d.); Li and Li (1999).

35 Shan hua pi jia you (n.d.); emphasis added.

36 H Chang (1987), pp. 29–30, 46–8; Tan (1984), pp. 215–6; Bellamy (1888).

37 Liang (1960c). This publication was foreshadowed in *Tung Wah News*, 13 March 1901.

38 *Tung Wah News*, 16 January 1901; Nichols (1986).

39 Liang's visit to Australia was sandwiched between a failed uprising in Hankow, a thwarted love affair in Hawai'i and plans to expand his political activities in Japan; Davies (1981).

40 J Fitzgerald (1996), chapter 3.

41 *South Australian Register*, 12 November 1900, cited in Davies (1981), p. 108.

42 *Tung Wah News*, 5, 9, 12 and 16 January 1901.

43 ——, 16 January 1901.

44 Translated selections were published in a reader for American (and Australian) students under the title *What is Wrong with the Chinese?*; see D Li (1978), pp. 22–29.

45 Liang (1960c), pp. 16–22.

46 Davison (1978).

47 *Tung Wah News*, 28 January 1899.

48 ——, 29 April 1899.

49 ——, 28 January 1899.

50 ——, 24 November 1999, cited in Davies (1981), p. 113.

51 Liang (1928a)

52 Liang (1903).

6 THE AUSTRALASIAN KUO MIN TANG

1 Chow (1933a), p. 470.

2 Yong (1977), p. 137. The English title, *Chinese Times*, was retained despite changes of Chinese title and editorship and lapses between titles. The Chinese titles

of the successive republican papers that appeared as *Chinese Times* were *Aiguobao* (1902–05), *Jingdong xinbao* (1905–07), *Jingdongbao* (1908–14), *Pingbao* (1917) and *Minbao* (1919–40); Yong (1977), p. 291; Z Chen (1935), pp. 76–77.

3   Yong (1977), pp. 123–24.

4   Z Chen (1935), pp. 34–35; on Sun Yatsen's reorganisations, see J. Fitzgerald (1996), chapter 5.

5   —— (1935), pp. 41–42, 50–51.

6   —— (1935), pp. 134–35.

7   —— (1935), pp. 14–15.

8   In 1931, after the Melbourne party school had closed, the Nationalist government's Melbourne consulate supported a Chinese Coaching School in the KMT building; ibid., pp. 71, 77.

9   Yong (1977), pp. 268–71.

10 The visit of Chan On Yan (*Chen Anren*) was jointly funded by the Australasian network and the Shanghai KMT headquarters; Luo and Huang (1969), vol. 2, p. 828. Before his arrival Chan stood unsuccessfully for election as county magistrate of Sun Yatsen's home county of Heungshan. He returned to China in 1923 to attend the First National Congress of the Nationalist Party in Canton as official representative of the Australasian branch network; see also Z Chen (1935), pp. 20–24.

11 Z Chen (1935), pp. 78–81, 84–85, 91, 95, 123–24.

12 ibid., pp. 16–20.

13 Of Chinese in North America and Hawai'i at the turn of the century, 70–90 per cent were members of the Chee Kong Tong (Masonic) order, Armentrout Ma (1990), p. 24; *Zhongguo guomindang tongxin*, 87 (1 July 1922), pp. 12–13.

14 Y Wu (1996), pp. 213–15; on Chen Jiongming, see L Chen (1999). Liang was himself a member of the Yee Hing; Armentrout Ma (1990), p. 24; *Tung Wah Times*, 13 January 1923.

15 Ramsay (2004), p. 56; *Tung Wah Times*, 22 March 1924.

16 By the 1930s all party cells around Cairns had dispersed; Z Chen (1935), pp. 91–92, 95, 126–29.

17 *Zhongguo guomindang zhoukan*, 12 (16 March 1924), p. 7. Table compiled from *Zhongguo guomindang* (1922).

18 By 1929 party membership in British Malaya and Singapore had grown to over 10000 members, despite the bans; Yong and McKenna (1990), pp. 49–55, 84–97, 243–45.

19 *Zhongguo guomindang zhoukan*, 12 (16 March 1924), p. 7; *Zhengzhi zhoubao*, 6/7 (10 April 1926), pp. 80–82. Declining membership was not confined to the US party network. In March 1923, the Shanghai party centre contacted all overseas branches requesting details of their institutional histories and current membership but very few responded. *Zhongguo guomindang benbu gongbao*, 8 (20 March 1923) pp. 14–15 and 30 (10 November 1923), p. 6.

20 J Fitzgerald (1996), chapters 4 and 5.

21 In 1931 Chen Yaoyuan visited Australia as head of the KMT Overseas Chinese Bureau in the company of Lin Sen, chair of the Nationalist government's Legislative Yuan; Z Chen (1935), pp. 49–50; for Chen Yaoyuan's position in the US party network, see *Zhongguo guomindang benbu gongbao*, 3 (30 January 1923) p. 4; for his hostile attitude to changing policies of the KMT in 1923 and 1924, see Luo and Huang (1969), vol. 2, p. 1049–050; *Zhongguo guomindang zhoukan*, 23 (1

June 1924), pp. 7–8.
22 Party membership exceeded 60 000 in 1926. *Zhengzhi zhoubao*, 6/7 (10 April 1926), pp. 80–82; Zou (1929), vol. 1, p. 360 ff.
23 Jiaolun (n.d.), p. 8.
24 *Guangzhou minguo ribao*, 11 April 1925; Haineiwai (1924–25). The opening donation was made by Liao Zhongkai on 5 August 1925, a fortnight before Liao was assassinated by right-wing opponents in the party, and the last dated 31 July 1926. Seeto Kwan returned to Australia in 1934 but later settled in the United States.
25 Z Chen (1935), p. 56. Seeto Kwan's colleague Chen Renyi, architect of the Canton Australasian Comrades Office, later joined the left-wing Revolutionary Committee of the Kuomintang.
26 ——— (1935), pp. 36–38; on membership, see ibid., p. 38.
27 ibid., pp. 27–33, 38–39; Yong (1977), p. 153; Chow (1933f), p. 439. Samuel Wong's Mandarin name was *Huang Laiwang*.
28 Yong (1977), pp. 30, 105. This episode is covered in chapter 8.
29 Isaacs (1967); Y Li (1966).
30 Z Chen (1935), pp. 40–41. In October 1949, after the KMT was defeated in China, Sam Wong stepped forward as local representative of the KMT Revolutionary Committee to claim the substantial KMT building that he had helped to fund; S Fitzgerald (1996), p. 142.
31 ——— (1935), pp. 41–42.
32 ——— (1935), p. 154.
33 ——— (1935), pp. 70, 76; Yong (1977), pp. 190–91.
34 *Zhongguo guomindang zhoukan*, 17 (20 April 1924), pp. 3 and 18 (27 April 1924), pp. 4–5.
35 Z Chen (1935), pp. 36, 155.
36 ibid., pp. 36, 59.
37 ibid., pp. 40, 155–56. The building cost over Y80 000 for land and construction. The imposing Australasian party headquarters off Broadway in Sydney cost £16 000 in 1921.
38 Peter Yee Wing, Chen Yansheng, Chen Renyi, Huang Pei, Xu Chengrui and Lei Geng were appointed to the committee, and Wu Hongnan, Huang Tongfa, Huang Zhihe, Yu Jin, Chen Cai and Wang Jianhai to an assisting committee; Z Chen (1935), pp. 22, 36, 45, 54–56, 156. The building's address is listed at the back of the same volume.
39 ibid., pp. 157–60.
40 ibid., pp. 55, 157–60.
41 ibid., p. 156.
42 *Guangdong xingzheng zhoukan*, 23 (20 June 1927), pp. 6–7.
43 Z Chen (1935), pp. 50, 155.
44 Chow (1933a).
45 ——— (1933f), p. 443.
46 ibid., p. 439; Yong (1977), p. 101; S Fitzgerald (1996), p. 170.
47 ——— (1933c), p. 456.
48 The four great Australian department stores are discussed in chapter 8.
49 Chow (1933f), pp. 436, 447; *Daily Examiner*, Grafton, 2 November 1932, reprinted in *United China* 1.11 (October 1993), p. 449.
50 This and the following quotations are drawn from Chow (1933f), pp. 434–41.

51   *Sun*, 22 December 1935. I wish to thank Philip Bramble for providing me with a copy of *Chinese Consulate-General* (1935); see also NSW Registry of Births, Deaths and Marriages, Deaths, Reg. No. 6657/1941.
52   Chow (1933c), p. 454.
53   Woollacott (2001); Hammerton (2001); Hammerton and Coleborne (2001), pp. 86–96.

7 THE PACIFIC SHADOW OF WHITE AUSTRALIA

1   S Chow (1933).
2   Jones (1999).
3   Yong and McKenna (1990), pp. 36–38; on Perth in this mercantile operation, see ibid., pp. 91–92, 95.
4   Yong (1977), pp. 48–53 and chapter 8 below.
5   C Guo (1961), pp. 4–5; Guo Le, *Huiyilu* (1949), p. 4; Yong (1977), pp. 48–50; Yong (1965–66). On Melbourne's banana trade, see Couchman (1995), pp. 75–87.
6   Deane (n.d.); Hudson (1978), p. 66; J. Fitzgerald (2004b).
7   Taplin (1988); Jan (1993). Alastair Kennedy brought this material to my attention.
8   An estimated 50 000 Chinese labourers were contracted to build trenches in France in 1917 and an additional 100 000 in 1918. Summerskill (1982); Stevens (1989).
9   May (1984), pp. 38–39; D Wu (1982), pp. 113–15.
10   Chinese growers pioneered and developed the sugar and banana industries in northern Queensland but were forced out by state legislation offering bounties to white growers (for sugar), limiting government assistance to white growers (for bananas), imposing dictation tests for property ownership and leases and, finally, through the Banana Industry Preservation Act of 1921, imposing a dictation test on banana growers. In light of decades of discrimination Cathie May argues that the 1921 Act was largely superfluous. May (1984), chapter 2; cf. Yong (1977), pp. 77–79 and Rolls (1996), p. 439.
11   Rolls (1996), p. 92; Ng Kumlin Ali (2002), p. 118. On reduction of Fiji production after the closure of Australian markets, see Scarr (1984), p. 122.
12   Yen (1998), pp. 61–64.
13   On Sun Yatsen's shares, see J Young (1998), p. 33. In 1922 Wing On loaned Y15 000 to the Shanghai KMT head office; Zhongguo guomindang (1922), pp. 19, 34. The loan was possibly negotiated by Sydney KMT leader George Biew who moved to Shanghai in the 1920s.
14   Z Chen (1935), pp. 27–43, 62–65, 156.
15   Comment from floor, Kuo Min Tang History Workshop, Sydney KMT Headquarters, 15 October 2005.
16   Z Chen (1935), p. 115.
17   ——, pp. 107–08, 134–35. Contrast German New Guinea and the Hawai'ian and Tahitian islands where Chee Kong Tong community halls were in place before the KMT arrived. Armentrout Ma (1990); McKeown (2001). Copies of the *Chinese National News* (*Guomin banyuekan*) are preserved in the National Archives of Fiji. Another branch opened in Tavua; Wilmott (1999), pp. 293–96; Ng Kumlin Ali (2002), p. 69.
18   Chow (1933f), p. 440.

19 Z Chen (1935), p. 107.
20 Ng Kumlin Ali (2002), pp. 14–17, 45; Yong (1977), p. 237, n. 96.
21 —— (2002), pp. 39–40; (2005).
22 Wilmott (1999); Ng Kumlin Ali (2002), p. 215. Figures for Huengshan native mobility are based on the table of applicants for the period August 1930–December 1931 in ibid., pp. 223–29.
23 Scarr (1984), pp. 122–23.
24 Z Chen (1935), pp. 107–08; Wilmott (1999), p. 293. Mandarin titles for each firm are Joong Hing Loong/*Zhongxinglong*, Kwong Tiy/ *Guangtai*, Sang On Tiy/*Shengantai*, Tiy Sang/*Taisheng*, Kwong Sam/*Guangshang*, and Zoing Chong/ *Yingchang*.
25 Ng Kumlin Ali (2002), p. 73, n. 43.
26 ibid., p. 45; Ng Kumlin Ali (2005), p. 80.
27 *Fiji Times*, 9 August 1879, cited in Ng Kumlin Ali (2002), p. 29.
28 Ng Kumlin Ali (2002), pp. 50–52.
29 ——, pp. 65–70.
30 ——, p. 81.
31 Z Chen (1935), p. 115. David Wu dates the establishment of the first KMT branch to 1921; D Wu (1982), p. 117.
32 D Wu (1982), p. 71.
33 ibid., p. 117–22.
34 ibid., pp. 11–13; Z Chen (1935), pp. 115–22. Twenty-seven of 72 new party recruits in 1947–48 were Hakka women from Huiyang County; Enlistment Records (1947–48).
35 ibid., pp. 69–72; C Inglis (1999).
36 Z Chen (1935), pp. 115–22.
37 Cf. D Wu (1982), pp. 18–19, citing European sources, and Z Chen (1935), pp. 114–15, citing Chinese sources; see also Ichikawa (2006).
38 Wilson et al. (1990), pp. 89–90; D Wu (1982), pp. 23–24.
39 Z Chen (1935), pp. 114–15; D. Wu (1982), pp. 25, 69.
40 D Wu (1982), pp. 29ff.
41 A Akun (1924); Wilson et al. (1990), pp. 89–90.
42 Z Chen (1935), pp. 114–15.
43 D Wu (1982), p. 108.
44 idem.
45 Wilson et al. (1990), pp. 91–94.
46 Rankine (1995); Wilson, Moore and Munro, 1990, pp. 91–94.
47 Wilson et al. (1990), pp. 91–94.
48 On Chinese indentured labour in the Pacific, see ibid., pp. 91–94, 100–03; Wilmott (2004).

8 ENTREPRENEURS, CLUBS AND CHRISTIAN VALUES

1 Cited in Yuan (2001), p. 204.
2 On Chinese-Australian business history, see Yong (1965–66), (1977); Yen (1998); W Chan (1998), (1999); Wilton (1998); Cai (2005); C Lee (2000); Z Li (1999); *Zhongshan ren zai aozhou* (1992), pp. 84–90, 198–219; Lian (2005), pp. 127–73.
3 Z Li (1999), p. 243.
4 ibid.; Cochran (2000); Faure (2006); W Chan (1998).

5 Carroll (2005).
6 Cochran (2006), pp. 5–6.
7 Sinn (1989); Carroll, (2005), pp. 60 ff .
8 Nanjing historian Professor Cai Shaoqing argues that the NSW Chinese Chamber of Commerce was the second in the world after Hong Kong; Cai (2005).
9 Yong (1977), pp. 80–83, 91.
10 ibid., pp. 82–83.
11 Cai (2005); on 1898 reforms, see Reynolds (1993); Karl and Zarrow (2002).
12 In 1902 the *Tung Wah News* was renamed the *Tung Wah Times*. Founders of the chamber included Thomas Yee Hing (*Liu Ruxing*), Ping Nam (*Ye Bingnan*) and Leong Cheong (*Liang Chuang*); Yong (1977), pp. 83, 117, 120 ff.
13 Yong (1977), p. 83; on White-Australian boycotts, see Wilton (1998).
14 Willard (1923); Rubenstein (2004).
15 *Tung Wah News*, 3 May and 6 September 1899.
16 Cited in Cai (2005), pp. 198–99. Yong refers to this organisation as the Chinese Merchants Society to distinguish it from the 'chamber of commerce' that emerged in 1912–13. Following Cai Shaoqing, I refer to both as chambers of commerce; Cai (2005).
17 Cai (2005); Chinese Chamber (1890–1950).
18 Mark Finnane brought this altar piece to my attention.
19 Yong (1977), pp. 88–91, 96. The resident Chinese population of Victoria declined from 24 732 in 1861 to 7349 by 1901, including about 1000 people of mixed Chinese–European descent; Australian Bureau of Statistics (1925).
20 Yong (1977), chapter 5.
21 ibid., p. 102; a contemporary source indicates £109 000; P Lee (1922).
22 Yong (1977) pp. 108–09.
23 P Lee (1922).
24 Yong (1977), pp. 106 and 108; Percy Lee estimated the loss at 'between £30 000 and £40 000 per annum'; P Lee (1922).
25 *Chinese Republic News*, 18 February and 18 March 1922.
26 The native places of board members are listed in Yong (1977), table V, p. 264.
27 See chapter 6.
28 Z Li (1999), p. 243.
29 W Chan (1998), pp. 66–68; Sincere (1924), pp. 2–3. Ma's major partners were *Zeng Guansheng, Chen Xia, Ou Bin and Huang Bingnan*; C Lee (2000), pp. 200–14; Z Li (1999), p. 243. Chung Wah was founded by *Chen Xiaoxia* and Jan Gwong and Gwong Seung by *Huang Zaiyang* and *Huang Zichao*.
30 Wilton (1998), pp. 92–94; Z Li (1999).
31 Kwan family stores were established in Glen Innes, Emmaville, Texas (NSW), Stanthorpe, Casino, Coffs Harbour, Ballina, Kyogle, Werris Creek and Bundarra; Wilton (1998), p. 106.
32 Sincere (1924), Chinese-language section, pp. 5–6, 11–12, 209–13.
33 W Chan (1998), pp. 66–7; on majority Australian investment, see Z Li (1999), p. 245.
34 Sincere (1924), English-language section.
35 W Chan (1998), p. 68.
36 Xianggang yongan (1932), p. 9.
37 C Lee (2000), p. 201.

38   The official history records that Ma was impressed that Hordern 'started out in life as a hawker'; Sincere (1924), Chinese-language section, p. 1.

39   Yong (1977), p. 83, Lian (2005), p. 133.

40   W Chan (1998), p. 84.

41   'Ma Yingbiao' (1975); Other sources cited list his date of birth as 1862 and 1863.

42   W Chan (1998), pp. 74–85. Sincere's capital subscription was matched in the same year by another Chinese-Australian company, the Wing On Company; see W Chan (1999), p. 27.

43   —— (1999), p. 31.

44   —— (1998), p. 72. Wing On (Shanghai) was registered with US authorities; see C Lee (2000), p. 12.

45   Yen (1998), pp. 61–64.

46   C Lee (2000), pp. 11–12, 209–13.

47   ——, p. 214; W. Chan (1999), pp. 32–33.

48   Yen (1998), pp. 47–65; C Lee (2000), pp. 22, 205; Z Li (1999), p. 247.

49   Wilton (1998), pp. 90, 100–111.

50   'Pan Gooey – Application for Certificate of Exemption from Dictation Test', National Archives of Australia (Victoria), B13/0, 1918/25405.

51   Yen (1998), pp. 47–65; Z Li (1999), p. 245.

52   S Fitzgerald (1996), pp. 170–71; Wilton (1998), p. 90. One family has preserved 500 letters from this period written in Chinese and sent by family and friends in Hong Kong and China. Other correspondence is held in local archives in China.

53   Kuo (2005).

54   C Lee (2000), pp. 2–10.

55   Sincere (1924), Chinese-language section, p. 9.

56   See 'Business Ethics', in Xianggang yongan (1932), pp. 320–46, and Wang Wenda 1932; cf. 'Letter of Paul to the Galations', 3: 28.

57   Xianggang yongan (1932), p. 7.

58   S Lee and Hill (2005), pp. 24–25.

59   'Ma Yingbiao' (1975), pp. 171–78; C Guo (1961), pp. 76–79.

60   Z Li (1999), pp. 247–48.

61   Austin (2004); on Chinese Christian communities in Melbourne, see Welch (2003).

62   Kuo (2005); A Chan (1990).

63   —— (2005); L Guo (1949), pp. 3–5; on Chinese-Australian attempts to master English, see Hayes (1995).

64   *Australian Christian World* (23 December 1910), Sydney KMT Archives newspaper clippings file; see also Austin (2004).

65   I wish to thank Kuo Mei-fen for this information.

66   Z Chen (1935), p. 46; Supplementary Volumes (1994).

67   Yu Junxian died in Taiwan in 1994 aged 92, an elder statesman of the Chinese Nationalist movement; ibid., pp. 18, 27–28.

9 BEING AUSTRALIAN

1   Cheong et al. (1888).

2   C Guo (1961), pp. 64–65.

3   idem.

4   On local discoveries of links with China, see J Fitzgerald (2001).

5   Love and Morse (2006), pp. 249–67.
6   Chung Martin (1988), (2004); on Freeman, see Preface.
7   For Chinese-Australian families' stories, see Ling (2001) and 'Stories', Chinese Heritage of Australian Federation website at <http://www.chaf.lib.latrobe. edu.au>.
8   Hokari (2000).
9   Murdock (n.d), pp. 232–33; Wise (1913), pp. 51–52; O'Farrell (2000); Woollacott (2001); Hammerton (2001); Hammerton and Coleborne (2001).
10   Hirst (2000), p. 15; emphasis added. Elsewhere Hirst argues that Chinese immigration did not figure prominently at federation as the issue had been resolved at the earlier intercolonial conference; Hirst (2004).
11   Russell and Chubb (1998), pp. 1–3.
12   Quartly (1999), pp. 221 ff.
13   Hirst (2000), p. 10.
14   Rasmussen (2004); Kuo (2005); Wong Hoy and Monaghan-Jamieson (2006).
15   O'Rourke and Williamson (1999). Studies of transatlantic migration generally overstate the importance of the Great War in relation to passports and immigration controls and underestimate long-term institutional trends beginning in the late 19th century; McKeown (2004b), p. 172 ff.
16   Murdock (n.d.).
17   La Nauze (1972), pp. 54–55; Irving(1999), p. 428.
18   For 19th century White Australian attitudes, see Price (1974), pp. 104, 116–17; for 20th century attitudes, see Strahan (1996).
19   McGowan (2004).
20   According to local legend, Joe Byrne was nicknamed 'Ah Joe' and spoke Cantonese; Corfield (2003), p. 83.
21   Lancashire (2004); McCalman (1985).
22   Chinese community leaders have often noted the discrepancy between local community acceptance and exclusionary official behaviour. Lack (2002); Gibbs (1990).
23   Horne (2000), pp. 75–76.
24   See chapter 1.
25   T Barker (1998), p. 14.
26   —— (1992), p. 216.
27   Price (1974), p. 81.
28   Yong (1977), p. 267.
29   Russell and Chubb (1998), p. 89.
30   *Rules of a Chinese Society* (1868).
31   Yong (1977), p. 128; Oddie (1959), pp. 115–16.
32   Price (1974), pp. 258–59.
33   Windschuttle (2004), pp. 174–78.
34   J Fitzgerald (1996); Ch'ien and J Fitzgerald (2006).
35   Z Li (1994), p. 38.
36   Brawley (1997).
37   Fitzhardinge (1979), p. 372.
38   Two drafts were proposed. The draft preferred by the Japanese delegation read: 'The equality of nations being a basic principle of the League, the High Contracting Parties agree that concerning the treatment and rights to be accorded to aliens in their territories they will not discriminate, either in law or in

fact, against any person or persons on account of his or their race or nationality.'
Fitzhardinge (1979), p. 401.

39   Cited in Fitzhardinge (1979), p. 405.
40   Piesse (1919).
41   That Hughes was seen in Japan as the 'typical Australian' was made clear to Australian delegates to the Institute of Pacific Relations in the 1920s; Brawley (1997), p. 97.
42   Brawley (1997), p. 33 and chapter 4; see also Hudson (1978), p. 58.
43   Tavan (2005).
44   Windschuttle (2004), p. 178.
45   Walker (2006).
46   Harris and Williams (2003).
47   Parliamentary Secretary for Immigration and Multicultural Affairs, quoted in *The Weekend Australian*, 29–30 April 2006.

BIBLIOGRAPHY

Ah Ket, Toylaan (2000), 'William Ah Ket', paper presented to the Chinese Heritage of
    Australian Federation Conference, Melbourne: Chinese Museum.
Akun, Alois (1924), 'Alois Akun's Petition to Colonel John Ainsworth, 1924 (Rabaul,
    11 June 1924)', in D Wu (1982), pp. 163–66.
Anderson, Benedict (1991), *Imagined Communities: Reflections on the Origins and Spread of
    Nationalism* London: Verso.
Andrews, EM (1985), *Australia and China: The Ambiguous Relationship*, Melbourne:
    Melbourne University Press.
*Aozhou zhigong zongtang yibai wushinian jinian tekan (Special commemorative publication marking
    the 150th anniversary of the general headquarters of the Chinese Masonic Association of
    Australia)* (2004), Sydney: Chinese Masonic Association.
Armentrout, LE (1976), 'The Canton Uprising of 1902–1903: Reformers,
    Revolutionaries and the Second Taiping', *Modern Asian Studies*, 10.1: 83–105.
—— (1990), *Revolutionaries, Monarchists and Chinatowns: Chinese Politics in the Americas and the
    1911 Revolution*, Honolulu: University of Hawai'i Press.
Atkinson, Alan (1997), *The Europeans in Australia: A History. Volume One: The Beginning*,
    Melbourne: Oxford University Press.
Atkinson, Anne (1988), *Asian Immigrants to Western Australia 1829–1901*, Nedlands:
    University of Western Australia Press.
Austin, Denise (2004), '"Kingdom-Minded People": The Contributions of Chinese
    Business Christians toward the Transformation in Society', PhD dissertation,
    St Lucia: University of Queensland.
AusAID (2006), *Australian Aid: Promoting Growth and Stability*, Canberra: AusAID.
Australian Bureau of Statistics (1925), 'International Relations Special Article – The
    Chinese in Australia. From Year Book Australia, 1925', at <http://www.abs.gov.
    au/ausstats>.
Bagnall, Kate (2004a), 'Going North to China as their Wives: The Experience

of Western Wives in South China', paper presented at the International
  Conference on Quong Tart and His Times, Sydney: Powerhouse Museum.
—— (2004b), 'He would be a Chinese Still: Negotiating Boundaries of Race, Culture
  and Identity in Late Nineteenth Century Australia', in Couchman et al. (eds).
Barker, Martin (1981), *The New Racism: Conservatives and the Ideology of the Tribe*, London:
  Junction Books.
Barker, Theo (1992), *A History of Bathurst*, vol. 1, Bathurst: Crawford House Press.
—— (1998), *A History of Bathurst*, vol. 2, Bathurst: Bathurst City Council.
Bate, Weston (1978), *Lucky City: The First Generation at Ballarat 1851–1901*, Melbourne:
  Melbourne University Press.
Bean, CEW (1933), *The Story of ANZAC from the Outbreak of War to the End of the First Phase
  of the Gallipoli Campaign, 4 May 1915*, 2nd rev. edn, Sydney: Angus & Robertson.
Beaumont, Joan (1995), *Australia's War, 1914–1918*, Sydney: Allen & Unwin.
Bellamy, Edward (1888), *Looking Backward: 2000–1887*, Boston: Ticknor & Company.
Berlin, Isaiah (1961), 'Rabindranath Tagore and the Consciousness of Nationality', in
  Berlin (1997).
—— (1972), 'Kant as an unfamiliar source of nationalism', in Berlin (1997).
—— (1997), *The Sense of Reality: Studies in Ideas and their History*, in Henry Hardy (ed.),
  London: Pimlico.
Booth, Martin (1999), *The Dragon Syndicates: The Global Phenomenon of the Triads*, London
  and New York: Bantam Books.
Bramble, Phillip (2000), '"Too muchee dam lallikin": Chinese and Larrikins in 19th
  Century NSW', *Locality*, 11.2: 19–23.
Brawley, Sean (1997), *The White Peril: Foreign Relations and Asian Immigration to Australasia
  and North America, 1919–1978*, Sydney: UNSW Press.
Brett, Judith (2005), *Relaxed and Comfortable: The Liberal Party's Australia, Quarterly Essay 19*,
  Melbourne: Black Inc.
Broinowski, Alison (ed.) (2004), *Double Vision: Asian Accounts of Australia*, Canberra:
  Pandanus Books.
Brumley, Linda, Bingquan Liu & Xueru Zhao (1992), *Fading Links to China: Ballarat's
  Chinese Gravestones and Associated Records 1854–1955*, Melbourne: University of
  Melbourne, History Research Series No. 2.
Bryan, William Jennings (1906), *Letters to a Chinese Official, Being a Western View of Eastern
  Civilization*, London and New York: Harper & Brothers.
Buck, Pearl trans. (1937), *All Men Are Brothers*, London: Methuen.
Button, James (2006), 'Ceremony Born from Wing and A Prayer', *The Age*,
  11 November.
Cai, Shaoqing (2004), 'From Mutual Aid to Public Interest: Chinese Secret Societies in
  Australia', in Couchman et al. (eds) (2004).
—— (2005), 'Aozhou niuxiuwei xueli zhonghua shanghui yanjiu 1901–1943' ('A Study
  of the New South Wales Chinese Chamber of Commerce in Sydney, Australia,
  from 1901–1943'), *Lishixue yanjiu (Historical research)*, 4: 198–204.
Calhoun, Craig (1994), *Social Theory and the Politics of Identity*, Cambridge, Mass. and
  Oxford: Blackwells.
—— (1997), *Nationalism*, Buckingham: Open University Press.
Callinicos, Alex (2000), *Equality*, Cambridge: Polity Press.
Camilleri, Joseph A (1998), 'Regional Human Rights Dialogue in Asia Pacific:
  Prospects and Proposals', *Pacifica Review*, 10.3 (October): 167–85.
Campbell, Persia Crawford (1923), *Chinese Coolie Emigration to Countries within the British*

Empire, London: F Cass.

Cannadine, David (2002), *Ornamentalism: How the British Saw their Empire*, Oxford: Oxford University Press.

Carroll, John M (2005), *Edge of Empires: Chinese Elites and British Colonials in Hong Kong*, Cambridge, Mass.: Harvard University Press.

Ch'ien, Yung-xiang & John Fitzgerald (eds) (2006), *The Dignity of Nations*, Hong Kong: Hong Kong University Press.

Chan, Adrian (1990), 'Young Wai, John (1847?–1930)', in *The Australian Dictionary of Biography*, vol. 12, Melbourne: Melbourne University Press.

Chan, Henry, Ann Curthoys & Nora Chiang (eds) (2001), *The Overseas Chinese in Australasia: History, Settlement and Interactions*, Taipei: Interdisciplinary Group for Australian Studies (IGAS), National Taiwan University; Canberra: Centre for the Study of the Chinese Southern Diaspora, Australian National University.

Chan, Wellington KK (1998), 'Personal Styles, Cultural Values and Management: The Sincere and Wing On Companies in Shanghai and Hong Kong, 1900–1941', in MacPherson (ed.).

—— (1999), 'Selling Goods and Promoting a New Commercial Culture: The Four Premier Department Stores on Nanjing Road, 1917–1937', in Cochran (ed.).

Chang, Hao (1987), *Chinese Intellectuals in Crisis: Search for Order and Meaning, 1890–1911*, Berkeley: University of California Press.

Chen, Hansheng (1980), *Huagong chuguo shiliao huibian (Historical materials on Chinese labourers abroad)*, 7 vols, Beijing: Zhonghua shuju.

Chen, Leslie H Dingyan (1999), *Chen Jiongming and the Federalist Movement: Regional Leadership and Nation Building in Early Republican China*, Ann Arbor: Center for Chinese Studies, University of Michigan.

Chen, Yong (2000), *Chinese San Francisco 1850–1943: A Trans-Pacific Community*, Stanford: Stanford University Press.

Chen, Zexian (1963), 'Shijiushiji chengxing de qiyue huagong zhidu (The Chinese indentured labour system in the 19th century)', *Lishi yanjiu (Historical Studies)*, 1: 161–79.

Chen, Zhiming (1935), *Zhongguo guomindang aozhou dangwu fazhan shikuang (Historical outline of the development of Chinese KMT party affairs in Australasia)*, Sydney: Zhongguo guomindang zhu ao zongzhibu.

Cheong, Cheok Hong et al. (1888), *Chinese Remonstrance to the Parliament and People of Victoria*, Melbourne: Wm Marshall & Co., reprinted in Welch (2003), Appendix.

Chinese Chamber of Commerce of New South Wales (1890–1950), Records 1890–1950, Canberra: Noel Butlin Archives, Australian National University.

Chinese Consulate General (1935), Correspondence from the Chinese Consulate General in Australia to the Right Honourable JA Lyons, 23 December.

Chinese Imperial Commissioners (1887), Chinese Imperial Commissioners to the Governor, Oriental Hotel, Melbourne, 13 June; enclosure, 'Petition by Lowe Kong Meng, Cheok Hong Cheong, Louis Ah Mouy & 44 others presented to the Victorian premier', Victorian Legislative Assembly, *Votes and Proceedings*, session 1888, vol. 1, Chinese Immigration, Part I. P87/1869, pp. 5–7.

Chinese Republic News (see *Minguobau*).

Chinese Society in Ballarat (1868), Rules of a Chinese Society in Ballarat 1854, in Reverend W Young, 'Report on the Condition of the Chinese Population in Victoria', *Victorian Parliamentary Papers*, Melbourne: John Ferres Government

Printer, pp. 45–49.

Choi, CY (1975), *Chinese Migration and Settlement in Australia*, Sydney: Sydney University Press.

Chou, Bon-wai (1995), 'The Sojourning Attitude and the Economic Decline of Chinese Society in Victoria, 1860s–1930s', in Macgregor (ed.).

Chow, SF (1933), 'The Chinese from Australia', *United China*, 1.11 (October): 453.

Chow, VY (1933a), 'Adventurous Chinese', *United China*, 1.11 (October): 470.

—— (1933b), 'Australia Acknowledges (A Compilation of Press Reports on the Official Historian's Visit to Australia)', *United China*, 1.11 (October): 448–52.

—— (1933c), 'China in Revolution (Broadcast lectures)', *United China*, 1.11 (October): 454–56.

—— (1933d), 'Early Revolutionary Crosses Great Divide', *United China*, 1.10 (May): 402.

—— (1933e), 'In 1850 the Revolution was Born', *United China*, 1.11 (October): 423–26.

—— (1933f), 'Odyssey in the South (A Diary)', *United China*, 1.11 (October): 434–47.

—— (1933g), 'On Writing a History of the Chinese Revolution (Radio Broadcast)', *United China*, 1.11 (October): 460–63, 491.

—— (1933h), 'Sun Yatsen's "Fatherhood" of New China', *United China*, 1.11 (October): 427–30, 491.

—— (1933i), 'To Lovers of Truth Throughout the World', *United China*, 1.11 (October): 421–22.

Chung-Martin, Helene (1988), *Shouting from China*, Ringwood: Penguin.

—— (2004), *A Lazy Man in China*, Canberra: Pandanus Books.

Clark, Prescott & JS Gregory (1982), *Western Reports on the Taiping: A Selection of Documents*, London: Croom Helm.

Clark, Anna (2006), 'Flying the Flag for Mainstream Australia', *Griffith Review* (Autumn): 107–12.

Cochran, Sherman (ed.) (1999), *Inventing Nanjing Road: Commercial Culture in Shanghai, 1900–1945*, Ithaca: East Asian Program, Cornell University.

—— (2000), *Encountering Chinese Networks: Western, Japanese, and Chinese Corporations in China, 1880–1937*, Berkeley: University of California Press.

—— (2006), *Chinese Medicine Men: Consumer Culture in China and Southeast Asia*, Cambridge, Mass.: Harvard University Press.

Commission (1855), 'Commission Appointed to Enquire into the Conditions of the Goldfields of Victoria', in McLaren (1985), pp. 6–14.

Cooke, Nola & Li Tana (eds) (2004), *Water Frontier: Commerce and the Chinese in the Lower Mekong Region 1750–1880*, Singapore: Singapore University Press.

Corfield, Justin (2003), *The Ned Kelly Encyclopaedia*, Melbourne: Lothian Books.

Couchman, Sophie (1995), 'The Banana Trade: Its Importance to Melbourne's Chinese and Little Bourke Street, 1880s–1930s', in Macgregor (ed.).

—— (2004a), 'Cobb & Co. Coach Dilemmas: Challenges Posed by Photographs and Chinese Australian History in the Networked Environment', paper presented to Computing Arts Conference, Newcastle.

—— (2004b), 'Oh I would like to see Maggie Moore again: Selected women of Melbourne's Chinatown', in Couchman et al. (eds).

—— (2004c), 'Not so mug mugshots: Behind the portraits of series B6443', *Crossings*, 9.3 (2004), at <http://asc.uq.edu.au/crossings/9_3/index. php?apply=couchman>.

—— (2006), 'Riding With the Best of Them: Chinese Australians and Cycling in

Australia', in C Simpson (ed.), *Scorchers, Ramblers and Rovers: Australasian Cycling Histories*, Melbourne: Australian Society for Sports History.

—— (2006), '"And Then in the Distance Quong Tart Did We See": Quong Tart, Celebrity and Photography', *Journal of Colonial Australian History*, 8.

——, Fitzgerald, John & Paul Macgregor (eds) (2004), *After the Rush: Regulation, Participation and Chinese Communities in Australia 1860–1940*, special edition of *Otherland*, Melbourne: Otherland Press.

Cronin, Kathryn (1982), *Colonial Casualties: Chinese in Early Victoria*, Melbourne: Melbourne University Press.

Crossley, Pamela Kyle (1999), *A Translucent Mirror: History and Identity in Qing Imperial Ideology*, Berkeley: University of California Press.

Cumming, G (1995), 'Mei Quong Tart (1850–1903)', *The Masonic Historical Society of New South Wales*, 23 (22 May): 6.

Curthoys, Ann (2001), '"Chineseness" and Australian Identity', in Chan et al. (eds).

—— & Andrew Markus (eds) (1978), *Who are our Enemies? Racism and the Australian Working Class*, Sydney: Hale & Iremonger, in association with the Australian Society for the Study of Labour History.

—— & Marilyn Lake (eds) (2006), *Connected Worlds*, Canberra: Australian National University E-Press.

Cushman, JW (1984), 'A "Colonial Casualty": The Chinese Community in Australian Historiography', *Asian Studies Association of Australia Review*, 7.3 (April): 100–13.

Darnell, Maxine (2004), 'Indentured Chinese Labourers and Employers Identified', at <http://www.chaf.lib.latrobe.edu.au/pdf/indentured.pdf>.

Davies, Gloria (1981), 'Liang Qichao and the Chinese in Australia', Honours dissertation, Melbourne: Department of East Asian Studies, University of Melbourne.

Davison, Graeme, John Hirst & Stuart Macintyre (eds) (1998), *The Oxford Companion to Australian History*, Melbourne: Oxford University Press.

Davison, Graeme (1978), *The Rise and Fall of Marvellous Melbourne*, Melbourne: Melbourne University Press.

Deane, PE (n.d.), 'Australia's Rights: The Fight at the Peace Table', at <http://www.abc.net.au/federation/fedstory/ep2/ep2_places.htm>.

Department of Foreign Affairs and Trade (2003), *Advancing the National Interest*, Canberra: Department of Foreign Affairs and Trade.

Dikotter, Frank (1992), *The Discourse of Race in Modern China*, London: Hurst.

Donghuabao (Tung Wah News), various issues. Initially published under the title *Donghua xinbao* in 1898, but abbreviated to *Donghuabao* in 1902.

Duara, Prasenjit (1997), 'Nationalists among Transnationals: Overseas Chinese and the Idea of China, 1900–1911', in Ong and Nonini.

Dundas, J. (1877), 'Notes by Mr. J. Dundas Crawford on Chinese immigration in the Australian colonies', September, London: Great Britain Foreign Office Confidential Prints, no. 3742.

Elvin, Mark (1974), 'The Administration of Shanghai', in G William Skinner (ed.), *The Chinese City Between Two Worlds*, Stanford: Stanford University Press.

Enlistment Records (1947–48), Enlistment Records New Guinea 1947–48. Archives of the Australasian Kuo Min Tang, Sydney.

Faure, David (2006), *China and Capitalism: A History of Business Enterprise in Modern China*, Hong Kong: Hong Kong University Press.

Ferrall, Charles, Paul Millar & Keren Smith (eds) (2005), *East by South: China in the*

Australasian Imagination, Wellington: Victoria University Press.

Fitzgerald, JD (1914), *The Rise of the Australian Labor Party*, Sydney: The Worker Print.

—— (1918), 'A Celestial Gentleman', in Turner (ed.), *The Australian Soldier's Gift Book*, n.p.

—— (1922), *The Ring Valley: A Novel of Australian Pioneering*, London: Hodder & Stoughton.

—— (1923), *Children of the Sunlight: Stories of Australian Circus Life*, Sydney: NSW Bookstall Co.

Fitzgerald, John (1986), 'Continuity within Discontinuity: The Case of Water Margin Mythology', *Modern China*, 12.3: 361–400.

—— (1996), *Awakening China: Politics, Culture and Class in the Nationalist Revolution*, Stanford: Stanford University Press.

—— (2001), 'Another Country', *Meanjin*, 60.4: 59–71.

—— (2004a), 'Gendering the Social Imaginary: Modernity, Nationalism, and Representations of Egalitarian Sentiment in 19th and 20th Century China', paper presented to the New Gender Constructs in Literature, the Visual and the Performing Arts of Modern China and Japan conference, Heidelberg: University of Heidelberg.

—— (2004b), 'Who Cares What They Think? John Winston Howard, William Morris Hughes and the Pragmatic Vision of Australian National Sovereignty', in Broinowski (ed.), *Double Vision*.

—— (2005), 'Legend or History? The Australian Yee Hing and the Chinese Revolution', *Studies on Republican China*, 8: 87–111.

—— (2006a), 'Nationalism, Democracy and Dignity in 20th Century China', in Ch'ien and Fitzgerald (eds).

—— (2006b), 'Revolution and Respectability: Chinese Masons in Australian History', in Curthoys and Lake (eds).

—— (2006c), 'The Dignity of Nations', in Ch'ien and Fitzgerald (eds).

Fitzgerald, Shirley (1996), *Red Tape, Gold Scissors: The Story of Sydney's Chinese*, Sydney: State Library of NSW Press.

Fitzhardinge, LF (1979), *The Little Digger Vol. II 1914–1952: William Morris Hughes, A Political Biography, Volume II*, Sydney: Angus & Robertson.

Fitzpatrick, David (ed.) (1992), *Home or Away: Immigrants in Colonial Australia. Visible Immigrants: Three*, Canberra: Division of Historical Studies and Centre for Immigration and Multicultural Studies, RSSS, Australian National University.

Flannery, Tim (ed.) (2002), *The Birth of Melbourne*, Melbourne: Text Publishing.

Foley, T & F Bateman (eds) (2000), *Irish Australian Studies: Papers Delivered at the Ninth Irish–Australian Conference Galway April 1997*, Sydney: Crossings Press.

Fraser, Andrew (2005), '"Racist" scholar's rejected White Australia essay', Higher Education Supplement, *The Australian*, 21 September.

Ganter, Regina (2006), *Mixed Relations*, Nedlands: University of Western Australia Press.

Gibbs, RM (1990), 'Way Lee, Yet Soo War 1853?–1909', in *The Australian Dictionary of Biography*, vol. 12, Melbourne: Melbourne University Press.

Goldsmith, Oliver (1762), *The Citizen of the World: Or, Letters from a Chinese Philosopher Residing in London to his Friends in the East*, London: Folio Society; reprinted 1969.

Gongfa xuehui xu (n.d.), 'Gongfa xuehui xu' ['Preface to Society for the Study of Public Law'], *Xiangbao*, no. 43.

Goodman, David (1994), *Gold Seeking: Victoria and California in the 1850s*, Sydney: Allen &

Unwin.

Grand Master of the Chinese Masonic Lodge (1933), 'Lung Hung Pung "The Great Leader"', *United China*, 1.11 (October): 433.

Guangdong Provincial Gazette Preparatory Editorial Committee (ed.) (1994), Supplementary Volumes of the Guangdong Provincial Gazette Preparatory Editorial Committee (ed.), 'Special Issue Commemorating Director Yu Chun-hsian (Yu Junxian)', *Research on Supplementary Volumes of the Guangdong Provincial Gazette*, 16 (20 May).

Guangdong xingzheng zhoukan (*Guangdong Administrative Weekly*) (1927), 23 (20 June): 6–7.

Guangyi huabao (*Chinese Australian Herald*), various issues.

Guangzhou minguo ribao (*Guangzhou Republican Daily*), various issues.

Guo Chuan (Phillip Gockchin) (1961), *Yongan jingshen zhi fazhan ji changcheng* (*The growth and ripening of the Wing On spirit*), Hong Kong: n.p.

Guo Le (James Gocklock) (1949), *Huiyilu* (*Memoirs*), Hong Kong: Wing On Publishers.

Gyory, Andrew (1998), *Closing the Gate: Race, Politics, and the Chinese Exclusion Act*, Chapel Hill: University of North Carolina Press.

Haineiwai (1924–25), Haineiwei dangwu xiaoxi jianbao diecunpu (Collection of paper clippings on party affairs at home and abroad), Historical Archives Commission of the Kuomintang (KMT Archives) 435/274, Taipei.

Hammerton, Anthony James (2001), 'Epic Stories and the Mobility of Modernity: Narratives of British Migration to Canada and Australia Since 1945', *Australian–Canadian Studies*, 19.1: 47–64.

—— & Catharine Coleborne (2001), 'Ten-Pound Poms Revisited: Battlers' Tales and British Migration to Australia, 1947–1971', *Journal of Australian Studies*, 'Scatterlings of Empire', 68 (Winter): 86–96.

Harris, Patricia & Vicki Williams (2003), 'Social Inclusion, National Identity and the Moral Imagination', *The Drawing Board: An Australian Review of Public Affairs*, 3.3 (March): 205–22.

Hayes, James (1995), '"Good Morning Mrs Thompson!" A Chinese–English Word Book from 19th Century Sydney', in Macgregor (ed.).

Heidhues, Mary Somers (2003), *Golddiggers, Farmers, and Traders in the 'Chinese Districts' of West Kalimantan, Indonesia*, Ithaca: Cornell University, Southeast Asia Program Publications.

Hess, Rob (2004), 'A Death Blow to the White Australia Policy: Australian Rules Football and Chinese Communities in Victoria, 1892–1908', in Couchman et al. (eds), pp. 89–106.

Hevia, James (1995), *Cherishing Men from Afar: Qing Court Ritual and the Macartney Embassy of 1793*, Durham: Duke University Press.

—— (2003), *English Lessons: The Pedagogy of Imperialism in Nineteenth Century China*, Durham: Duke University Press.

Hirst, John (2000), *The Sentimental Nation: The Making of the Australian Commonwealth*, Melbourne: Oxford University Press.

—— (2004), 'The Chinese and Federation', in Couchman et al. (eds).

Hobsbawm, Eric (1985), *Bandits*, Harmondsworth: Penguin.

Hokari, Minoru (2000), 'Does Size Matter? Aboriginal Relations with Other Asian Populations', paper presented to Lost in the Whitewash: Aboriginal–Chinese Encounters from Federation to Reconciliation colloquium, Centre for Cross-cultural Research, Canberra: Australian National University.

Horne, Donald (2000), *Billy Hughes: Prime Minister of Australia 1915–1923*, Melbourne: Black Inc.

Howard, John with Kerry O'Brien (1999), transcript of 7.30 *Report*, ABC TV, 11 August, at <http://www.abc.net.au/7.30/stories/s43234.htm>.

Huang Jianda (1999), *Zeng Jiale zhuan (Biography of Arthur Lock Chang)*, Shijiazhuang: Huashan wenyi chubanshe.

Huck, Arthur (1960), 'A Note on Hwuy-Ung's Letters from Melbourne 1899–1912: A Chinaman's Opinion of Us and of His Own Country', *Historical Studies*, 9.35: 316.

—— (1968), *The Chinese in Australia*, Melbourne: Longman.

Hu-Dehart, Evelyn (2005), 'Opium and Social Control: Coolies on the Plantations of Peru and Cuba', *Journal of Chinese Overseas*, 1.2 (November): 169–83.

Hudson, WJ (1978), *Billy Hughes in Paris: The Birth of Australian Diplomacy*, Melbourne: Thomas Nelson.

Hummel, Arthur W (ed.) (1943), *Eminent Chinese of the Ch'ing Period (1644–1912)*, Washington: United States Government Printing Office.

Hwuy-Ung (1927), *A Chinaman's Opinion of Us and of His Own Country*, trans. JA Makepeace, London: Chatto & Windus.

Ichikawa, Tetsu (2006), 'Chinese in Papua New Guinea: Strategic Practices in Sojourning', *Journal of Chinese Overseas*, 2.1 (May): 111–32.

Inglis, Christine (1999), 'Papua New Guinea', in Pan (ed.), *The Encyclopedia of the Chinese Overseas*.

Inglis, Ken S (1992), 'Going Home: Australians in England 1870–1900', in Fitzpatrick (ed.).

Irving, Helen (ed.) (1999), *The Centenary Companion to Australian Federation*, Cambridge, New York, Melbourne and Madrid: Cambridge University Press.

Isaacs, Harold (1967), *The Tragedy of the Chinese Revolution*, Stanford: Stanford University Press.

Jan, Gilbert (1993), 'Honour List of Australian Ex-Service Personnel of Chinese Descent who Served in WWI, WWII, Korean War and Vietnam War', unpublished paper, Sydney.

Jiaolun (n.d.), *Jiaolun renwen ziliao – Jiaolun yuebao zengkan (Materials on Jiaolun personalities – a supplement to the Jiaolun Monthly)*, 2.

Jones, Paul (1999), 'Alien Acts: The White Australia Policy, 1901 to 1939', PhD dissertation, Melbourne: University of Melbourne.

—— (2001), 'Chinese in Modern Australia', in Jupp (ed.).

—— (2004), 'What Happened to Australia's Chinese Between the World Wars?', in Couchman et al. (eds).

—— (2005a), *Chinese–Australian Journeys: Records on Travel, Migration and Settlement, 1860–1975*, Canberra: National Archives of Australia.

—— (2005b), 'The View from the Edge: Chinese Australians and China, 1890 to 1949', in Ferrall et al. (eds).

Jubilee History of Lodge Wentworth 1881–1931 (n.d.), Archives of the United Grand Lodge of New South Wales and the Australian Capital Territory, Box 171.

Jung, Moon-Ho (2006), *Coolies and Cane: Race, Labor, and Sugar in the Age of Emancipation*, Baltimore: Johns Hopkins University Press.

Jupp, James (ed.) (2001), *The Australian People: An Encyclopedia of the Nation, Its People and their Origins*, Melbourne: Cambridge University Press.

Just, P (1859), *Australia: or, Notes Taken During a Residence in the Colonies from the Gold Discovery in 1851 till 1857*, Dundee: n.p.

Karl, Rebecca A & Peter Zarrow (eds) (2002), *Rethinking the 1898 Reform Period: Political and Cultural Change in Late Qing China*, Cambridge, Mass.: Harvard University Asia Center.

Kee Pookong, Chooi-hon Ho, Paul Macgregor & Gary Presland (eds) (2002), *Chinese in Oceania*, Melbourne: Association for the Study of the Chinese and their Descendants in Australasia and the Pacific Islands, Chinese Museum, Centre for Asia–Pacific Studies and Victoria University of Technology.

King, Russell (1978), 'Return Migration: A Neglected Aspect of Population Geography', *AREA*, 10.3:175–76.

Kok, Hu Jin (1996–2005), *Chinese Cemeteries in Australia*, vols 1–8, Bendigo: Bendigo Chinese Association Museum.

—— (2003), *Hung Men Handbook*, Bendigo: Bendigo Chinese Association Museum.

—— (2005), 'The Followers of Hung Xiu Quan in Australia', paper presented to the Eight Biennial Conference of the Chinese Studies Association of Australia, Bendigo Golden Dragon Museum.

Kuang Qizhao (1889), Correspondence from Kuang Qizhao to the Zongli Yamen Regarding the Report by Chinese Merchants of Harsh Treatment in Australia (19th day of 8th month of Guangxu 14), Beijing: First National Archives.

Kuo, Mei-fen (2005), 'The "Imagined Chinese Community" in the Carnivals of 1897', paper presented to Postgraduate Conference, School of Social Sciences, La Trobe University, Melbourne.

Kuo Min Tang (1921), 'Memorandum and Articles of Association of the Chinese Nationalist Party of Australasia 1921', reprinted in CF Yong (1977).

La Nauze, John (1972), *The Making of the Australian Constitution*, Melbourne: Melbourne University Press.

Lach, Donald F (1985), *Asia in the Making of Europe*, 3 vols, Chicago: Chicago University Press.

Lack, John (2002), 'Wang, David Neng Hwan (1920–1978)', in *The Australian Dictionary of Biography*, vol. 16, Melbourne: Melbourne University Press.

Lai, Him Mark (2004), *Becoming Chinese American: A History of Communities and Institutions*, Walnut Creek: Altamira Press.

Lake, Marilyn (2003), 'On Being a White Man, Australia, Circa 1900', in Teo & White (eds).

Lancashire, Rod (2004), 'Blanche Street, Wahgunyah: A Pre-Federation Australian Chinese Community on the Border', in Couchman et al. (eds).

Lea-Scarlett, EJ (1974), 'Mei Quong Tart (1850–1903)', in *The Australian Dictionary of Biography: 1851–1890*, vol. 5, Melbourne: Melbourne University Press.

Lee Sui-ming & Emily M Hill (eds) (2005), *A Phoenix of South China: The Story of Lingnan (University) College, Sun Yat-sen University*, Hong Kong: Commercial Press.

Lee, Charles Cheng-Che (2000), *Li Chengji xiansheng fangwen jilu (The Reminiscences of Charles Cheng-Che Lee)*, interviewed and recorded by Lai Chi-Kong, Taipei: Institute of Modern History of Academia Sinica.

Lee, Percy (Li Xiangbo) (1922), 'Jiu zhongao gongsi zhi da heimu' ['Behind the great black curtain of the old China–Australia Mail Steamship Line'], *Chinese Republic News*, 11 and 18 February.

Li Tana (2006), 'Canton and Southeast Asia's Water Frontier in the 18th Century: New Data and New Insights', paper presented in the Division of Pacific and Asian History, Canberra: Australian National University.

Li Yumin & Bin, Li (1999), 'Wuxu shiqi weixinpai dui pingdeng tiaoyue de renshi' ['Recognition of the Unequal Treaties among the reform faction in 1898'],

Hunan shifan daxue shehuikexue xuebao (*Journal of the School of Social Sciences of Hunan Normal University*), no. 2.

Li Yunhan (1966), *Cong ronggong dao qingdang* (*From the admission of the communists to the purification of the party*), 2 vols, Taipei: Zhongzheng shuju.

Li Zhigang (Lai Chi-kong) (1999), 'Jindai Guangdong xiangshan shangren de shangye wangluo chutan' ['Preliminary analysis of the commercial networks of the modern Huengshan merchants of Guangdong'], in *Zhongguo haiyang fazhan shilun wenji* (*Essays on the history of Chinese maritime development*), 7 (March): 233–55.

Li Zhisui (1994), *The Private Life of Chairman Mao: The Inside Story of the Man Who Made Modern China*, London: Random House.

Li, Dun J (trans. & ed.) (1978), *From Mandarin to Commissar*, New York: Charles Scribner's Sons.

Lian Lingling (2005), 'Qiye wenhua de xingcheng yu zhuanxing: yi minguo shiqi de shanghai yongan gongsi wei lie' ['The formation and transformation of commercial culture: The case of the Shanghai Wing On Corporation'], *Zhongyang yanjiuyuan jindaishi yanjiusuo jikan* (*Journal of the Modern History Institute of Academic Sinica*) 49 (September): 127–73.

Liang, Qichao (1903) 'Bai aozhou zhi fanduilun' ['A theory to counter White Australia'], *Xinmin congbao* (*New Citizen*), 34: 69–70.

—— (1928a) 'Aozhou xin neige yu ershi shiji qiantu zhi guanxi' [1904] ['The new Australian cabinet and its significance for the future of the twentieth century'], in *Yinbingshi quanji* [*Complete works of the Ice-Drinker's Studio*], n. p.

—— (1928b), *Yinbingshi wenji* (*Collected essays from the Ice-Drinker's Studio*), 22 vols, Shanghai: Shangwu yinshju.

—— (1960), 'Zhongguo jiruo suyuanlun' ['Tracing the source of China's weakness'] [1990], in Liang Qichao, *Yinbingshi wenji*, Vol.2, Taipei: Zhonghua Shuju.

—— (1978), 'What is Wrong with the Chinese?', in Dun J Li (trans. & ed.), *From Mandarin to Commissar*, New York: Charles Scribner's Sons.

Lei Dehong *et. al.* (1889), Report to Zongli Yamen from Chinese Merchants regarding exorbitant taxes imposed on Chinese in Australia (1st day of 7th month of Guangxu 14), Beijing: First National Archives.

Lim, Irene (1999), *Secret Societies in Singapore*, Singapore: National Heritage Board.

Ling, Chek (ed.) (2001), *Plantings in a New Land: Stories of Survival, Endurance and Emancipation*, Brisbane: Society of Chinese Australian Academics of Queensland and Cathay Club.

Liu, Daren & Tian Xinyuan (eds) (1958), *Aozhou huaqiao jingji* (*Chinese Australian Economy*), Taipei: Haiwai chubanshe.

Lloyd, Longfield (1935), Inspector, Investigation Branch to Director, Commonwealth Investigation Branch, 7 March, Canberra: National Archives of Australia, Series C32091 Item CIB 676.

Lo, Hui-min (ed.) (1976–78), *The Correspondence of GE Morrison*, 2 vols, Cambridge: Cambridge University Press.

Loong Hung Pung (1933) 'Loong Hung Pung, "the Great Leader", by the present Grand Master, Chinese Masonic Lodge', *United China*, 1:11 (October): 433.

Love, Graeme Campbell & Neil Wynes Morse (2006), 'The Re-Formed Triad League', *Transactions of Quatuor Coronati Lodge*, 116: 249–67.

Lowe Kong Meng, Cheok Hong Cheong & Louis Ah Mouy (eds) (1879), *The Chinese Question In Australia*, 1878–79, Melbourne: FF Bailliere.

Luo Jialun & Huang Jilu (eds) (1969), *Guofu nianpu zengdingben* (*Chronology of the Father of the Country*, 2 vols, rev. edn, Taipei: Zhongzheng shuju.

Lyman, Stanford M, WE Willmott, & Berching Ho (1964) 'Rules of a Chinese Secret Society in British Columbia', *Bulletin of the School of Oriental and African Studies*, 27.3, pp. 530–39.

'Ma Yingbiao' (1975), in Liu Shaotang (ed.), *Minguo renwu xiaozhuan (Brief biographies of republican figures)* , vol. 17, Taipei: Zhuanji wenxue chubanshe.

Macgregor, Paul (ed.) (1995) *Histories of the Chinese in Australasia and the South Pacific*, Melbourne: Museum of Chinese Australian History.

Macintyre, Stuart (1986), *The Oxford History of Australia, Volume 4, 1901–1942, The Succeeding Age*, Melbourne: Oxford University Press.

—— (1999), *A Concise History of Australia*, Melbourne: Cambridge University Press.

MacPherson, Kerrie L (ed.) (1998), *Asian Department Stores*, Richmond, Surrey: Curzon.

Markus, Andrew (1979), *Fear and Hatred: Purifying Australia and California 1850–1901*, Sydney: Hale & Iremonger.

—— (1998), 'White Australia', in Davison et al. (eds).

—— (2001), *Race: John Howard and the Remaking of Australia*, Sydney: Allen & Unwin.

—— (2004), 'Reflections on the Administration of the "White Australia" Immigration Policy', in Couchman et al. (eds).

Mason, CW (1924), *The Chinese Confessions of Charles Welsh Mason*, London: Grant Richards.

May, Cathie (1984), *Topsawyers: The Chinese in Cairns 1870 to 1920*, Townsville: James Cook University History Department.

McCalman, Janet (1985), *Struggletown: Public and Private Life in Richmond 1900–1965*, Melbourne: Melbourne University Press.

McClain, Charles (1994), *In Search of Equality*, Berkeley: University of California Press.

McGowan, Barry (2004), 'Reconsidering Race: The Chinese Experience on the Goldfields of Southern New South Wales', *Australian Historical Studies*, 124 (October): 312–31.

McKeown, Adam (2001), *Chinese Migrant Networks and Cultural Change: Peru, Chicago, Hawaii, 1900–1936*, Chicago: University of Chicago Press.

—— (2003), 'Ritualization of Regulation: The Enforcement of Chinese Exclusion in the United States and China', *American Historical Review*, 108.2, pp. 377–403.

—— (2004a), 'Global Chinese Migration', paper presented to the Fifth Conference of the International Society for the Study of Chinese Overseas, Helsignor, Denmark.

—— (2004b), 'Global Migration 1846–1940', *Journal of World History*, 15.2: 155–89.

McLaren, Ian (ed.) (1985), *The Chinese in Victoria: Official Reports and Documents* Melbourne: Red Rooster Press.

Meadows, Thomas Taylor (1856), *The Chinese and the Rebellions*, London: Smith, Elder.

Minguobao (Chinese Republic News), various issues.

Mo, Yimei & Mo Xiangyi (1991), *William Liu OBE 1893–1983: Pathfinder*, Sydney: Australia–China Chamber of Commerce and Industry of NSW.

Molony, John (2000), *The Native Born: The First White Australians*, Melbourne: Melbourne University Press.

Moore, Clive, Jacqueline Leckie & Doug Munro (1990), *Labour in the South Pacific*, Townsville: James Cook University Press.

Morrell, WP (1940), *The Gold Rushes*, London: n.p.

Morrison, GE (1895), *An Australian in China*, London: Horace Cox.

Murdock, Walter (n.d.), *The Making of Australia*, Melbourne: Whitcombe & Toms.

National Multicultural Advisory Council (1999), *Australian Multiculturalism for a New Century: Towards Inclusiveness*, Canberra: Commonwealth of Australia.

Ng Kumlin Ali, Bessie (2002), *Chinese in Fiji*, Suva: Institute of Pacific Studies, University of the South Pacific.

—— (2005), 'Quong Tart and Early Chinese Business in Fiji', *Journal of Pacific Studies*, 28.1: 78–88.

Nichols, Bob (1986), *Bluejackets and Boxers: Australia's Naval Expedition to the Boxer Uprising*, Sydney: Allen & Unwin.

Nickless, Brother OU (1961), 'Forward and Narrative in Two Parts of the History of the Lodge of Tranquility No.42 UGL of NSW for the Period January 1874 to 11 May 1961', typed manuscript dated 11 May, Archives of the United Grand Lodge of New South Wales and the Australian Capital Territory, Box 517.

Noonan, Rodney (2006), 'Grafton to Guangzhou: The Revolutionary Journey of Tse Tsan-Tai', *Journal of Intercultural Studies*, 27: 1–2 (February–May): 101–15.

Nye, Robert (1993), *Masculinity and Male Codes of Honor in Modern France*, Oxford: Oxford University Press.

O'Farrell, Patrick (2000), *The Irish in Australia: 1788 to the Present*, 3rd edn, Sydney: UNSW Press.

O'Rourke, Kevin & Jeffrey Williamson (1999), *Globalisation & History: The Evolution of a Nineteenth Century Atlantic Economy*, Boston: MIT Press.

'Obituary' (1933), *United China* 1.10 (May): 402.

Oddie, Geoffrey A (1959), 'The Chinese in Victoria, 1870–1890', MA dissertation, Melbourne: University of Melbourne.

Ong, Aihwa & Donald M Nonini (eds) (1997), *Ungrounded Empires: The Cultural Politics of Modern Chinese Transnationalism*, New York and London: Routledge.

Owenby, David & Mary Somers Heidhues (eds) (1993), *'Secret Societies' Reconsidered: Perspectives on the Social History of Early Modern South China and Southeast Asia*, Armonk: ME Sharpe.

Palfreeman, Anthony (1967), *The Administration of the White Australia Policy*, Melbourne: Melbourne University Press.

Pan, Lynn (ed.) (1999), *The Encyclopedia of the Chinese Overseas*, Cambridge, Mass.: Harvard University Press.

Pearl, Cyril (1967), *Morrison of Peking*, Sydney: Angus & Robertson.

Pelissier, Roger (1963), *Chine entre en scene (China takes the stage)*, Paris: R Juillard.

—— (1967), *The Awakening of China*, trans. Martin Kieffer, London: Secker & Warburg.

Perdue, Peter (1987), *Exhausting the Earth: State and Peasant in Hunan, 1500–1850*, Cambridge, Mass.: Harvard Council on East Asian Studies.

Petition (1891), Petition Regarding Chinese Immigration from Y.S.W. Way Lee, on Behalf of the Chinese in South Australia to the South Australian Parliament, Parliamentary Papers, no. 128, South Australia, at <http://www.chaf.lib.latrobe.edu.au>.

Piesse, Major (1919), March 24, Naval Office, Melbourne, MP, NAA 1049/1, 1918/049.

Price, Charles (1974), *The Great White Walls are Built: Restrictive Immigration to North America and Australasia, 1836–1888*, Canberra: Australian National University Press.

Qingyibao (Pure Talk), various issues.

Quartly, Marian (1999), 'Victoria', in Irving (ed.).

Quong Tart & others (1888), 'To the Honorable the Representatives of the Australasian Colonies, meeting in Conference upon the Chinese Question in Sydney,

June, 1888', petition presented by Quong Tart & others, New South Wales Legislative Council, *Conference on Chinese Question: Proceedings of the Conference held in Sydney in June 1888*, Minutes of the Proceedings, papers laid before the conference, Sydney: Government Printer.

Ramsay, Guy (2004), 'The Chinese Diaspora in Torres Strait: Cross Cultural Connections and Contentions on Thursday Island', in Shnukal et al. (eds).

Rankine, Wendy (1995), 'From Nauru to Nowhere: Pacific Island Chinese Evacuee Workers in Central Australian Wolfram Mines, 1942–1943', in Macgregor (ed.).

Rasmussen, Amanda (2004), 'Networks and Negotiations: Bendigo's Chinese and the Easter Fair', *Journal of Australian Colonial History*, 6: 79–92.

Reddy, William M. (1997), *The Invisible Code: Honor and Sentiment in Postrevolutionary France 1814–1848*, Berkeley: University of California Press.

Reid, Anthony (ed.) (1996), *Sojourners and Settlers: Histories of Southeast Asia and the Chinese*, Sydney: Allen & Unwin.

Reynolds, Douglas R (1993), *China, 1898–1912: The Xinzheng Revolution and Japan*, Cambridge, Mass : Council on East Asian Studies, Harvard University.

Richards, Eric (1992), 'Return Migration and Migrant Strategies in Colonial Australia', in Fitzpatrick (ed.).

Rolls, Eric (1992), *Sojourners: The Epic Story of China's Centuries–Old Relationship with Australia*, St Lucia: University of Queensland Press.

—— (1996), *Citizens: Flowers and the Wild Sea*, St Lucia: University of Queensland Press.

Rowe, William T (1989), *Hankow: Conflict and Community in a Chinese City, 1796–1895*, Stanford: Stanford University Press.

Royal Commission (1891–92), *Royal Commission into Alleged Chinese Gambling and Immorality*, New South Wales Votes and Proceedings, Legislative Assembly.

Rubenstein, Kim (2004), 'The Influence of Chinese Immigration on Australian Citizenship', in Couchman et al. (eds).

Rule, Pauline (2000), 'Challenging Conventions: Irish–Chinese Marriages in Colonial Victoria', in Foley and Bateman (eds).

—— (2002), 'A Tale of Three Sisters: Australian–Chinese Marriages in Colonial Victoria', in Kee et al. (eds).

—— (2004), 'The Chinese Camps in Colonial Victoria: Their Role as Contact Zones', in Couchman et al. (eds).

Russell, Rosslyn & Philip Chubb (1998), *One Destiny! The Federation Story: How Australia became a Nation*, Ringwood: Penguin.

Ryan, Jan (1995), *Ancestors: Chinese in Colonial Australia*, Fremantle: Fremantle Arts Centre Press.

Said, Edward (1978), *Orientalism*, New York: Pantheon.

Sakai, Naoki (2006), 'Equality, Hierarchy and Identity in Modern Japan: Reflections on The Nationalist Ethics of Fukuzawa Yukichi', in Ch'ien and Fitzgerald (eds).

Scarr, Deryck (1984), *Fiji: A Short History*, Sydney: Allen & Unwin.

Schama, Simon (2005), *Rough Crossings: Britain, the Slaves and the American Revolution*, London: BBC Books.

Schiffrin, Harold Z (1970), *Sun Yat-Sen and the Origins of the Chinese Revolution*, Berkeley: University of California Press.

Schlegel, Gustav (1973), *The Hung League*, New York: AMS (Batavia 1866).

Secretary (1908), Secretary of Department of External Affairs to Collector of Customs Fremantle, 27 October, Registers of Correspondence 1901–42, Collector of Customs Western Australia, National Archives of Australia PP4/4.

Select Committee (1856–57), *Report of the Select Committee on the Subject of Immigration 1856–57*, Votes and Proceedings of the Legislative Council, Victoria, vol. 2, pp. 3–4.

Selle, Earle Albert (1948), *Donald of China*, Sydney: Invincible Press.

Shan hua pi jia you (n.d.), 'Pingdeng shuo' ['Egalitarianism'], *Xiangbao (Hunan Journal)* 58: 229, 59: 233, 60: 237.

Shen, Congwen (1982), *Alisi zhongguo youji (Alice in China)*, in *Shen Congwen wenji (The Collected Writings of Shen Congwen)*, first published 1928, vol. 1, Hong Kong, n.p.

Shen, Yuanfang (2001), *Dragon Seed in the Antipodes: Chinese–Australian Autobiographies*, Melbourne: Melbourne University Press.

Shnukal, Anna, Guy Ramsay & Yuriko Nagata (eds) (2004), *Navigating Boundaries: The Asian Diaspora in Torres Strait*, Canberra: Pandanus Books.

Sincere (1924), *The Sincere Co. Ltd Twenty Fifth Anniversary*, Hong Kong: Commercial Press.

Sinn, Elizabeth (1989), *Power and Charity: The Early History of the Tung Wah Hospital*, Hong Kong: Oxford University Press.

—— (1995), 'Emigration from Hong Kong before 1941: General Trends', in Skeldon (ed.).

Skeldon, Ronald (ed.) (1995), *Emigration from Hong Kong: Tendencies and Impacts*, Hong Kong: Chinese University Press.

Skinner, G William (ed.) (1974) *The Chinese City Between Two Worlds*, Stanford: Stanford University Press.

Sleeman, John HC (1933), *White China: An Australasian Sensation*, Sydney: Alert Printing & Publishing.

Spence, Jonathon D (1996), *God's Chinese Son: The Taiping Heavenly Kingdom of Hong Xiuquan*, New York: WW Norton.

Stephenson, Peta (2005), 'Beyond Colonial Casualties: Chinese Agency in the Australian Post/Colonial Endeavour', in Ferrall et al. (eds).

Stevens, Keith (1989), 'British Chinese Labour Corps Labourers Buried in England', *Journal of the Hong Kong Branch of the Royal Asiatic Society*, 29.

Strahan, Lachlan (1996), *Australia's China: Changing Perceptions from the 1930s to the 1990s*, Melbourne: Cambridge University Press.

Summerskill, Michael (1982), *China on the Western Front: Britain's Work Force in the First World War*, London: M Summerskill.

Sun Yatsen (1943), *San Min Chu I, The Three Principles of the People*, trans. Frank W Price, LT Chen (ed.), first published 1924, Chungking: Government Printing House.

Tan Sitong (1984), *An Exposition of Benevolence: The Jen-Hsüeh of Tan Ssu-t'ung*, trans. Chan Sin-wai, Hong Kong: Chinese University Press.

Taplin, Harry (1988), 'Shang, Caleb James (1884–1953)', *The Australian Dictionary of Biography*, vol. 11, Melbourne: Melbourne University Press.

Tart, Margaret (1911), *The Life of Quong Tart*, Sydney: WM Maclardy.

Tavan, Gwenda (2005), *The Long, Slow Death of White Australia*, Melbourne: Scribe.

Taylor, Charles (1975), *Hegel*, Cambridge: Cambridge University Press.

—— (2004a), *Modern Social Imaginaries*, Durham & London: Duke University Press.

—— (2004b), 'Modern Social Imaginaries', *Public Culture*, 14.1: 91–124.

Teo, Hsu-ming & Richard White (eds) (2003), *Cultural History in Australia*, Sydney: UNSW Press.

The Argus, various issues.

The Australian Christian World, various issues.

The Bendigo Advertiser, various issues.

The Daily Examiner, various issues.
The First 90 Years of Lodge Wentworth (n.d.), 'The First 90 Years of Lodge Wentworth No. 89 UGL of New South Wales', typed manuscript. Archives of the United Grand Lodge of New South Wales and the Australian Capital Territory, Box 171.
The New York Times, various issues.
The Richmond River Free Press, various issues.
The Sun, various issues.
The Sydney Morning Herald, various issues.
Thompson, Peter & Robert Macklin (2004), *The Man Who Died Twice: The Life and Adventures of Morrison of Peking*, Sydney: Allen & Unwin.
Tongwen (1889), article translated by Tongwen Publishing House on Australia's Harsh Treatment of Chinese (27th day of 8th month of Guangxu 14), Beijing: First National Archives.
Travers, Robert (1981), *Australian Mandarin: The Life and Times of Quong Tart*, Sydney: Kangaroo Press.
Trevarthen, Cora (2006), 'After the Gold is Gone: Chinese Communities in Northeast Victoria 1861–1914', *Journal of Chinese Australia*, 2 (October), at <http://www. chaf.lib.latrobe.edu.au/jca>.
Trocki, Carl A (1990), *Opium and Empire: Chinese Society in Colonial Singapore 1800–1910*, Ithaca: Cornell University Press.
—— (1993), 'The Rise and Fall of the Ngee Heng Kongsi in Singapore', in Owenby and Heidhues (eds), *'Secret Societies' Reconsidered*.
—— (1997), 'Boundaries and Transgressions: Chinese Enterprise in Eighteenth- and Nineteenth-Century Southeast Asia', in Ong and Nonini (eds), *Ungrounded Empires*.
—— (2005), 'A Drug on the Market: Opium and the Chinese in Southeast Asia, 1750–1880', *Journal of Chinese Overseas*, 1.2 (November): 147–68.
Tse Tsan Tai (1924), *The Chinese Republic: Secret History of the Revolution*, Hong Kong: South China Morning Post.
Tseng, Marquis (Zeng Jize) (1887), 'China, the Sleep and the Awakening', *Chinese Recorder and Missionary Journal*, 18.4 (April): 146–53.
Tung Wah News (see *Duonghuabao*), various issues.
Turner, Ethel (ed.) (1918), *The Australian Soldier's Gift Book*, Sydney: Voluntary Workers' Association.
Vattel, Emmerich de (1883), *The Law of Nations, or, Principles of the Law of Nature, Applied to the Conduct and Affairs of Nations and Sovereigns: From the French of Monsieur de Vattel* (1758), Joseph Chitty (ed.), with additional notes by Edward D Ingraham, Philadelphia: TW Johnson & Co.
Vivian, Helen (1985), *Tasmania's Chinese Heritage: An Historical Record of Chinese Sites in North East Tasmania* (2 vols), Launceston: Australian Heritage Commission/Queen Victoria Museum and Art Gallery.
Viviani, Nancy (ed.) (1992), *The Abolition of the White Australia Policy: The Immigration Reform Movement Revisited*, Brisbane: Centre for the Study of Australia–Asia Relations, Griffith University.
Walker, David (1999), *Anxious Nation: Australia and the Rise of Asia 1850–1939*, St Lucia: University of Queensland Press.
—— (2006), 'Strange Reading: Keith Windschuttle on Race, Asia and White Australia', *Australian Historical Studies*, 37.128 (October): 108–22.
Wang Gung-wu (1992a), 'The Origins of the Hua-Ch'iao', in Wang (1992b).

——— (1992b), *Community and Nation: China, Southeast Asia and Australia*, Sydney: Allen & Unwin.
——— (1996), 'Sojourning: The Chinese Experience in Southeast Asia', in Reid (ed.) (1996).
——— (2000), *The Chinese Overseas* Cambridge, Mass: Harvard University Press.
Wang, Sing-Wu (1978), *The Organisation of Chinese Emigration 1848–1888: With Special Reference to Chinese Emigration to Australia*, San Francisco: Chinese Materials Center.
——— (2001), 'Chinese Immigration 1840s–1890s', in Jupp (ed.) (2001).
Wang, Wenda (1932), 'Qianti' ['On the above topic'], in *Xianggang yongan youxian*, p. 342.
Ward, JSM & WG Stirling (1925), *The Hung Society*, 3 vols, London: Baskerville.
Ward, Russell (1958), *The Australian Legend*, Melbourne: Oxford University Press.
Wasserstein, Bernard (1998), *Secret War in Shanghai: Treachery, Subversion and Collaboration in the Second World War*, London: Profile Books.
Weale, BL Putnam (Lennox Simpson) (1905), *The Re-Shaping of the Far East*, London: Macmillan.
Welch, Ian (2003), 'Alien Son: The Life and Times of Cheok Hong Cheong, 1851–1928', PhD dissertation, Canberra: Australian National University.
Will, Pierre-Etienne (1990), *Bureaucracy and Famine in Eighteenth Century China*, trans. Elborg Forster, Stanford: Stanford University Press.
Willard, Myra (1923), *History of the White Australia Policy*, Melbourne: Melbourne University Press.
Williams, Mark. 'Sentimental Racism', in Ferrall et al. (eds).
Williams, Michael (2001), 'Destination Qiaoxiang – Pearl River Delta Villages & Pacific Ports, 1849–1949', PhD dissertation, Sydney: University of New South Wales.
Wilmott, WE (1999), 'Fiji', in Pan (ed.).
——— (2004), 'Chinese Contract Labour in the Pacific Islands during the Nineteenth Century', paper presented to the International Conference on Quong Tart and His Times, Sydney: Powerhouse Museum.
Wilson, Margaret, Clive Moore & Doug Munro (1990), 'Asian Workers in the Pacific', in Moore et al. (eds).
Wilton, Janis (1998), 'Chinese Stores in Rural Australia', in MacPherson (ed.) (1998).
——— (2004), *Golden Threads: The Chinese in Regional New South Wales*, Armidale: New England Regional Art Museum in association with Powerhouse Publishers, Sydney.
Windschuttle, Keith (2004), *The White Australia Policy*, Sydney: Macleay Press.
Wise, BR (1913), *The Making of the Australian Commonwealth 1889–1900: A Stage in the Growth of the Empire*, London: Longmans Green & Co.
Wong Hoy, Kevin and Patricia Monoghan-Jamieson (2006), 'Chinese Feasts and Festivals in Colonial Australia', *Journal of Chinese Australia*, 2 (October): 1–9.
Woollacott, Angela (2001), *To Try her Fortune in London: Australian Women, Colonialism, and Modernity*, Oxford and New York: Oxford University Press.
Wu, Yucheng (1996), *Guangdong huaqiao shihua* (*Historical notes on Cantonese overseas*), Hong Kong: Xianggang shijie chubanshe.
Wu, David YH (1982), *The Chinese in Papua New Guinea: 1880–1980*, Hong Kong: Chinese University Press.
Xianggang yongan (1932), *Xianggang yongan youxian gongsi ershiwu zhounian jinianlu*

(*Commemorative record of the twenty fifth anniversary of the Hong Kong Wing On Company*), Hong Kong: Wing On Publishers.

Yarwood, AT (1964), *Asian Migration to Australia: The Background to Exclusion 1896–1923*, Melbourne: Melbourne University Press.

—— (ed.) (1968), *Attitudes to Non-European Immigration*, Sydney: Cassell.

Yen, Ching-Hwang (1998), 'Wing On and the Kwok Brothers: A Case Study of Pre-War Chinese Entrepreneurs', in MacPherson (ed.).

Yong, CF (1965–66), 'The Banana Trade and the Chinese in New South Wales and Victoria, 1901–1921', *ANU Historical Journal*, 1.2: 28–35.

—— (1977), *The New Gold Mountain: The Chinese in Australia 1901–1921*, Adelaide: Raphael Arts.

Yong, CF & RB McKenna (1990), *The Kuomintang Movement in British Malaya, 1912–1949*, Singapore: Singapore University Press.

York, Barry (1995), *Admissions and Exclusions: Asiatics and other Coloured Races in Australia 1901 to 1946*, Canberra: Centre for Immigration and Multicultural Studies.

Young, John D (1998), 'Sun Yatsen and the Department Store: An Aspect of National Reconstruction', in MacPherson (ed.).

Young, Reverend W (1868), 'Report on the Condition of the Chinese Population in Victoria', *Victorian Parliamentary Papers*, Melbourne: Government Printer.

Yuan, CM (2001), 'Chinese in White Australia 1901–1950', in Jupp (ed.).

Yung, Luther (n.d.), 'Reminiscences by Luther Yung', handwritten manuscript, recorded by Glen Hall, Lismore: Richmond River Historical Society.

Zhengzhi zhoubao (*Political Weekly*), various issues.

Zhongguo guomindang (1922), 'Zhongguo guomindang benbu caizhengbu tonggao' ['Report of the Finance Bureau of the Chinese Nationalist Party'], Historical Archives Commission of the Kuomintang (KMT Archives) 415/25.

Zhongguo guomindang benbu gongbao (*Chinese Nationalist Party Centre Bulletin*), various issues.

Zhongguo guomindang tongxin (*Chinese Nationalist Party Gazette*), various issues.

Zhongguo guomindang zhoukan (*Chinese Nationalist Party Weekly*), various issues.

Zhongguo liguo (1912), 'Zhongguo liguo da fangzhen shangque shu' ['On the greater goal of state-building in China'], *Tung Wah News* (*Donghua shibao*), part 2, 22 June, and part VI, 27 July.

Zhongshan ren zai aozhou (*Zhongshan People in Australia*) (1992), *Zhongshan wenzhi* (*Records of Zhongshan*), 24, Guangzhou: Zhengxie guangdongsheng zhongshanshi weiyuanhui wenshi weihuanhui.

Zou Lu (1929), *Zhongguo guomindang shigao* (*Draft History of the Chinese Nationalist Party*), 2 vols, Shanghai: Zhonghua shuju.

ACKNOWLEDGMENTS

Part of Chapter Four is reprinted with permission from my earlier publication 'Transnational Networks and National Identities in the Australian Commonwealth: The Chinese-Australasian Kuomintang 1923–1937,' *Australian Historical Studies*, vol. 37, no. 127, April 2006, pp. 95–116; part of Chapter Six from 'Revolution and Respectability: Chinese Masons in Australian History' in Ann Curthoys and Marilyn Lake, eds, *Connected Worlds: History in Transnational Perspective* (Canberra: Australian National University E-Press, 2006), pp. 89–110; and part of Chapter Nine from 'Who Cares What They Think? John Winston Howard, William Morris Hughes and the Pragmatic Vision of Australian National Sovereignty' in Alison Broinowski, ed., *Double Vision: Asian Accounts of Australia* (Canberra: Pandanus Books, 2004), pp. 15–40.

INDEX